ADVANCE PRAISE FOR *SACRED LINK*

"... sent chills up my spine—what a compelling, empowering story!"

—Christiane Northrup, M.D., author of *Women's Bodies, Women's Wisdom*

"One of the great teachings ... in modern literature."

—Nancy London, co-author of *Our Bodies, Ourselves*

"Compelling storytelling ... vibrant, spellbinding, revolutionary."

—JoAnne Dodgson, author of *Gifts of the Grandmother* and *Cocoonin*

"I read *The Reluctant Shaman* ... re-read it many times over the years ... but THIS BOOK ... I do not think I have been as profoundly effected by a book in my life!"

—Phyllis King, Health Practitioner

"This well-written tale is much more than a story—it illuminates the way home."

—Alan Cohen, author of *The Dragon Doesn't Live Here Anymore*

"*Sacred Link* ... is like eating a box of truffles ... you savor every bite!"

—JoEllen Koerner, author of *Mother, Heal My Self*

"This book redefines ... 'spiritual sensuality.'"

—John Perkins, author of *Shapeshifting* and *Spirit of the Shuar*

"*Sacred Link* ... [where] ... our everyday lives become prayers to Creator."

—Eve Bruce, MD, author of *Shaman MD*

"A hauntingly beautiful and profound journey."

—Patricia West-Barker, co-author of *Healing Spirits*

"Politically challenging ... thought provoking—Kay Cordell Whitaker's work will be revered and honored for generations to come."

—Leslie Botha-Williams, author of *Holy Hormones Honey!*

SACRED LINK

JOINING FORTUNES WITH THE UNKNOWN

KAY CORDELL WHITAKER

THE WRITERS' COLLECTIVE
Independent Books for Independent Readers

Cover Designer: Robert Aulicino
Interior Design: Mary Jo Zazueta

ISBN-13: 978-1-59411-108-2
ISBN-10: 1-59411-108-1

Library of Congress Control Number: 2004098504

Printed in Canada

10 9 8 7 6 5 4 3 2 1

Published by The Writers' Collective ▲ Cranston, Rhode Island

Made from Acid-Free 100% Post-Consumer Chlorine Free Recycled Paper

This book is dedicated in respect and gratitude to my son
and daughter and to all the children now and yet to come.

CONTENTS

PREMISE

AFTER several years studying with Chea and Domano Hetaka, my two Peruvian teachers, it became apparent to me that they purposefully and creatively used our language in a very different arrangement and emphasis than what is normally considered standard American English even when they had known what the common phrasing was. Their usage was carefully and precisely chosen to best portray their unique, native perspective of life.

Throughout the writing of these books about the Hetakas, I have maintained their patterns of speech and rhythm, the only alterations being to minimize the extreme brokenness of sentences in order to ensure clarity.

The Hetakas had often talked with me about the power that knowledge carries when one does not hold it in fear, but relates to it and uses it to find and hold onto one's Song and center—to wake up and stay awake. I cannot say that this or that is "THE KNOWLEDGE" or "THE TRUTH." I can only present the view of the world as I have lived it and, in the tradition of a *kala keh nah seh* (medicine storyteller) of the Hetakas' tribe, show you this way to experience for yourself. As Chea and Domano have often said to me, it is for each person to objectively re-examine deep inside themselves, their beliefs, their values, and their world, to find their own truth—whatever that may be.

The Hetakas advised in their parting words to me to suggest to the readers that they read with more than their thoughts, that they enjoy the pages slowly, and that they experience with their whole selves as they proceed.

~ Kay Cordell Whitaker

PRELUDE

THE ALL-MIGHTY-MOST-IMPORTANT-THING

"OK, you old hallowed teachers, you," I blurted out. "I'm sure not getting it here. What is this all-mighty-most-important-thing?"

I don't think they were expecting me to say anything. Their heads popped up like two Jack-in-the-boxes. Domano stared at me through his right eye like a giant parrot. "You are saying your elders are wallowers? No French coffee for you. Don't they teach you respect in this country?"

"'Fraid not."

"She's just talking about your big old holes in your head," said Chea. Domano looked at her with disbelief. "Holes," she repeated. He laughed and they smiled at each other.

"Kay," he said turning to me. "Sometimes I sure have to tell you many times. It is a good thing I am so patient." Chea poked him with her elbow. "This is serious here." He looked as though he was shooing a fly the way he was flapping his hand at her. "I have to be serious."

"This thing," the smile slipped off Domano's face, "is something nobody *wants* to see. Its importance must step in front of everything. If you really 'see' this, nothing will be the same. I tell you again. This thing is about your world. You know very well your world is collapsing in a cycle that feeds on itself: disrespect-force-revenge. How does that happen?"

"Yeah." I was fishing for their sympathy. Maybe they would take pity on me and just tell me the point. "That's kind of hard to not admit to. About our world and all."

"How does that happen?" Domano asked again. "Think. Look at it. What do you feel in there?"

"Ugly."

"No," he directed. "You are letting it suck you in and control…"

"There's nothing I can trust there." I interrupted him, a habit that was getting worse with time, not better. I always felt so childish when I did it.

"Underneath. Under all that garbage. Not splashing around *in* it." Domano thrashed his hands as though he were digging something out from under a huge, smelly mess. "Playing *in* the pucky is not it."

I couldn't help laughing. While he was busy teasing I wondered what he meant by "underneath the garbage." What could possibly be under there?

Chea and Domano had always said that to perceive something accurately one needed to clear the jabber out of the mind by turning one's attention into the feeling experience of one's own spirit or essence, "one's own Song" as they called it. This feeling state then becomes one's center and place of clear perception. I tried to clear away my thoughts once again and feel my Song, to perceive from there. My mind kept burping up a long parade of ridiculous items that could be under that garbage. It was hard to be serious. I tried to hold back the giggles but couldn't.

Domano just ignored me. After a few moments as I watched him digging away at his slime heap it seemed as though there was something heavy in the air above his arms. I strained and refocused my eyes and it was still there. I could actually see his slithering mountains of garbage. There were thoughts inside—millions, no billions, of people's thoughts woven as the fabric of this cycling creation. And there were many thoughts and ideas outside the amassment feeding it—an endless trail appearing and moving eventually into the great bulk that was our culture.

Bits of haze from the refuse began to drift through the air. It was disgustingly foul. I couldn't avoid the taste of it getting in my mouth. My tongue twinged. It was pushing my gag reflex.

I was starting to feel very uncomfortable. The noise of it was relentless, grating, assaulting. It made me feel dirty just watching it but I was so mesmerized at what I was seeing I couldn't stop. Unexpected scenes popped into my head complete with driving, insistent emotions.

Inside the scenes of the weaving there was strong agreement to purposefully take actions for personal convenience or gain at the expense of others, even when it meant their victim's total annihilation. Images of wanton destruction with no notice or remorse were disturbingly common. Condemnation was used to manipulate people, sometimes overtly but more often in the most constant and subtle of ways. I detected purposefully and strategically placed fear and paranoia worming its way through the mass. I couldn't find any feelings of respect for one's self or anything else. Everywhere I looked there was a desperate craving, like the withdrawal of an addict, for enforcing control over others. Everything bent toward gratifying the grasp for control, convenience and wealth in the present with no concern for what would be left behind for the future. To think outside this "box" was not an option. There was purposefulness here. Deliberateness.

"Ugh!" I gasped. "Ugh! It's been planned! Directed! It's all been orchestrated!"

Domano calmly asked again, "How does that come about? How do they succeed?"

"I don't know. Why would anybody create that on purpose?" As I broke away from the experience my own feelings came to the surface. I felt tricked and violated by my culture. My sadness distracted me.

"How do they do it?" Domano persisted.

"Who cares?" I knew our society was unstable and had a lot of problems, but I had never seen it quite from this perspective before. I felt like I didn't want to waste my time with this endeavor any longer. "What's the point?"

Chea held up a pen. "When you know the workings of a thing, you know how to control it or change it." She wiggled the pen in front of my face. "You have its power."

I was feeling especially powerless and impotent at that moment. We were all caught, stuck in the middle of this perpetual garbage heap. "That cultural construct is immense. I'm small. End of story."

Domano tapped his fingers on the table. He wasn't at all concerned about what I said. "How do they make it?" he said again to me. "How do they keep it going? What is under the garbage?"

Right. Underneath. The image came back in my mind even though I was fighting it and as I contemplated its structure and movements my attention kept returning to how the participants of the weaving adhered to its tenets with such fervor and without question. The mounds behaved like a living creature consuming the forms outside the main body. Then I realized that the forms outside the weaving were actually being emitted from the main body in what began as barely visible precursors to their final shape. As more of this ethereal material was emitted the precursors assumed their final form and were eventually assimilated.

I mumbled out loud, "There must be a correlation."

"You are not making sense," Chea said.

I was too deep in the experience to answer her. The picture was making sense. The woven mounds were thoughts. The outside forms were thoughts. The participating people created these thoughts. The thoughts were full of ideas and the participants held to the ideas as if it meant their very existence. These ideas were all they knew. This was their entire world, a world created from their unshakable belief in these ideas. This was carefully nurtured, dogmatic, *blind belief*—a believing that kept them in a kind of unaware, drugged half-sleep. This was an ingenious machine systematically maintained by a knowing elite.

"I got it," I said. "The controlling factor sees that the necessary ideas are always fresh on the minds of the participants and that they hold such a charged belief in them that they can't see anything else."

There was silence.

Chea finally asked, "What are the workings? Where is the power?"

"The power, the key to the workings of the machine is blind belief. The stronger the better. That way the people won't be able to wake up," I answered. The full experience, the full understanding, of it all was still hitting me. I think I was slipping into shock. "Why?" I added. "Why would anybody create this?"

"That's the lesson for a later time." Domano patted Chea's leg. "Let's go now. Let's find some of that French espresso coffee."

~ Kay Cordell Whitaker

ONE

FIRE, CLAY, BONES AND CAVES

SOMETHING jolted me awake. There was darkness and the smell of wet dirt. I did not know this place I was standing in or how I got here. It was altogether strange. There was something completely odd about it, like I might imagine the land of the dead would be. It had an unfamiliar…oldness. It frightened me. I didn't want to be here.

In my grogginess I had trouble keeping on my feet. I staggered a few steps toward a small torch burning to my left. There was stone behind it. This seemed to be a large cave of some kind and there were sticks and straw all over the ground.

It took a tremendous struggle to stay awake. Pieces of dream memories were enticing me of a trail on a cliff and flying excitedly through the clouds. But this cavern seemed alarmingly empty. I was all alone and the only sound was from the flame on the torch. The crackle echoed faintly down into the darkness.

How did I get to this place? What on Earth had I been doing asleep standing up? Or had I been unconscious? Perhaps someone brought me here. But to what purpose? I decided I'd better take the torch now and try to find my way out.

As I reached for the light a figure moved from the shadows. It appeared to be a woman but she didn't feel like a woman. She grabbed the torch before I could. She was odd like this cave: not quite alive but more than alive. Her face was old and her clothes were dark and flowing. I was more terrified than I ever thought possible. My breath left me and my mind began to sink as though I were falling asleep.

"Wake up!" she screamed at me and waved the torch in my face. Her voice was shrill and grated. "Wake up! Wake up! Look at this flame. Here! Right here!"

I reached out for the torch and then everything around me changed. I saw a sunset sky and green mountains. My old friend and teacher, Chea Hetaka, was to my left and her husband, Domano, was to my right. I tried to get them in focus but they warped the way things sometimes do in a dream.

"What's happening to me?" As soon as I tried to talk I felt a crackling that ran from my head to my toes and I was suddenly back in the cave with the odd woman.

"No! No! No!" I was frantic. "Stop this! Oh, please stop!" I could barely make the sounds. I had no breath. My legs fell under me and I lay crumbled and scratched on the sticks. The fear was uncontainable. I would have done anything to get out of there.

"Control your mind." Her voice scraped into the cavern walls. "Where is your attention? Breathe." She stomped the shaft of the torch hard onto the ground. The sound shook through the chamber. "Observe. Here!" She stomped it yet again. "Now!"

I opened my eyes. The shaft was only inches away. I was sure she was going to hit me with it. I tried to force my body to roll away. My vision was blurring out of control and my limbs felt boneless. A memory ached inside me of walking on a forest path with Chea and Domano. We were traveling some place special but I couldn't remember if that happened moments ago or months ago.

The woman gave a horrific scream and slammed the torch violently onto the ground by my face. It was as though I was being swept away by a current of fear. I began to yell involuntarily and found myself snapped into yet another scene. Chea and Domano were sitting on the ground with me in front of a rocky outcropping in a mountainous part of a jungle. They stared at me, stone-faced, as I hollered at the top of my lungs. I suddenly realized that I no longer felt the fear and I had nothing left to scream about. The sound finished and left my mouth of its own accord.

I reached out and took their hands. Their peacefulness calmed me. I began to hear the sounds of birds and smell the nectar in the air. Then out of everything surrounding me came another devastating shriek and crash and with no warning I was back in the cave. Terror had me by the throat. Inside me I felt I could get up and run out of the cave. But my body was crippled, broken with fear. I didn't know what to do. This must be some kind of traditional training or testing from the Hetakas and it looked like I was failing badly.

I stared up at the woman. It was dark and the flame flickered wildly, but it seemed that she wasn't entirely solid, as though I could see the rock wall through her at moments. I struggled to get control of my breath, to breathe the way the Hetakas had taught me, filling myself as though I were an empty vessel.

I couldn't hold onto any image or feeling. I slipped and snapped from one place and dream to the next. I became groggy again and the sensations and ecstasy of the flying came back to me. I remembered the freedom of moving through the air with no obstacles, the troubles of my world removed, on my way to a mysterious and ancient ceremony of the eastern Andes Indians. But I couldn't place if it had been real or not.

The odd woman took a few steps toward me, and leaning over just slightly, glared into my eyes. She grumbled and gestured to herself before she stepped back and, without any compunction at all, touched her flame to the brush around my feet. If I thought I was afraid before it could not compare to the nightmare I felt now. I was stuck. I couldn't get up and run away or even roll off the straw and branches. I hoped this was a dream and the scene would change again or I would wake up. Only this was crystal clear and holding fast.

I screamed and screamed but the woman paid no attention to me. She diligently walked around the pile of brush to light the fire from the other side. I could feel the heat from the flames as they flashed toward me. I was going to die.

FIRE, CLAY, BONES AND CAVES

"Oh! My god!" I cried at her. "What about my life? What'll happen to my babies?"

Every feeling, unpleasant and pleasant, that I'd ever had was rising with the flames and consuming me. I was burning with the fire, the guilts and regrets, the loves and passions. The images of my world went up with the steam and smoke as the flames took each part of my body.

Then I remembered. A feeling of great failure came over me. I was indeed on my way to a legendary ceremony just moments ago, one said to have been revered most highly by these mountain Indians for countless centuries. Domano and Chea had guided me on this spirit journey to the Andes. But something went wrong. I must have fallen into sleeping on my way into the cave. This couldn't possibly be the ceremony. This wasn't right at all.

My god, where had I ended up? Was I being crushed at the hands of what the Hetakas called an adversary? Was this odd woman my adversary?

My sadness was excruciating. I was devastated by my own loss and the overwhelming feelings of self-pity for an inadequate life. As I sobbed I thought I saw two figures through the smoke. I managed to move my head only slightly. There in the distance were my old horrifying acquaintances, Death and Destiny. I actually felt a strange comfort in their presence. At least there was something here that was familiar. I could hear Destiny singing. It was as haunting and eerie as ever. It seemed quite beautiful in the midst of my wallow. I loved that Song. I wanted that Song.

I listened through my sadness for her melody. I felt deeper and deeper inside my pain, and there, like a seed hiding at the core of a decaying apple, was her gentle persistent voice and with it my own inner sounds.

I had forgotten about the strange woman until she laughed. She pushed the coals in toward me from around the fire with the shaft of the torch. The fire rose. The smoke was suffocating and the flames were painful beyond description. I cried, laughed, screamed, felt sorry for myself and thankful. Then the airs that pass through all the forms of our world could no longer pass through me. And hidden underneath it all, I listened to the Songs.

The fires had taken my world and my flesh and when there was none left my bones fell scorched in a pile on the ashes. I stayed among them until they were cold and I could no longer hold any thought.

The woman had been sitting patiently against the stone wall with her elbow resting on her raised knee. She rose and came over to me. With great care she picked up each of my bones, one by one, blew them off, and arranged them in a fine net bag. Then chanting quietly she carried me down deep into the dark cave.

The woman walked for a long time. I watched as though trailing along behind her, and it felt natural that all my perceptions seemed to be intact. When we came to a faint sound of water bubbling she stopped and lit a tiny clay lamp. We were in a small cavern rich with mineral deposits on the walls. It smelled of sulfur and hot, wet air. There wasn't much room to stand or move around in, only the little pool against the modeled wall and the bank of dried clay just big enough for the two of us. I liked this tiny chamber. It was delicate and charming and its many undulating forms were some of the most beautiful in nature. Even in this dim light I could see swirls of blues and pure yellows among the gray. Something about it was like the wise woman's cauldrons in the old fairy tales and myths that were read to me as a child.

She set her bag down and gently took out each of my bones, lining them carefully on the ground in order from my feet to my head. The words she mumbled while dusting and rubbing every piece gave me a sense of safety even though all my awareness of anything before this chamber was drifting away.

I remained peaceful, very curious and unusually alert. I watched her as she scooped up handfuls of the sulfury, mineral-rich mud from under the water of the hot spring and packed it on my bones. It seemed that hours had passed, maybe even days. But she never paused or hesitated, and out of that young flesh of the Earth, with the artistry of a surgeon, she molded and attached every new fiber that was to be part of my body.

Once finished she sat motionless watching me. Then an unexpected thing happened. I began to have awareness through this body. I realized that I was observing her from inside this meticulous form she had just built. The steamy clay on my bones wrapped me in the soothingness of "home." My sense of my own unique individual identity was becoming uncharacteristically strong. I knew myself in a primeval way. This was everything to me at this moment and my body was my focal point.

Strength was coming back to me and sensations of muscle tension. I could stretch my toes, when not long before I thought that I'd never be moving again. I wanted to yell with excitement, to tell the woman of my great luck, but I was unable to make a sound. She just looked blankly at me. I couldn't figure out what she was doing there, or what sort of person she was. I wondered about her greatly.

I knew now that I soon should be able to move my whole body and I wanted to make that happen more than anything. I wanted to be able to experience and express with agility. As the time passed on I worked without rest to make my muscles respond.

The woman got up and placed the little lamp onto a ledge of rock behind her. Then she reached over into the pool and filled her cupped hands with the water from the spring. It was wonderfully hot as she poured handful after handful on me, from my feet to my head and back again. I could feel the mud underneath me and the warm freshness of the air on my bare skin.

It was then I realized that I was now looking at her through my eyes. As she passed in front of the flame I could see the light and the shape of the rocks through her body. That shook a memory loose of an earlier time in a bigger chamber when I had thought I'd seen her as transparent, and I remembered the flames of the torch and the burning of my flesh. The way I had known myself was burnt away and here, now, I was something new, something to be cherished and carefully attended.

The more she poured the mineral waters on me the better I was able to flex and stretch my muscles. I could feel every tiny fiber moving and filling with a blood that was excited with life and action. It was as if every cell in my body was electrified with a passion all its own to live and experience life for itself. As I concentrated on every part of my body, I could hear this excitement that was the identifying signature of each of these cells and the organs they formed. They were like a tremendous chorus of many harmonies and melodies all blending perfectly together. Then I noticed a larger, encompassing Song in their background. I knew this elusive symphony. I was struck at its astounding complexity. It was my own identifying signature sound and it was orchestrating and directing all the others in an ever changing poem.

"Stretch," the woman said. "Stretch all your muscles over and over. They are new. They need to be worked to break them in. You will have to give them the knowledge you have about how they should work."

I still couldn't make any sound but I nodded my head. As I relished every sensation I wondered how I would accomplish that knowledge giving, and if I would ever be able to speak again.

The woman seemed to know what I was thinking and cocked her head to the side, "Shhh. You will talk soon. Don't struggle with it yet. The voice takes time to build. This will help." And she scooped up more spring water and poured it on my neck and face.

It ran inside my mouth and ears and down my nose. I choked and tried to blow it out. It tasted of sulfur and clay. She held my head up and wiped my face. "Pay attention to the moment. You are losing the present. Look how hard you work to be scattered already. Those ways are gone for you. Now pay attention so you will not be trying to breathe the water." The woman laughed lightly at me and continued pouring water over my face and body.

The feeling of her, like the cave, was primal. She was destroyer, creator, keeper of secret knowledge and places, a spirit living in a spirit world. I didn't fear or glorify her; but I trusted her.

I worked out every muscle. The feeling was of wonderful relief, as though I were moving for the first time after being long restrained. And I could hear the many Songs of my body change with every movement I made. I was conducting an entire orchestra that I was not only creating but feeling dynamically throughout my whole being.

"Sit up," the woman pulled me by my arm. "You can do it. You know you can do it."

As I sat up all the Songs faded and the blood left my head. The cavern wobbled and I gulped the air to keep from losing consciousness.

"There. There you are," she said. "Breathe long and slow. Keep moving. Push that blood back through your body." Then she rubbed a handful of scorching hot mud up my back and onto my head.

"Ahhh!" The shock of it made me jerk and noise came out of me involuntarily.

"You see?" she said. "You work."

That seemed funny to me and I laughed. The sound was fragile and bounced across the cavern against the rock walls. I twisted my head back and forth as if trying to watch the sounds as they leaped from crevice to overhang. Looking around this tiny chamber was a delight to my eyes. It contained every shape, texture, and color arrayed in patterns that teased the imagination. I reached out to touch the mineral formations. They were hard like stone but felt somehow the same as the boiling mud in the edge of the pool.

"What is this place?" I pushed myself up onto my knees. My arms were weak and gave way under the weight of my body. I leaned over on the mud. "How did I get here? You seem familiar. Am I supposed to know you?"

"Do you?" she asked.

I couldn't place her. I struggled, trying to remember something about her and realized that I couldn't recall anything but the time in these caverns. It seemed to me that I had had experiences outside this place but no details or images would come to mind. I dropped my head to the ground and took the weight off my arms.

"Be careful in that position. You'll have gas," she said, smirking.

I laughed and the thought of noisy gas loosened a memory of talking and laughing with my son about a man on the beach who had had remarkable flatulence and I couldn't laugh out loud about it at the time without being outrageously rude. I realized then that I had a young son and a little girl who were the greatest delight of my life and I was raising them alone. I remembered taking classes at a university and the man on the beach and his wife were my dearest friends and had been my teachers and mentors for the last several years.

They were an elderly Indian couple from the western Amazon of Brazil and were instructing me in their traditions and customs. I remembered how I first met the man, Domano, on the beach cliffs of Santa Cruz in a violent storm. From that moment on he and his wife, Chea, had forced me by their mere presence to re-evaluate all of my world and myself.

Their demeanor and knowledge as shamans had challenged everything I held as true and worthy of pursuit. Since I had met them several years before my life overflowed with passions and terrifying challenges. The unexpected haunted my every turn, and I had grown to need and love it all.

My mind filled with the preparations that we had made for a quest. We had traveled far in a spirit journey to the great forests of the Amazon and then a long and hard climb up into the Andes to a craggy cave Chea said was the very one that she had had ceremony in. She said that they would wait for me at the entrance. I had asked her what kind of ceremony it was going to be, what was the purpose. She said there was nothing she could say, no way to describe it or prepare myself as I had often been able to do with the other quests they had sent me on, that each person's experience here was far too unique to do that.

As I was leaving them to walk into the jagged hole in the rocks, there was the smell of wet dirt and a sensation that made my flesh vibrate. I was becoming afraid. Chea instructed me to breathe through the fear and let it be my helper or it would pull me all the way off my quest and I would find myself drifting from dream to spirit walk to dream. I nodded to her and then stepped into the darkness of the opening.

"This is the right ceremony that I've been in. Isn't it?" I asked the odd woman. "This is it. The quest. The thing I came for."

"I remember coming into the cave. I must have gotten swept up with my fear and fallen into sleeping. I remember now, plummeting in and out of dreams. What is all this?"

"This is how a kala keh nah seh, a storyteller, is born," she answered. "Born from the heart of the Mother, from her flesh. This is what you asked for."

"What do you mean, 'this is what I asked for'?"

She just shook her head.

"But…"

The woman smiled and put her finger to her lips. "Stay present. It is good that you remember. Now be here, in your body. There are things we have to do here."

She helped me up and over to the edge of the spring and began to rinse me with the clear water.

When most of the loose mud was off my skin she stopped and moved around in front of me. "Soon it will be time for you to go. But before you can, I must tell you how you return to this underworld and gain knowledge to help your people."

"But...I'm not a kala keh nah seh," I said. "I can't do those things. What are you telling me for?"

"You have been born, here, as those before you were born. Your life from now on can no longer be 'ordinary.' No matter what you do, the knowledge of this world will come to you. We give this because you have asked."

"You keep saying that." I was puzzled but felt no anxiety or anger. "What do you mean, 'I asked for this?' I never asked for anything like this. I never asked to be burned, or to forget everything, even my name."

"Stop wasting your time concentrating on being confused. Just pay attention to what is happening now, to what I tell you. Eventually you will have enough of the pieces for it to make sense to you. You will see. Now you make sure you keep relaxed. *Enjoy things.*" She waited for me to respond but I didn't. "Just trust your Song—pay attention and remember all this."

I nodded but I still didn't understand why she was telling this to me.

"You are from the white culture. Aren't you?"

"Yes."

"Ahhh," she nodded and laughed. "That explains your determination to be confused again, even after it was all burned away. Remarkable people." She chuckled and patted my arm.

"Now, Kay, to get back to this place, first you must spirit journey through the forest up the same path that you took to get here. Your purpose must be clear in your mind and heart. Then you enter the cave. Bring nothing with you. Light no lamps or candles. You must make your way to the first chamber in the dark by yourself. Here you will find a torch lit or maybe a small fire. Here you wait. You will wait for a spirit woman to come. She will be your guide and teacher and will show you whatever you came to find, whether it is a special story or the answer to a problem or some particular knowledge that you seek. She and her spirit companions of this world can show you many things or take you many places."

"Will you be here? Can I see you again if I come back?"

"Yes. This is my home. Ask for me, the one who was your midwife. I will come.

"But you must have your attention pulled together. You must be able to hold onto your concentration and not give yourself to fear. Or you will not be able to get here or stay. Or maybe you won't remember anything, flipping back and forth through sleeping and spirit walking. You almost didn't make it here this time. You entered the cave very sloppy. You will have to do better than that. And you can, you know."

I nodded. More and more details of this whole quest were continuing to come back to me. I could see how I let my fear and lack of self-confidence pull me off center, giving my power away to them until I had nothing left to keep me in my quest.

"You must hunt for your power from now on." Her raspy voice was stern but I could hear the kindness. "Wherever you are, whatever you are doing. Watch how you spend your power. Who do you give it to? Where have you carelessly left it behind? Or never bothered to pick it up? You are different than when you first entered this cave. You are not the same person. That person that entered the cave was consumed in fire. You have been formed from the Earth. This is your birthplace now and life for you will be as the storyteller. You will live and hunt as a storyteller. That means an exploration for beauty and knowledge and caring that takes up a lifetime. You must be willing to accept your own power—to own it—to live it."

"But what is power?" I asked. "What do you mean by saying, 'power?'"

"It is what allows you to make every movement, to think a thought, to dream a wish. When we come into this world we are perception stretching out into action. We desperately want to experience 'aliveness'—from each moment to the next—a whole lifetime of moments. So to choose your action and cause it to happen, you aim yourself. You collect yourself and focus. That is power. You collect all the pieces of your attention and put them toward your goal. This is your task. And now you must take it seriously. No more of this on-again-off-again stuff. This is for real. It is full time for you, now, ever since you walked into this cave."

So this was the quest: to die and live again, to be made into something new, something able to perceive and move through life with

FIRE, CLAY, BONES AND CAVES

greater and clearer intensity, beauty, purpose, and peace. No wonder Chea and Domano had not told me the nature of this quest. Either I was ready or I wasn't. And it seems that I made it this far only by the skin of my teeth.

I remembered the seizures of dying once before, when I met Death and Destiny in a clearing near the Hetakas' home. There was the absolute horror of losing all that I could say was mine, and the irresistible, intoxicating lure of the potentials within my future. Hearing Destiny's calling and knowing that I was dying and would never be able to taste any of these promised triumphs that were being dangled in front of me was more than I could ever hope to bear. I had crumbled under the grief and terror of it. I couldn't tell which was worse, the dying and losing of all that I had known and had or the losing of everything that I *could* have had and been. And now, here it was again, only the dressings were a little different; this time I'd been meticulously prepared to take the future, by the throat if necessary. I felt strong and alive and ready.

I knew Destiny was out there waiting for me, just daring me to follow her. I could hear her singing somewhere far off in the caverns. It's as though I was given another chance, and now there were guideposts to help me along. The draw to follow her was impossible to ignore. I looked over at the woman who called herself my midwife.

"You must go now." She smiled up at me with her lips closed, scooped up a handful of mud out of the spring and rubbed it down the front of my chest and belly. "Remember."

I sucked a breath in from the shock of the heat and nodded. There was nothing left to say. I had to go out the little tunnel that led back to the rest of the cave. Destiny's Song was out there moving farther away into the distance and I couldn't afford to lose it. I looked back at the cavern walls and the spring and the woman. And then I left.

I had to stoop over to walk through the shaft. The light was soon too far away to make anything visible. I held my hands out to feel my way. It was a long, tight shot to the next chamber, and as I stepped out into it I could no longer hear Destiny's Song. I groped around the room to find a way out and realized that I was depending on her singing to lead me. I had expected it to be there for me. Why would it have stopped?

I clambered and stumbled around the circumference but could not even find the tunnel I had entered by. A fatigue was wearing me down. I sat on the ground to rest and think of what to do next. The rock underneath me felt smooth and warm, so I stretched out, laying my face on the surface, and fell asleep.

I dreamed of a nude woman with a large belly and dozens of breasts. She was holding fruits and grains in one hand and a cup of liquid in the other. Part of her long hair was piled up high on her head with flowers. Birds were nesting there. Creatures of every kind surrounded her, many of them suckling. Her smile held the raptures and pains of an ageless maternity. She was humming and the creatures hummed with her. It was a gentle, quiet collection of sounds that ebbed and swelled like the seas. There was something ancient and very familiar about her and the music, but I could not place them.

She offered me her food and the drink from her cup. I felt as though I hadn't eaten for days and I was very thirsty. Her meal contented me. I thanked her and she held out her arm to make a place for me in her lap. I curled up and closed my eyes, restful and lulled by her voice.

When I awoke I found myself alone in the dark. The dream was strong with me and I could still feel the warmth and comfort of the lap I had been in. I thought about the Many Breasted Woman as I sat there and then, faintly, in the distance was Destiny's Song. I scrambled to my feet and felt my way toward the sound, down another craggy passage. These tunnels felt endless and I wondered if I would ever live on the surface again.

My eyes were becoming accustomed to the dark. I could make out faint shapes and get an idea of the size of the chambers that I was in. Sometimes I heard variations of sounds that it seemed the cave itself was making, and I felt huge waves of energies not unlike electrical fields. They felt like they must be special places in the body of the Earth, similar to nerve bundles or vital organs. On several occasions, what little I could see moved in great tall spirals. Some of these spirals seemed to be pouring out the world on their current and others seemed to be collecting pieces of the surroundings and sucking them away through their center.

I recognized them. They were what the Hetakas called gates, natural phenomena that tied the webs of the worlds together and could be used to travel from one location to another. But then I'd hear the seductive Song again that was pulling me and I was off, following it down tunnels that seemed to be shaped along lines of force running between the spirals.

I kept thinking of the Many Breasted One that I had dreamed about. There was something remarkably similar about how she felt and the way the whole of these caverns with their spring and even the rock walls themselves felt. They were both nurturing and sensuous. And each of them, being filled with tremendous energies, seemed deeply impassioned with form. In the cave I was being cradled by the two of them, cared for and secure.

As I walked on I could see a faint light up one of the long, inclining shafts. The voice that I was seeking came from there. I hurried toward the light as fast as I could and found myself in the same large chamber where I had been burnt. The light was coming from the old torch which had been propped up in the rock wall. My ashes were still on the ground. I walked over to the pile and bent down to touch them.

There was a memory of the destruction and terror in this place, but the feeling was different now. This was a part of the whole, a part of the cycle of things here, and fit naturally and harmoniously into its balance. There was no further need for burning, that was behind me now. I was not afraid or repulsed, but found myself admiring this room and its history.

"Kay."

I turned to see who had called me but no one was there.

"Kay."

This time I walked back and forth through the chamber looking and listening.

"Hello? Is somebody here? Where are you? Is it the midwife?"

There was a long silence. I stood still, in the middle of the hall.

"Kay!" It echoed around the cavern. I couldn't tell where it was originating from.

I stepped backward until I bumped the wall and realized that I was not far from the torch. I walked over and grabbed it. It seemed now that the best thing to do might be to search the edge of the room for tunnels leading out.

I examined the rock wall carefully as I walked around the big cavern. There were so many passages. I was reluctant to pick one and thought perhaps I should wait here for a while longer until I heard a voice that I could follow. As I stood arguing with myself the familiar, eerie Song came clearly from the tunnel to my right. She sang and called my name and sang again. It was Destiny who had been calling me.

Holding the torch before me I made my way up the tunnel after the sound. There were many curious things in the rocks and I thought I saw ruins. As much as I wanted to stop and investigate, I didn't dare. I was too worried that I might lose the trail I was following and thus lose what was propelling me into my future—my best future I thought. Perhaps as the midwife had said, I would return someday and could investigate these things to my heart's desire. The cave floor rose steeply. Running became climbing. I was panting hard, making it difficult to keep up with the voice.

The chase labored on for hours upon hours, until there, like something almost forgotten, was the light from the coming dawn outside. The voice melded with the brightness. I walked out into the open sky where the wind was blowing freely. It was herby sweet from the plants in the forest. Smiling at me from the rocks that reached all the way out into the brambles sat Chea and Domano. They motioned for me not to speak.

"This was good," said Domano. He took my right hand and pulled himself to his feet. The breeze rustled into my hair and there were little birds everywhere calling up the sunrise.

"Set the torch in there." Chea pointed to the stone floor just inside the entrance. Then she took my other hand and led us to a narrow path not far from where they had been sitting. Monkeys ran screeching around the treetops and as the first light darted through the branches everything woke up and moved.

We started into the foliage. I turned to look, one last time, and there in the opening stood the spirit woman who was my midwife. She picked up the torch, raised it in the air to me and then disappeared back into the darkness.

Chea tugged my hand, "It is time we must return now."

TWO

TRAPPED IN A BROKEN WORLD

THE next few days were like a fog for me. I didn't know how long I had spent in the cave with the midwife. My thoughts lay heavy on those experiences, which left my whole life seeming out of focus. I dreamed about the Many Breasted Woman each night. She was familiar and comforting. I knew her well, yet I could still not remember from where or how. Deep in the night she sang to me and told me about her home and her children.

It was March and spring was already showing itself in the meadows and forest floor. New green grasses were everywhere and delicate, tiny flowers of white and pink and red. It was difficult to take a step without injuring them. The Sun was out. The sky was crystal clear and the air fresh and warm. I was back on campus and walking to all my classes and it seemed a shame to go indoors and miss it all. As fate would have it though, finals were in a few days. I couldn't afford to lose any class time.

Integrating my new experiences into the rest of my life was always difficult, and the last few days even more so. Time with the

Hetakas was so intense. It was passionate and vital and riddled with the unexpected. It always pushed me beyond my limits, while my conventional life was predictable, redundant and ordinary. I felt I was splitting in two. I wanted to somehow blend the two, to enrich each of them with the other, to live one through the other. But I didn't know how.

It was Friday and I took the long path around the campus through the meadows and forest to my English composition class. We had spent the entire quarter writing hundreds of small assignments of descriptions. They ranged from single sentences to paragraphs and now to several pages. I had written about everything from the smell of burnt toast to the sound of an old, troubled car. I was running out of ideas to write about. As I entered the classroom I hoped the instructor had something else in mind for us to work on.

I had no such luck. He assigned us a complex description, five to six pages long, to be ready to hand in on Monday, and as was the case with all his assignments, we were not allowed to work from anything that we had already written. I was drawing a blank. I couldn't think of anything new to write about.

Then the thought occurred to me to write about some experience I had had with the Hetakas. My mind was always on events that had taken place with them over the years. These were the things in my life that propelled me and inspired me from a very deep level. If I was supposed to draw from the best of my life experiences and try to capture their moods, feelings and surroundings, then it made sense to try to write about some of these as well as the domestic events. The instructor was the only one who ever saw the papers and, if I took the event out of context and changed the names of any people or places, what harm could that do? Would that still fall under the rule for silence about anything concerning the Hetakas or their traditions? He wouldn't really know what I was talking about and I would have an opportunity to try to express something that was important to me. I was also very curious to see if I could tell a story even partially as well as Domano. There was a sense of challenge in the prospect.

The more I thought about it the more I wanted to try it, and the guiltier I felt about possibly breaking the rule of silence. Perhaps this would be a way to help integrate the factions of my life. I was, here again, trying to catch any opportunity to interact with or think about my worlds that would help the two influence and highlight each other. But I'd had very little success.

Well, I would have to give this serious consideration. As soon as class was over I was due at an appointment with the Hetakas. Perhaps I would ask them about the question and settle the whole issue.

I arrived at their home on schedule and the Sun was shining in through the curtainless window onto the wicker bench where I always sat. The Hetakas were as friendly and casual as ever. Domano was in the kitchen fixing French roast coffee and Chea was in the bedroom folding laundry. She hollered at me to come in and help her. I really wanted to sit in the sunlight while it still shone in through the window but I went into the bedroom to give her a hand. I hadn't been in that room very often. It felt like a very private space.

Chea turned her head to smile at me and then reached over their bed and pulled up the window shade. These were the only two furnishings in the room.

"There," she said and hugged me. "That should take care of your worries about the light. Hello, young one. You've been doing well."

The golden light covered me and flooded the room. It was like a shot of vitamins. I soaked in as much as I could while I helped Chea fold the laundry. I had no idea they had so many clothes. I'd always thought of them as having so few possessions, living the austere life. To look around their sparse apartment I would never have guessed that hidden back in the closets were all these things.

"What did you find in the cave, Kay?" Chea spoke without looking up.

I couldn't breathe for a moment. I didn't know what to say. I tried to catch her eyes to perhaps get some idea of which part I should talk about. All the many events of the quest jolted around in my head and my stomach and I didn't have a clue which one was the most important.

I folded the T-shirts. There was only the sound of the fabric moving and this old woman's breathing.

The feeling of the cave was still strong in me. Chea opened the window and the musk from the ground outside had the same smell as the wet air in the big cavern. Since the quest I felt different inside my body somehow. My mind was very active with concepts and memories, but thoughts as words and sentences were not fighting

TRAPPED IN A BROKEN WORLD

to crowd out everything as they had in the past. It was as though they had less of a grip on my muscles and organs. They weren't digging in and festering there but rather drifted lightly on around and through.

I pulled a pile of socks over to my side of the bed and copied the way Chea had rolled the others.

She still had not spoken. Thinking of the burning in the cave now, with her focus on me, made my innards roll. I did not feel afraid; it was more like a nervous anticipation that I could put no words to. It just tumbled through my gut and faded into a dull buzz. I thought about the fear that I had had when my body was burning.

"Chea," I finally said. "I was so terrified in that cave. I've never felt that much fear before. I don't think that I will ever be that afraid again. Ever."

"Hmm," she still did not look up.

"It feels as though I won't ever have to be that terrified again. That was like the grand finale. The first prize in the fear contest."

"And you won, did you?"

"I think so," I answered. She glanced up and we laughed. I loved the way the wrinkles on her face softened and turned up around her eyes when she laughed. There was just a small slit left for one dark eye to peer out of. It caught the sunlight like a prism.

"Chea..." I hesitated to bring up what was really bothering me about my experience. "This is going to sound really bizarre. I had a really bizarre reaction to my fear in there. I mean, I'm really shocked at it. It seems kind of sick, you know?" I knew that I should tell her and perhaps she would help me understand. But voicing it seemed to give it even more realness. "When I was burning in the cave and unable to move, I didn't just feel fear. I felt all kinds of pains, and... pleasures. All kinds of things in my life that had been intense and important to me. Horrors. Sensual delights. My god, Chea, even sexual feelings. And they didn't even seem weird at all at the time."

I looked at her for a reaction. She remained her usual stone-faced self. She was silent, waiting for me to continue.

"The fear was so consuming. And the loss! I was so miserable. I hurt in my body and my feelings more then I ever thought possible. And at the same time came all these other feelings. Enjoyable feelings and sensations. They were separate, but somehow there was something connected about them. At the time it was so natural feeling. It seemed like the most obvious and natural response in the world. When I thought about it a day or so later it looked a bit masochistic to me. Is that as perverted as it appears?"

Chea's face remained plain except for the slight raising of one eyebrow. "Is that all?" she asked.

"That's not enough?" I smiled a little, trying to avoid the seriousness that I felt about it.

She didn't laugh. Her face was still unchanged.

"No. That's not all. I...uh." I coughed and cleared my throat and thought, Oh, what the hell. Here it goes. "While I was in the middle of feeling all those things, I felt my Song. The stronger, the more intense the experience was, the more intense my Song was. The more intense the ecstasy of the Song was. Even in the midst of the most horrible pain and terror! I felt so alive! Chea! It was as though I was feeling my whole life's aliveness all at once. It's as if everything there is about me that is alive cried out all at once. As loud as it could, crying out its sorrow and desire and pleasure and its pain and ecstasy. I hated it...and I loved it."

Chea grinned and nodded at me knowingly. Her eyes became transparent, as though I could see into their darkness to somewhere deep inside her. "Yes. That is the way it is. That is a secret about Humans. At the bottom of the most tragic of pains there moves the Song. Always. The more intense the pain, the stronger the Song is felt; but not everyone identifies it as such." She looked satisfied and proud for me.

"But that doesn't make any sense to me. Your Song is your joy. A feeling of passion. It's beautiful. How can we feel it in our pain? That's a contradiction."

"Not really." Chea picked up a stack of shirts and walked to the closet to put them away. "The Song of a thing is like its signature, its identity. This aliveness has a feeling to it. And everyone's 'feeling' is different from everyone else's. It is there at the heart of a thing, with all its life's events and properties coming from it. Like a wellspring. Whatever we experience, there underneath it, almost as if it was hiding, but so alive, sings our Song. You see, even through great tragic pain one can come to find their Song, their center, their passion. If they can grab it and hold on, they can ride the waves of pain, like an anchor in a storm, a light to steer by. They can come to truly know themselves."

I had no idea how to think about this concept. It seemed so foreign to me. I was going to need much more time with it.

"There are many roads to *ka ta see*, to the balance. Sometimes we need a more drastic one. Be careful not to judge the paths to god. It might be the one you are standing on."

I laughed and looked down at my feet. "Speaking of god, there was something else about my Song that I noticed, Chea. I don't know why I didn't catch this before. You and Domano never mentioned it and that kind of makes me wonder why, 'cause it seems so central, so basic. Well, when I felt my Song, and sometimes it was pulling me toward my center, it felt like a calling out to Creator, I think—like a cord that I can talk to Creator on."

"Ah!" She nodded slightly.

"Why didn't you tell me before?" I just stood there and kept holding the jeans that I had started to fold. "It seems like kind of an important thing to know."

She took the pants from me and finished folding them. "You would not have learned it. It is a knowing that one has to come across for themselves, or it never has any reality or power. This understanding of sending your voice into the Great Mystery, of what prayer really is, this is yours now, never to be shaken. You have lived it. That is true knowing."

Domano yelled from the kitchen, "I think these cookies are real done now. And French roast coffee, too. Come you two. Come and sit in the sunlight. We can get fat together."

Chea and I laughed. We left the rest of the laundry on the bed and went into the living room to join Domano.

Domano and I hugged and greeted each other. He was wearing a T-shirt and blue jeans and his feet were bare. He held the plate of cookies he had just baked as though they were something that might be a source of ridicule and, with a forced smile on his face, he set them in the middle of the floor. I walked around the plate and sat in my usual spot on the little wicker bench next to the window. There were a few more minutes of direct light left to come in before the Sun sank behind the Pacific Ocean. I picked up my coffee and a cookie and leaned back against the glass.

The cookies looked scrambled and overcooked but they smelled good. They stuck together when I tried to pick up a piece. I wasn't sure if they were supposed to be chocolate chip or what. The color was all wrong, as though he had accidentally added something to the batter. As I started to take a bite Domano wrinkled his face slightly and twitched his upper lip.

I had to laugh. Chea remained tightly straight-faced as though this was all very serious and we had to maintain our most polite face forward. However, I noticed that she had not yet taken a cookie. She just sat there being overly mannered.

As I put the cookie to my mouth again, Domano looked truly embarrassed. Now I wasn't sure if I wanted to take a bite, but with the two of them staring at me I was socially committed to sampling Domano's hard work. It was obviously his first baking attempt. I couldn't help but think of the first things my kids had baked. Domano's cookies made them look like culinary masterpieces.

I took a sip of my coffee instead and looked again at the plate on the floor. It really did look bad. Actually, disgusting was more to the truth. I couldn't remember ever seeing anything cooked come out so badly. Politeness insisted that I not wait any longer to taste the cookie. I lifted it to my mouth and bit.

It crunched delicately and melted over my tongue. The sweet, sensual smell rose up in my face. There was vanilla and deep chocolate with the flavors of many roasted nuts, each light and full unto itself. It could very well have been the best tasting cookie I had ever eaten. I felt joyful just in the chewing and tasting of it. How he ever managed to get something that tasted that good to look so bad was a mystery to me.

I looked up at both of them. Their expressions hadn't changed.

"Well?" Domano asked. "You don't have to be polite. Tell what you really think."

"The flavor and texture are fabulous!" I said. "Really." He acted like he didn't believe me. "They are truly an experience of joy and... awe, not to be missed."

"Oh," he laughed as though he knew something marvelous that I didn't. "Like many things in life, I suppose.

"What were you two talking about so quiet in the other room? I could not hear any of the good parts."

"Is that what happened to your cookies?" Chea laughed. "You were straining so hard to hear us instead of paying attention to them."

He raised his hands in the air and tilted his head.

"She wants to understand the Song," Chea said. "Go ahead, master chef. Tell her something about the Song. The gift of the south."

"Oh." He reached down for a cookie. "I better get one fast here, now, before Kay eats all these."

When he said that I realized that I had eaten nearly half the plateful already. I had to laugh.

"Grab now or forever hold your peace," Chea reached down quickly and took several big hunks. We all laughed.

"The Song is always there." Domano tapped his chest. "It is just people don't pay any attention. They always find a way to have themselves looking in some other direction.

"You know how to feel your Song. You know what that feeling is like. But you still do not understand what that feeling really is.

"It is the core of what you are. Inside. It is what your aliveness feels like. That drive to live. The yearning to experience. That is the mysterious you that is left after the masks have been eased aside." He reached down to get another cookie. "These do taste kind of good, don't they?" And he grinned at me like a sly old fox.

"But now, don't confuse these. The masks and thoughts are another bunch of 'melodies' separate from the Song. We are real familiar with our masks. They are what makes us who we think we are. They are how we hide, how we shut out the rest of the world so it can't hurt us. But through any thought and feeling, even the most worst, our Song is there, underneath. We can feel this. Is this not what you felt? In the cave?"

I nodded. "It was kind of like those feelings, even the awful ones, were the catalyst to finding my Song. After I had gotten home and thought about it, it seemed so strange to me. It scared me. I always thought it was the exciting, the joyful, things that brought up your Song. This just doesn't fit for me."

"Even in bloody battle," Domano licked his fingers, then wiped them on his jeans, "men can come the closest in their whole life to feeling their Song because Death is at their side and in their nostrils. They slaughter. They risk their existence. And that is the moment when their livingness is felt the strongest to them. That is when their real identity is the closest at hand. Do you see? They are feeling everything that is horrible and righteous and fearful and glorious. They are valiant in defense of their god. They are the worst their minds can imagine—and the greatest. Everything is at its most intense. In the strength of that aliveness they feel their Song."

"Domano," I said, "have you ever been in battle?"

"Yes." He replied so matter-of-factly. I wondered when that was and with what people. But I didn't ask.

"When we feel our Song," he said, "it carries with it the flavors of what brought it to our attention. Don't confuse this feeling with the Song. Do you see?"

"Yeah," I answered.

Chea studied my face. There was a long silence before she spoke. "Aliveness, the Song of things, has a feeling to it all its own. It feels like love. Like being in love. It is clear and moving and alert. It is a pleasant feeling. That is why we can find it so easily by concentrating on feelings that are joyful and loving."

Domano reached for the last cookie and looked up at me through the corners of his eyes. "The more you feel this Song of yours, the better you truly know who and what you really are. You know all your masks and the superstitions that drive them. You are able to live without the masks controlling you. Then this is when you can choose to put a behavior on, like a costume, to serve your purpose—if you choose. When you truly understand and know yourself then you have your attention in your heart and under your control. To know yourself is to know power.

"You see, a people who know their Song have no use for starting war. But a people who live without their Song in their life live in self-importance and fear, separated from all things. Trapped in a broken world. Our elders used to say that those people 'live in death,' because to them life *is* a brutal war."

"Sounds lonely," I said.

"Yes. It is." Domano picked up the empty plate and took a few steps toward the kitchen. He stopped and said, "I ask you this. Just what sort of people are we? What is our place among the peoples of the stars?"

I didn't think, the answer stumbled out of my mouth automatically. "An embarrassment."

"That's closer than you know," he said almost inaudibly as he turned and went into the kitchen. Silence followed his footsteps. I looked out the window to find the Sun setting. It was red and the color came out across the western sky like the spreading of blood on a pool of water.

It was late. I needed to get home to my kids. I got up and said goodbye, making arrangements for meeting them on Sunday.

The next day I studied for finals. By late evening I was ready to work on my English assignment and realized that I had forgotten to ask the Hetakas whether or not I could use images out of context from any of my experiences.

I was running out of time. It was Saturday. I had already made arrangements for all of Sunday and I had to turn in the English assignment on Monday. I needed to make a decision very soon so that I could write the whole paper that night. I argued the pros and cons back and forth until I finally managed to talk myself into writing a description from my journey through the jungle to find the "masks." I concentrated on the time we spent crawling through the mud in a hidden tunnel cut out from underneath an impassable thicket.

It was great fun. I went over and over each phrase and word, playing with it first one way then another until I had it just right. I was up most of the night. I felt I had done a fantastic job, possibly the best I had ever written for a class.

When I woke up the next morning I was beginning to feel guilty. Should I have written it? Maybe I should tear it up and burn it. It was just a description of the hardships of crawling through bugs and thorns and other exotic difficulties. It wasn't as though I had written about the ceremonies or the teachings, or analyzed the events in any way. It was just a fragment of a physical description. But the farther in the day it got, the guiltier I felt.

I decided to put it away for the moment and get ready to meet the Hetakas. It was really something I should be asking them for advice on. I had just enough time to shower and still catch the bus to Capitola for our meeting.

I had been so busy preparing for finals I hadn't spent much time during the last days thinking about the burning in the cave and my confusion about that experience. While in the middle of a questing experience I often feel that I have some understanding. But when

I contemplate the events later that quality of things making sense sometimes fades.

When I arrived at our agreed upon location near the beach, Chea and Domano were waiting for me. We walked over the ice plant and down onto the rocks along the water's edge. The glare of the sunlight off the waves almost hurt my eyes. The tide was low and the sea had left behind many beautiful little pools scrambling with life and activity. We stopped at each one to see who was there and what they were up to. Domano picked up a variety of old snail and hermit crab shells as we went along.

Chea touched my arm and asked, "On your spirit journey where the burning took place, where was that? Tell me, where were you?"

I wondered why she would ask such an obvious question. I looked up at her and stuttered, "Well...we went to South America, to the Andes...right?"

"Stop whining. Not the geography, Kay." She picked up a handful of sand and held it out to me. "Where was the place you were in? What was there? What kind of place? Think back and remember the feeling of the place. What was that feeling?"

"The feeling?" I stopped walking to think. "It was a cave. It was dark and kind of dank."

She held out the sand again. "Maybe it would be better to ask who was that feeling?"

I shook my head. "Who? The midwife? The midwife was the only other one there."

"What was that cave?" She shook her fist with the sand in it. "What did you feel in that cave? It has a Song all its own. Whose Song was that?" And she opened her hand and let the sand fall.

She was right. Now that she pointed it out I could remember a very strong presence throughout the entire cave. There was something familiar about it but I could not identify it.

"Then you must search for this one whose Song you felt," she said. I tensed up. She broke into a big smile. "Ease up. You act like I just sentenced you to Siberia. All you have to do is to pay attention and watch for that Song. And then feel where it is coming from and who it belongs to. Like a game. Can you remember when you felt it before?"

I couldn't. She coaxed me and led me to think of many other experiences that I had had, but I could not place the feeling.

"This is OK," she assured me. "This will be a quest. No matter how long it takes, or where you go. This will be a task for you."

"That is a good one." Domano poked me in the side and laughed lightly. "You are getting real heavy again. This is play. It is serious, but it is play too. Let yourself enjoy it. A quest is a challenge. Pay attention to what your senses are telling you, feel your Song and hunt in excitement and joy. Not dread. Come on now. Lighten up."

I nodded.

"Domano," I said as we sat down around a tiny pond full of hermit crabs. "If our Song is, as you said Friday, something different than our masks and our thoughts, even different than the thoughts that can call our Song to our attention, then how do you tell them apart? What is it that makes up our identity? Aren't we all of the things that we feel and that have happened to us? Our habits and our quirks? Don't these things make us who we are?"

"Sure they do." He reached in the water to grab one of the crabs that was running across the bottom. It was bigger than most of them and had a slightly spotted shell. "But these things change each day you live. Each hour. When I say 'identity' I am talking about the part of you that is never distorted by all the storms and currents and chaos of the daily life. The thing that is the source of your livingness—your Song. That is your true identity. The others are unreliable. They are your masks. It's kind of like we 'rent-a-face' for every occasion.

"When masks run your life, they war among themselves to take control over you. You act on automatic. You build your image of yourself out of them. This is like trying to walk on a floor that is made of paper. That web is clumsy and falls apart very easily. Masks are very superstitious characters. They are shallow, incomplete, unstable, and they limit you more than what you can imagine. A thing goes wrong in your world and all of a sudden you do not know who to be to deal with it. Your confidence is shaken. Your reality does not have a ground to stand on."

A warm wind came up hard off the water from the south. It had been soft and chilly most of the day. "Like a screwy automatic pilot, huh?" I asked.

"Something like that." He chuckled and grabbed again into the water for the crab. "Ah! He is a little booger, this guy. I'll catch him this time. You see." And he splashed from one end to the next until he pulled up a hermit crab and held it out with a big proud smile.

"That's not the same one." Chea shook her head. "That's a different one. You're cheating. That little fellow is too tricky for you." He let the smile sink off his face and put the crab back in the water. "You're going to have to do better than that."

Domano looked into the water. "Where is he? Hey, you little guy. Where are you? Come out and meet your challenge. This is no time to hide. Your adversary is here. And I say, 'I challenge you today. Come. Come and face me.'" He watched the water as though he expected the crab to have heard and understood his words.

Chea leaned over and watched the pool with as much care as he did. I didn't know what to expect. I felt a little silly. I looked back and forth between each of them and the water. After a few moments the crabs had scuttled off to the sides of the pond, leaving the center area relatively clear. Then some of the crabs moved aside from a little crag in the rocks, and out from underneath came the hermit crab in the spotted shell. He walked to the middle and stood defiantly with his claws up and ready to strike.

Domano nodded and shifted his position so that his legs were squarely and stably under him. Then, reaching over the pond from the side so his shadow did not cross over the crab, he eased his hand in the water and made a remarkably fast lunge.

"Ah!" Domano yanked his hand out. "That fellow is a worthy opponent. He got me." I could see a scratch on his fingers as he reached back down into the water. There was shuffling and splashing and I could see the crab as it darted from spot to spot avoiding Domano's grasp. The two of them were very fast and concentrated. I wouldn't have laid bets on either one at this point.

Domano suddenly yanked his hand out of the water again. There was another scratch down the outside of his little finger. He took the shells out of his pocket and sprinkled them in the pond around his opponent. "Now I've got him. He will not be able to keep from trying out these new shells for a house. He will forget about me and run out of his shell and then in and out of all the other shells. It is their weakness. They can't help themselves."

He sat poised over the water as we watched. The spotted crab stood unmoved in the middle of the pool with his claws out. He didn't

TRAPPED IN A BROKEN WORLD

seem to care at all about the empty shells. The other crabs however, became quite curious and inched their way toward the center. Then, like crazed shoppers at a garage sale, they began to leave their own shells behind, scrambling from one new shell to the next, just as Domano had said. But the spotted crab remained still and waiting.

"Ah. Yes." Domano nodded very slightly. "He knows. He is truly worthy." He slid his hand into the water to approach the crab from the front. They were motionless for a long time. Each waiting for the other to falter. Finally Domano lunged at the spotted crab. He was able to touch him but not grab him, while the crab managed to strike Domano's hand for a third time. They backed away from each other and Domano said, "You meet your challenge in a good way my little friend. You have won well today. I honor you and your family."

The spotted crab retracted his claws and Domano removed his hand from the water. The other crabs were still unconcerned with the battle, running from shell to shell. I glanced up at Chea and Domano. They were looking softly at each other. I was going to ask about the challenge but I didn't want to interrupt.

We got up and walked in silence to the other tide pools. There were starfish, sea urchins, kelp and many other things I did not know the names of.

Chea turned her face into the wind. It was now intermittently warm and cold. "Can you say that you know your identity, Kay?"

"I know what my Song feels like," I answered. "And if that's my identity then I can say I know what my identity feels like. I know my masks. I mean I know at least what my masks are. The details of who they are, how they work, I don't see all of that. I certainly felt them all in the cave. Like old friends. I felt each one leave as it went up in the smoke and steam. You know I actually grieved for them. I was finally free of their entrapments, and yet I actually grieved for their leaving me. But, to answer your question, no, I don't think I 'know' my identity."

Chea's face seemed stern but caring. I felt like she could see right through me. "That is the trick of it all. To learn what and who you truly are. What your place is. What does it mean to you to be on this planet, under that star? That is what it means to walk the spiral path. To stand in the center at the foot of the Great Tree. That is your center. That is what your Song teaches."

They had said these things many times before, but they were difficult concepts for me. "Even after all this time I have to say that this is so hard for me. Why am I still so overpowered by my masks? I stop and turn around and look at my day, and it's as though I was bumbling along in my sleep."

"It is simply a matter of choice," Chea said. "We choose from one moment to the next to be asleep or aware. And to live in pain and fear, or in pleasure and aliveness. If you are so afraid to relate to yourself, how can you relate to anything else?"

I plopped down in the sand. It was wet under the surface. Now I was becoming frustrated. "You're confusing me. Are you saying to turn away from my pain, like ignore it?"

"Not at all," Domano answered. "One always has to look at all of their life and their experience straight in the face. Head on. Know it. Understand it. Grow. And then leave it behind. Don't dwell in it like you were stuck in some broken record. That is what masks do. They replay the same pain or fear or numbness or reaction—over and over. It becomes our habit to feel this lie over and over, totally blind to what is really there, really happening, in that moment. It blocks out the Song. You see?"

I hesitated. "Yeah."

He clapped his hands. "Good. Let's get on our way back. It gets late now. I have to get home to take care of my duties. I'm going to cook something again, you know."

Chea and I looked at each other and laughed.

"What are you laughing at? How rude. You two show no respect. No respect."

"Yeah," I said. "You and that comedian on TV. 'I don't get no respect.'" We laughed and joked. I walked all the way into Santa Cruz with them along the beachfront road to their apartment near the Boardwalk and took a bus back home from there.

I got to my apartment after sunset and spent the evening with my kids. I was very tired. It was too late to write something new for my English class and I realized that I had again forgotten to ask the Hetakas whether I could use the description or not. I decided to turn it in anyway.

The next day I expected to hand in the assignment as the first activity of the hour. But as we were all preparing to pass our papers to the front, the instructor announced his intentions for a new process. We were to take these descriptions and pass them to the person to our left. We were going to read and comment on our peers' work.

I was mortified!

I quickly tried to think of any way I could get out of having to hand my paper to another student. Maybe if I feigned illness and asked to hand in my paper later—which wouldn't have been entirely untruthful. I was fast becoming quite sick to my stomach. I shook involuntarily. Perspiration was forming on my whole body.

When I asked the instructor if I could please be excused, he thought my request was "cute," and said he realized I had been just a housewife and he respected the fact that I was very shy, but we all have to learn to face the adult world sooner or later. He said if I hadn't come to college to learn that, what had I come here for? He refused to accept the paper late. I wished I could have thrown up all over his designer-hippie shoes.

My current grades for the class couldn't afford an F to be averaged in. I was trapped. I sat back in my chair and handed my paper to the young woman to my left. At least she seemed innocuous enough and almost as scared as I was.

We spent a quiet thirty or forty minutes examining and writing comments on the papers in front of us. Then the instructor suggested we talk to the owners of the description and voice our opinions. I stiffened and turned slowly to the left. I thought if I acted as uninterested and distant as I could she would be too uncomfortable to say much, and I would be able to interact as little as possible.

She looked at me with her eyes almost bugging out of her head and said in a remarkably loud, shrill voice, "Did you really do this? Where was this? Did you really crawl through the jungle?"

It was all I could do to shut her up. Everyone turned around and looked. I made as little of it as possible. "Of course not. Don't be silly. I just made that up."

Still just as excited and loud she kept on, "Oh! This is so real! Where did you go? Was it some kind of safari? It's so right there. You know this description. I can tell. Was this in Africa or the Amazon?"

My stomach pushed its contents up against my throat. I swallowed hard. My heart was beating like it was on a racetrack. My shirt was becoming wet under the arms. "Be realistic," I said as calmly and quietly as I could, trying to make her settle down and lower her voice, the way I do to hush my children. "I'm flattered that the writing impressed you. But I'm just a housewife. I made it up. You know, like something I make up to tell my kids at bedtime. This is just California. Remember? Just old planet Earth?"

I think I finally convinced her. I turned around to talk to the person whose paper I had read. The first woman waited a moment as though she had something else to say, then turned to her other partner. I was so thankful that was over, I swore to the powers that be that I would never, ever, do anything like that again. I felt I was starting to get a picture of why the silence rule was there.

I hadn't quite finished giving my comments to my other partner when the teacher instructed us to pass our descriptions to the person second to our left for yet another reading and comments.

I couldn't believe it. It was worth it to me at that point to take the F. I almost got up and left. I don't know why I didn't. I was on the verge of gagging. My head throbbed. My bladder felt extremely full and I could feel a good case of the runs building in my gut. I passed my paper on to the next person.

The reading of the papers dragged on unbearably long. Finally, it was time to change seats and talk. I braced myself. This woman looked a little older than the last, more conventional and subdued.

She rushed over to my chair before I could move and said almost as loudly as the first woman, "When did you go to the Amazon? You don't look old enough to have done all this kind of wild stuff! Was this some kind of ceremony?"

I gagged involuntarily. A bead of sweat ran down my face. I tried to keep the shaking of my hands from being noticed.

"Are you all right?" she asked. "You look awfully pale."

This was my chance. If she thought I was contagious maybe she would keep her distance and cut our conversation to a minimum.

"I have a flu. I couldn't afford to miss this class, though. I hope I don't infect you. I'm really sorry. Really. You don't have to stay here and make your comments. They're all on the paper aren't they?"

It worked. She set my assignment down on my desk and wished me well.

As class was ending the instructor asked for our descriptions with all their comments to be handed in. I plopped it down on his desk, incredibly relieved the whole thing was over and rushed out into the sunlight and fresh air. My symptoms faded away as I walked across the cow pastures on the long path back to my student apartment.

The next day in English class I avoided eye contact with the two women and did my best to be invisible. Our papers came back with the instructor's observations. He corrected my grammar and said this piece would make a fine short story. He wanted to know what the details were to have propelled me into such an adventure and where it ended up. What was its purpose? At least he agreed with me it was the best thing I had written to date.

I thought, now, with my paper in hand, I could take it home and burn it.

"Don't put those papers away yet," the instructor shook his finger at the class. "You guys get a special treat. You finally get to do some rewriting. Today in class and for your assignment tonight, you are to rewrite your long descriptions. Do a good job, people. This is going to be part of your final."

This wasn't possible. It was starting all over again. I couldn't think of any way to get out of it. My stomach turned sick. I wanted to crawl away and die in a hole somewhere. I tried to sit there in class and work on the paper. The entire time I was half expecting to be interrupted by the two women or to have to pass my work on to yet another person for evaluation again. The period turned out to be uneventful and I staggered out and on to my next class. That night I spent as little time as possible on the rewrite. The guilt was so uncomfortable that I could not bear facing my own words on the page. I slept little, tossing in and out of dreams of the burning cave.

The next day in class I felt as though someone had betrayed me and I was cornered into a vile and dangerous position. I wanted to strike out and retaliate, take revenge. Except I had no one to blame but myself. At that moment I wanted to be anyone else but me. I was repulsed at my own shortsightedness and lack of honesty. How I could have done such a thing I did not know or understand. I felt very undeserving of all the incredible things that had been given to me on my path. I suspected my time with the Hetakas was now going to come to an unfortunate end.

As I sat down the instructor ordered us to pass our rewritten papers to the person to our right. This was completely intolerable. My stomach began to turn again. I tried to think of something to do as fast as I could. I jumped up and slammed my paper down on the desk of the young woman who had read it the first time.

She started to object but I leaned over and told her I really wanted her to do the evaluation because I thought she had done such a good job before and I wanted to take advantage of her skills. She was flattered and consented as I had hoped she would. I really wanted her to read it so I didn't have to worsen my broken commitment any further. She took her task very seriously and made a number of excellent suggestions. We worked quietly until we were instructed to pass our work on to another student.

Again I raced to the second woman who had examined the paper before. She gave me no resistance and asked if I would be so kind as to do the evaluation on her work. I was more than happy to agree to the arrangement. We spent the rest of the period together barely saying a word.

Our evening's assignment was to rewrite the description yet a third time and hand in all the copies with all their respective comments. By now I was so mortified I was numb. This whole series of rewrites and evaluations was our final exam. If I wanted to pass I had no choice but to take the rewriting seriously, applying everything I could that I had learned in the class. I had no other finals the next day so I spent most of the night reworking and reworking the description and fell asleep on the couch, pencil still in hand.

This was our last class session and someone had brought cookies and coffee to share. We handed in our papers and were free to spend the rest of the time as we desired. I accepted a cookie and left early. I had an appointment with the Hetakas later that day and wanted the time to walk through the meadows and along the beach to their home. I was terrified it was going to be the last time I would ever see them.

When I arrived Chea opened the door and invited me in. She greeted me as usual and then turned away and went into the kitchen. She almost looked as if she were restraining herself from laughing. I wondered if I looked in particularly bad shape or if maybe there was something unsightly on my face. I had been blowing my nose a lot on the walk over; perhaps I had missed with my hanky.

I sat down on the bench and wiped my nose with my sleeves. They left me alone for a long time. I could hear them clanking around on the counter. I didn't know what I should say to them. Should I confess to them right away or wait? Should I tell them at all? What would happen if I never told them? How would they ever know about it if I didn't bring it to their attention? And if I did, it could mean the end of my training with them. They would probably disappear into the world somewhere and pick another student. I couldn't bear the thought of losing them and the experiences we had had together. But even harder was the feeling of not saying anything to them and trying to continue together as though nothing had happened. It would be the same as lying to them every time I saw them. I might as well be stabbing them in the back while taking all the richness they had so lovingly and carefully given to me.

No. I had to say something. Right away. The sooner I got it out the sooner I could stop waiting for the floor to fall out from under me.

Domano came into the room. I could smell the coffee being brewed. Chea opened the back door in the kitchen and a draft of cold air came past me. Domano hugged me and we said our usual hellos. He gave me a quizzical side glance. His eyes were playful and penetrating—they never left me.

I took a deep breath to begin to talk, but he laughed in bursts as though he was trying to hold it back. "Been doing some writing? Hmmmmm?" And he broke out in delighted laughter.

I must have been going into shock. My body wouldn't move. I couldn't figure out how he knew. My limbs started to shake. I felt cold yet I was perspiring and my heart was beating erratically. He should have been furious. Why was he laughing?

My body slumped back against the glass. Chea came into the room. I couldn't look at her. I was deathly afraid of whatever she would do. She said nothing and sat on the other bench.

Domano faced me square on. "You see the kind of webs our masks make? They have no ground. They twist and tear out of our control. They are formed from fibers of fear and they weave things like greed, dishonesty, self-importance, two-mindedness, guilt, dishonor. A person feels empty and separate, then binds the web up tighter and tighter trying to get control, trying to fill that hole in the web that has no bottom. And they can't.

"Learn your Song. Learn your masks. Refuse to take part in these broken webs and they pass into death of their own weight. Hold to your center and dance on your Song instead. It is the only way you can stay alive."

I began to cry. For the first time I could see what it really was I had been so careless with. It wasn't just a promise whose definition I muddled and misused, it was a whole way of life, a way of actually living in beauty and health. It was my truest friend. It was my very future.

Chea spoke from across the room, "The spiral path is a very narrow one. In the beginning it is difficult to walk on day after day. It will be the hardest thing you have ever done. But in time it will be more natural for you. Except by then the path is even narrower. You go from direction to direction as the spiral gets smaller and closer to the center. It seems faster and faster. Sometimes it is harder and harder."

Domano added, "Each direction has its own things to teach, its own way to see the world. Its own pitfalls." He smiled at me with all his teeth showing.

I didn't understand why he wasn't mad. He should have been yelling at me and kicking me out of his house. "Why are you so nice to me? Have I ruined it for myself? Are the teachings over now?" Tears ran down my face. I felt as though I had stabbed my most precious friends in the back. "Why are you smiling? I hurt you."

"You only hurt yourself, Kay," he said softly. "For your culture honesty and commitment are some of the hardest things to learn. It's like having big holes on the side of the path. You have to watch carefully with every action so you don't fall. The path is narrow. It's up to you to pick yourself up and continue the journey on the path or off. You learn from it or not. This is your choice. We are here to help you. It is not up to us to turn away from you."

Chea got up to get the coffeepot and turned at the kitchen door. "Commitment means a different thing for you now. Yes?"

"Yes," I answered. In a way I was relieved but I felt so awkward and ugly. I didn't deserve this chance.

She went into the kitchen. Domano stood up and looked out the window toward the Sun and said, "I will tell you some stories about the directions. The pillars. This is a good time for this.

"We look around our circle." He pointed all the way around the room. "They are the forces that weave together to build our world. The First Ones. The Oldest. They are the Wheel out there and the Wheel inside. Our people say they are the oldest of the old Grand-parents that sit with each direction and watch. We say Grandparents because for us this is the greatest respect. They are the Watchers, the helpers of each direction. The Grandmothers and Grandfathers of the directions. I'll tell you something about them.

"There is this Grandmother of the West and she is real harsh. But she loves the Humans. She guards the gate to the West. No one gets past her that does not turn their eyes to themselves, to their world inside themself. She sits in council with Death and Destiny. To one who walks in truth to themself she makes sure they see the ugly inside, all the ugly, as well as the beautiful. She is relentless but she makes a warrior very strong and persistent.

"One day a warrior came to her door. He said, 'Grandmother, I seek to be wise and worthy. Help me, please. I have nothing to offer to you but my respect and gratitude and my love. This is not much, but it is all I have. This is the desire in my heart. I want nothing else more in my life.'

"She looked at him and said, 'This is a difficult thing you seek. Are you sure this is what you want?'

"'Grandmother,' he says, 'I know nothing of your ways. I know only that I seek to be worthy.'

"'Then my door is open to you.' And she lets the warrior in and the door shuts behind him with a huge bang.

"He is about to thank her when she grabs him and tosses him into her mouth. He screams and fights for his life but it is no use. She just chews and laughs and says to herself how good he tastes. She says this one is a real wriggler. She enjoys him a lot, rolling him around in her mouth and crunching him with her teeth, swallowing the best parts, then she spits him into the big river that lives over in the West corner of the world.

"There is nothing in this deep water but him. A long time goes by. A real long time. And his body floats to the top of the water. The old Grandmother walks by the bank that day and sees him. She pulls him out and there is still a little spark of life in him. She shakes him real good until he opens his eyes, and she says, 'Why are you still alive? Why do you come to my feet again?'

"And he struggles to find thoughts and says, 'Because I seek to be worthy and wise.'

"'Well,' she tells him, 'I cannot help you any more right now. You will have to go find the elders of the North. But I will see you again someday.' And she throws him hard into the wind toward the corner of the North.

"Now these North Grandparents are full of compassion and kindness. The warrior comes crawling across their land calling to them, crying for their help. This one Grandmother who sees him runs over and carries him to her hut. She washes his body, gives him food and drink of his ancestors and a place to lay down. Her little humble home is full of the smells of food cooking and herbs drying. She is happy to care for him and sings to him until he falls asleep.

"He stays with her many seasons. She walks in council with the Mother Earth and they bring the life and strength back to his body. She teaches him the fixing of herbs, and the tending of the fields and animals. He works long and hard for the Grandmother. They love each other very much but the day comes when they know he must leave. It is time that his seeking takes him somewhere else. She tells him he must hunt for the Grandparents of the East and gives him what he will need for the quest.

"He sets out for the long journey to the corner of the East. Many things happen to the warrior as he travels and he becomes confused and loses his way. He is having a real hard time. One day he looks up from the ground and in front of him stands the old harsh Grandmother from the West. He knows now that he has come a great way off his path and is on the opposite side of the world from where he thinks he should be.

"She picks him up and says, 'You again? What are you doing here? So, you are no longer seeking to be worthy, hmm?'

"'But Grandmother,' he says, 'I do still seek. I've lost my way. Can you help me?'

"'Maybe,' she says. 'I bet you taste as good as ever.' And she bites off pieces of his flesh and throws him back into the river.

"He struggles and swims for a long time when Turtle finds him and gives him a ride down the river to the East. Turtle takes good care of the warrior, helping him heal from his wounds, and they share many tales of their lives on the long journey.

"When he gets to the corner of the East many years have passed since he first began his search. He wonders if he ever will be worthy and wise. But his dream is still in his heart and he can think of no other thing he would rather put his efforts to. So he asks to speak to the Grandparents of the East. They are very wise and see everything that goes on. There is no hiding anything from them.

"This Grandmother came to him and took him to her hut on the top of the nearby mountain. This house was open to the Stars and he could see far, far away into the valleys below. The air was clear and sweet. The sounds of the villages and the forests and the meadows moved through the sky with the calls of birds and the voice of the winds. The Grandmother said, 'Don't speak. Listen.' She pointed all around the land and the sky. 'Live among us here. Watch. And feel.'

"The Sun came and went, came and went. The seasons came and went, and came and went. She saw to his needs but would not spend time with him. One day she came to him and asked, 'Why do you sit here warrior? Don't you miss your people? Why don't you go home to them?'

"'I still seek to be worthy and wise, Grandmother. Every day my dream gets clearer. I will follow what you say.'

"'Then listen and watch and feel,' she says. And she left him there again. The Suns and the seasons passed. And the warrior's hair grew long and white.

"Now she came again to him one day in a dream and tells him it is time for him to take his quest to the South. He was afraid the journey was very long and hard and he was old now and might not make it to the end. She said to him, 'If your mind is full of only your purpose then you will succeed.' So, he sets out the next day.

"When he reaches the corner of the world in the South he is very happy. He goes to the elders and tells them of his quest. An old Grandmother takes him into her care. She puts her arm around him and they walk through the village. The children are laughing and playing and the old Grandmother laughs with them.

"'It is good to be alive,' he says touching the leaves of the trees and plants.

"'Yes,' says the Grandmother. 'Life feels good. It fills my heart and makes it sing. Like these little children. They know only their aliveness. They are so full it bounces out of them.'

"'Grandmother,' he says. 'Can I stay with you awhile and learn from you?'

"'Spend your time here, with these children. Enjoy yourself.'

"So this is what he did. The old warrior had lots of fun. And one day he and the old Grandmother were talking and he says, 'Grandmother, I've been to the four corners of the world. Where do I go next? What is left?'

"She says, 'There is the Spirit Place Above, and the Mother Below whose body is made from the four corners and the Above, and there is the Tree at the Center of All. Go to the Tree. There you can learn about all things.

"This was the old warrior's last walk. It was only a short ways to the Great Tree. The Sun was warm. Birds were singing around and there were many kinds of living things. He could taste the sweet of the flowers on the air. He looks around and takes a deep breath, 'Ahh!' he says. 'Yes.' He knows this place. It is the home he left those many long years ago."

The Hetakas had never told me exactly what the significance was behind the directions no matter how many times and ways I had asked for them to be explained. They would only tell me about them in story form. This story today was the clearest one yet, describing their meanings and functions as archetypal. I thought about how the other direction stories they had told me through the years compared to this one. And I wondered how it related to my life and my current struggles with commitment.

Even though they had taught me in story and in action of the difficulties of staying on the spiral path I felt very unprepared for this pitfall, both in not having seen it coming and in not knowing how to deal with it now that the mistake was done and over with. I was extremely uncomfortable. I felt stupid and morally deficient. It would have been easier if they had gotten angry and punished me. I didn't know how to act. I didn't know what was the proper thing for me to do now. Should I withdraw myself from the instructions out of respect and shame? Or would the correct thing to do be to remake my commitment to learning these traditions with more determined persistence, pursuing them now as a way of thinking, feeling and living with honor and equity?

"You said that you would not kick me out." I had to cough and clear my throat. "But does that mean that I should be the one to withdraw? I would rather stay and keep trying. I don't know what the proper thing is in your culture. What would be done in your tribe?"

Chea nodded. "Your questions show honest concern, Young One. This is a good thing." I felt something exciting and wonderful from her that wouldn't let my attention stray away. "You already made the decision of your direction when you chose to learn this way. This is your path. For the rest of your life this is the path you will walk. How you walk it, or stumble around it, is up to you. Whether or not we are together is for the spirit people to say. You will still be on this path, one way or the other."

This old woman was an enigma to me. She was not angry or disappointed or stressed in any way. Her face looked so beautiful. Sometimes it was almost as though she was observing me from some other world. The lines of time that carved her dark skin spoke of the thousands upon thousands of years that her people have lived and loved and gained. There was such knowing and curiosity, sternness and softness. She walked in pride but never arrogance. Her face was mystery itself. A steadiness in her eyes was always there. I wondered what she saw, what she had seen through her life. Would I have a chance to see even half as much before I died?

Domano picked up the coffee pot, "This is kind of cold now. But it still will taste good. Who wants some more? You want a little more?"

I looked at him blankly. He interrupted my train of thought and it took me a few seconds to understand what he had said. "Oh. Yeah. Have I ever turned down French roast?"

"No," he answered. "Never."

I thanked him and looked out the window. The few clouds that were in the sky were breaking away from the Sun. "Do we have time today to walk on the beach for a while?" I asked. "It sure would feel good."

Chea slapped Domano lightly on the back, "I want to go too. Come on. Let's go get our feet wet."

"OK," he said. "But no throwing sand, and no pushing in the water."

I took off my shoes and left them by the door. Chea shoved Domano in the side as she took off her socks and ran for the door ahead of him. They giggled and pushed each other all the way down to the water's edge.

"So what do you think of the directions? The pillars?" he asked, splashing water as hard as he could with every step.

"What?" His question took me completely by surprise. He would never allow me to discuss it before. "I don't know." The tension inside me was growing again and I had trouble putting words together. I felt like I was being put on the spot; I was so afraid of being wrong. I wanted to show them I was able to be coherent and stuttered the first thing that came to my mind. "I think I'm getting a little idea of what they are. But the Tree is what I can't figure out. And I guess I really don't understand what they are all together. What is the Great Tree?"

"The Tree is in the center," he said. "It's there at the place where all things meet at the center of the circle—the 'Center of the World.' Where the forces of the directions come together. The male and the female come together. It is also a great mystery that they all come from the center too. This wheel is what the whole of existence is. It is what each one of us is inside. The wheel's hub is the garden."

He squatted in the water's edge and dug into a little hole in the sand. "What sort of fellow do you think lives down here? Look at this bubble coming up out of the sand."

"I don't know," I answered. "Maybe you should be careful. He might bite." We all laughed, and he looked up like a little boy about to be naughty. "But really," I asked, "what is the difference if you go around the circle or around the spiral? Don't you still go from one direction to the next? What difference does it make? And what difference does it make to be in the center or go up the Tree? It's still the center."

The wind was blowing hard and Chea tucked a loose strand of hair back into the bun she always wore. I had never seen it come down before. It was barely long enough to stay in the tie that she used to hold it up. She shook her head at Domano digging in the sand and smiled. She said, "Walking the outer circle is the everyday life. We feel the influence of the directions as they weave into our daily lives. Walking on the spiral is touching the directions from a different place. You are closer to the Tree and the directions feel different, stronger. You are in a portion of the directions that you don't always feel from the outer circle. Their Songs have changed like new harmonies added; they are sung in a new range of tones. As you go to the center and up the Tree, each branch up the Tree is singing with yet another harmony and another range of sounds and tones. The web that we use on the outer circle is woven light and simple. Up the spiral and up the Tree the web grows more and more intricate and layered, passing through many other webs and worlds, weaving and unweaving as the need comes.

"Different peoples talk about this in different ways. This is just a way to talk about things that can not be explained with the words and logic of your culture. For some they say that each of these changes is a god, or maybe a new time in the god's life."

The cuffs of my jeans were getting wet. I thought of rolling them up but it was already too late. I just walked out a little farther into the water anyway. The cold felt good. It reminded me that I was alive.

Domano spoke and waved his finger in the air at me, "In the ways of our tradition those Grandparents I told you about have gifted you. From each direction a tool, a special gift, to help you reach the spiral to the Great Tree. From the south you know how to feel your Song. From the north they gave you healing and the life energy of the Earth Fire Serpent from the Mother Earth. From the west you danced at your own death and tasted your destiny; you felt the loosening of your thoughts that bind and imprison you. And from the east, in the larger part of your mind, the place inside that connects to everything else was shown to you. These put you on the spiral path, they teach the balance and equity with all things. And together they put you in the center, the Center of the World, at the base of the Great Tree of Life. This is what we call *wanowa ka ta see* —building a world that is in balance. You see?"

As he spoke I remembered the time in the Cowell courtyard and how I experienced an event from the perspective of each direction and the center. When I was there I understood what that meant. But now, away from the experience, the memory of the feeling of it had faded. I found myself grasping again to piece together the understanding and application of it.

"We are Humans," he said. "And we make mistakes. The path is rough and narrow. Each direction has its own kind of snares and troubles. There will always be problems to overcome. How you avoid them, fall into them, or climb back out, is how you walk your path. Life is not always a piece of cake, no matter which path you walk."

I hesitated, not knowing what I should say. "I had moments when I knew. I mean I really knew. But now I can't remember it all. It's as if it is just outside of my remembering."

"Yes," he nodded as though that was all perfectly logical. "This will happen until you can stay closer to the Tree all the time. The memory is there inside you. The knowing is there. It helps you in spite of your downfalls. You will see."

I nodded and looked back and forth at both of them. I still felt awkward and full of remorse for having broken my commitment. It didn't make any sense to me that they were suddenly so willing to explain many things they usually would not talk about. It made me uneasy. And even though I felt undeserving I wanted to be respectful and show that I wanted to learn from them. So I quickly asked, "What is the south? What does the south mean?"

"I cannot answer that for you," Domano said. "You will have to come to know this for yourself. Think on the stories. Remember what you have learned from experience. This is not something that can be learned from explaining. This is not something from memorizing. It is from experiencing.

"You have goose bumps on your arms, Kay. You getting cold yet? I'm cold yet. I think it is time." He jumped up shaking and shivering all over.

I looked out to sea. The Sun was moving low and the air was cooling off fast. I needed to get home to my kids soon. We turned around and headed back to the Hetakas' apartment.

On the way Domano asked me how I was doing with my concentration exercises and told me to double the number of times a day I

TRAPPED IN A BROKEN WORLD

was practicing them. Then he began describing a new one to add to the others.

"As we walk here," he said, "find a fist sized rock with many patterns and colors. And ask it if it wants to come and help you."

I looked intensely at all the rocks near my feet as we walked along. I picked one up and asked it if it wanted to come. I felt silly, but they encouraged me to be still and feel for the answer. I didn't expect to have any perceptions or feelings from the rock but I became positive that this was not the right one. I put it back and kept looking. One after the other I picked them up and asked. And each one felt wrong. I was getting frustrated.

"Slow down," Domano said quietly. "Find your Song. Let the Earth energy come and let the other gifts come. Get your center. Then you look."

I took a deep breath and let the gifts of the directions fill my attention as I had been taught. I felt the beauty of being alive and the excitement of the cold sand and water around me. Holding this feeling I opened my eyes and looked at the rocks. One rock a few feet away stood out from all the rest. It was just fist sized and complex in design as Domano had instructed. I picked it up and asked. This one felt different from the others. I think if I had not taken it, I would surely have missed not having it in my life.

"Now," Domano said. "Don't do anything else with this rock but look at it. Just study the way it looks and memorize it. Don't let anyone else see it. Don't even talk to it. Just study only the one side that you see right now. Do this two, three, four times a day if you can. The more the better."

"Should I offer something here?" I asked. "To thank...?"

He interrupted me, "Offer your sincereness from your heart. Let it pour out of your heart as a gift."

"Do you ever offer gifts in return or thanks?" I asked.

"Sure," he smiled. "Our people offer many different things, such as tobacco, grain, honey, pollen. All kinds of things."

"I only have the gum that's been in my pocket." I had to laugh at the thought of offering that old mangled up piece of Dentyne.

"What counts is the Song and the truth that comes from your heart." He touched his chest. "That's what makes the difference. If you want to offer something, and the piece of gum is all you have, then offer it proudly, with all the caring that can come. Yes?"

I took out the piece of gum and looked at it. We all laughed. It was half out of its wrapper, a little damp in places, suffering from heat exposure and speckled with bits of dirt and sand. They both smiled gently but showed no judgment. I took off the wrapper and rubbed off the dirt. It felt like the right thing to do so I found my center again and let the feeling of the joy and love from my Song pour out onto the rock and the place on the ground where the rock had been and set the gum down there.

Domano took Chea's hand as we began to walk away and said softly, "This was good."

THREE

SECRET LIAISONS

SPRING vacation went quietly without event. I spent the time with my children and working on some art projects that were interesting me. The intensity and craziness of the world of the Hetakas seemed far away. Aside from their exercises that I did almost every day as part of my normal routine, I thought very little else about the old shamans and the unusual experiences I had had with them.

I was finding the latest exercise they had given me on the observation of a rock very appealing. I didn't know why, but it gave me a sense of consistency and stability. I felt I was coming to know that rock very well.

I would sit myself down in a secluded place and use the gifts of the directions to find and hold my center for as long as I could. I'd stare at the rock for a time then look away and try to remember what I had seen.

Usually it was daytime and I was in the sunlight. Sometimes I would take it out late at night after the kids were in bed. And once

I took it outside under the full Moon. There was something about the rock that was always unchanged. The surface design appeared different with the alteration of the light, almost as if it was showing me another aspect of itself with each new environment. But there was something about it that was always the same.

My ability to concentrate and visualize was improving little by little. I noticed the difference in all the exercises and in my art work for my classes. I was finding that I could build pictures in my mind and hold them with increasing clarity and ease. I didn't really understand why the Hetakas felt this was so important, but it was fun and satisfying and I trusted their instructions.

The evening before our next meeting I was walking in the field below my apartment as the Sun was setting. The sky was lightly streaked with clouds that were turning incredible shades of pinks, reds, purples, and for a moment, clear across the southern horizon, a band of earthy green. I couldn't recall ever having seen that color in the sky before. I wondered if I would remember it well enough to paint it.

Suddenly, out of the south, racing across the grasses came a concentrated wind. It pounded against me. The pressure in my ears changed. It blew so hard I couldn't hold my footing and fell. Even on the ground it was relentless. I looked around at the bushes nearby and I quivered all over. They were unmoved. They were staying perfectly still. The wind was on only me. I had to fight my fear and struggle to keep clarity.

Then down underneath the fright was a familiar feeling. I turned my face into the flurry. Something inside me knew it was all right and the fear melted aside. It was my old friend the wind keeper. It had been a while since I had seen her last. Her power and vastness always startled me and caught me off guard.

I realized that she was trying to tell me something and I couldn't understand her. I tried to make my body stop shaking by breathing deeply. And I waited.

But still I couldn't understand. There was only a feeling of anticipation, as though something exciting was about to happen.

I kept trying until I knew she was going to leave. I thanked her and watched her move off through the bushes to the west. The sky had lost its brilliance and was settling into darkness. A few stars were coming out between the clouds.

I sat there feeling the dirt with my hands, watching the last of the ants disappear into a small hole a few inches away. My mind began to wander over many different things the Hetakas had said to me. As I ran the soil through my fingers I thought of the time Chea held out a handful of sand and told me to remember the feeling of the cave. I had forgotten about that little quest she had given me until now. The Song of the cave was so familiar. The identity of its maker was almost solid enough for me to grab hold of. Soon I would have it.

When it got too cold to stay outside I returned to the apartment to clean up the dinner dishes and put the kids to bed. I was filled with a warmth of being in love. The sunset was my lover, and the soil and the wind. I carried that sensation all through the night and into my dreams.

The next day I got to the Hetakas' home as scheduled. It was Saturday morning and I had the whole day free to spend with them. We talked about the unusually overcast weather and how my children were doing in school. I told them about a man I had just met and was thinking about dating. They were interested in him and wanted to see him. So I said I would arrange it as soon as possible.

The wrenching feelings of guilt about breaking my promise were beginning to mellow into new perspectives and the Hetakas didn't mention the subject. We made coffee from the African beans I had brought them and sat down in the last rays of the fleeting sunlight before it disappeared completely behind the dark ominous clouds.

"I sure like the rock I found on the beach," I said. "I'm getting better at remembering how it looks. That exercise is great, it has a really neat feeling. You know, I can picture my art work better now, too. I can change things around in my mind and examine whether I like it or not, before I ever touch the piece. It's saving me hours of time. But making the pictures in my mind just feels so good. It feels so satisfying. I know you're having me do it for more than that, though. So what is it? In terms of your traditions, I mean, why am I really doing it?"

They smiled and teased me about making huge, elaborate sculptures in my mind. Domano said that my head would get so full and heavy with them that it would start pulling me over and I'd have to scoot it around in a wheelbarrow.

Chea sat back on her bench against the wall and laughed. "It pleases us that you are doing so well with this rock. Using the mind

SECRET LIAISONS

is supposed to feel good—when you know how to use it and not stress it. It's like exercise. You need to exercise your mind. Both the logical side and the side that has no words, what is called the mind of the heart. It feels good, like stretching and building the muscles. That is what you are doing.

"To be a kala keh nah seh you have to build and strengthen both parts of your mind. It has to be kept active and alert. A kala keh nah seh always has to keep building it as long as they live."

"I see," I said. "Sometimes when I'm doing it, I lose all my other thoughts. The thoughts that are words just drift away, and I'm left with my mind filled with the image and the feeling of the rock."

"Yes," she pulled her feet up under her and sat cross-legged, "good. Memorizing the feeling of it, too, is how the mind of the heart works. You are exercising this when you remember the feeling as well as the image. Good."

Domano and Chea looked at each other for a long moment. The room seemed to get tense. I felt a buzzing on the top of my head and my stomach rolled. It reminded me of other times when I'd been with them just as they were about to teach something extraordinary. I wondered what they were up to. Fear began to literally climb up my legs and into my belly.

Chea turned to look at me. "We are going to teach you about the oldest sacrament. It takes a long time to learn this way. But it is worth it. Through the eons the ones who walk the spiral path have always met in a hidden way, an uncorrupted way, with the other forms we share this world with. We will teach you this. It is the developing and honoring of the sacred links of life between all beings.

"The walker always strives to be pure in heart, humble and worthy. You have been given and can use the gifts of the directions. You are learning the truth of your masks, and can see the narrowness of your path. And you understand, now, when you feel your Song or experience your center that it is a prayer to Creation, the Great Mystery. You know in your heart how hard it is to catch the nature of honesty and commitment. Now you will learn the use and meaning of your senses."

The fear eased away but the tingling was still there. I stretched the tension out of my neck and shoulders. This new step sounded intriguing. Secret liaisons with other beings. I felt a little like I was in an adventure movie. I wondered what it meant to meet in the way they had described—"the oldest sacrament." I knew very little about the white world's traditions of sacrament or even what the word really meant. It sounded mysterious, ancient.

Domano grinned at me, "Our teachers sent us off to learn about the secrets of each of our senses, one at a time. We will do the same for you, but to teach you, sometimes, is a different thing than the way we were taught. Our cultures are so apart from each other. The way we are shown what the world is when we are young, your people compared to our people, is so different. Our people are not taught to be numb and blind to the world. Your people teach you to close off your senses and feelings to protect yourselves, so your world cannot hurt you."

"But what does that have to do with hidden meetings?" I interrupted. "What does that mean, a 'sacrament?'" I went to take another drink of coffee but my cup was empty.

"The senses are the first steps," he answered. "You have to learn how to pay attention. How to watch for what the world is telling you, both the body and the spirit. This information is what you must rely on, not the superstitions of your culture. Then you will be prepared to make these links with your neighbors, your relatives. You will be able to make the contact you seek and understand what these different folks are about and what they are telling you.

"Sacrament is the opened sharing of your Songs with each other. Intimate. Bonding. Sometimes even merging. This is a sacred thing. Learning is shared. Medicine is shared. Gifts given. Oaths are even traded. They have so much they want to give to us. This is very sacred. And one never comes to it without great care."

"Is it dangerous?" I had to swallow to clear my throat. The buzzing was spreading now into my elbows and knees. I tried to hold the fear down.

Chea leaned forward. "Of course. Where do you think you are? The wonderful land of Oz? Any time you are working with medicines and the spirit people there is danger there. Remember the wind keeper?"

My stomach flinched and the buzzing increased. I thought back on the time I was on the mountain top in ceremony seeking to meet the wind keeper. The power of that being was unspeakable. She could have crushed me at any time if I had done things incorrectly, without the proper respect. I remembered the terror I felt in the pursuit and also the incredible joy when I was able to succeed at contacting her.

"Is this different than seeking a wind keeper?" I asked. "Wasn't that a meeting like you describe?"

"Yes," Chea answered. "They were interested in you. Your nature is suited well to seeking the wind keepers. They came to you to help shake you loose of your culture. The bonding succeeded, but the training of your culture is so deep and so thorough, it keeps you almost as blind and deaf as before, in spite of the bonding. Do you see?"

"But why?" I asked.

"Because your culture's grip is that complete and strong on your people, on you."

I remembered the wind keeper coming to me in the meadow below my home the night before. Chea was right. I knew the wind keeper was telling me something important but all I could understand was a feeling of anticipation. Now, reflecting on it, I think she was telling me this training was coming.

I was excited that I could even perceive what I had, but very frustrated that it was so piecemeal. I wondered if I would ever be able to learn all of what the Hetakas offered, if my cultural handicap would always prevent me.

Chea seemed to understand and tried to explain further. "In order to make contact with different kinds of beings we have to be sensitive in different ways. We have to be strong within ourselves in different ways. Each person's abilities are different from each other. And these beings we seek are all different from each other. Some are easier for one Human and not for another. There is no prescription. Each person's path is special. This is your path. There are no footprints to step in but yours."

Domano pulled a little tie out of his pocket and wrapped his hair back out of his face in a pony tail. "This questing," he said. "This contacting, is very sacred to the native peoples. You must be walking your life with equity, honesty and respect. You must prepare yourself like this, in these ways of being, and be strong in your own Song."

"Your commitment to honor the nations you seek," Chea picked up on his words as though she was finishing his thought, "and the entire globe that you share with them must be complete. The preparing could take a long time."

Domano added, "And these are the things that are done. For everyone, it takes great persistence. Nothing in the world of the spiral path is instant. There are no fast service drive-up windows here. No express lanes." We all laughed.

The smile still warming her face, Chea turned her eyes to me. "And it is dangerous, yes, if you don't follow the strict tradition of respect and equity. If you seek without honor. If you try to shortcut. It is damn dangerous. You could get hurt. Die. Or worst of all, those you love could get hurt."

Now even the bottoms of my feet tingled. "Why are you having me do these new things? I don't think I'm ready for this. I can barely use the gifts all at once. I don't hold my center but for a few moments at a time. I'm not ready for this. It scares me. It really scares me."

"No," Chea answered. "You are not ready for the questing. But you are ready to learn how and why to quest. It is more than just learning a technique. It is learning a whole way of life. Be thankful that you have the good sense to be frightened. It will keep you alert and honest. It will keep things in perspective for you." She smiled like the Cheshire cat.

The fear kept creeping up and down my legs to my stomach. I struggled to stay logical and calm and asked slowly, "Is the training dangerous?"

Chea's expression softened. She chuckled a little and answered, "Not unless you are a complete idiot. Training teaches you how to watch, listen and feel. How to understand what the physical is telling you, and what the spirit, the medicine, is telling you. Many things are picked up by our senses that we usually ignore. It's a habit. To ignore it. Your culture is particularly good at it." That seemed funny to me and I laughed nervously. I was afraid my laughter was going to be out of place but they laughed with me.

Domano jumped up and walked toward me. "Let's go downtown," he said. "We can take the bus down at the Boardwalk. You need to move your body. It will help the fear leave to move yourself around, walk. We can show you what we are talking about out there much better. This will be fun." He clapped his hands together and looked at me with a side glance. The mischief bounced off his eye with the glint of the light. "You will see. Come. Where's my shoes? Let's go raise some hell."

We laughed and scuffled around to get ready to go. I was still nervous. I could feel the fear poised somewhere out of my sight just waiting for an excuse to assault and devour me. Domano looked like he was up to his old tricks and was about to do something that would tease and embarrass me. On the one hand I really didn't want to be embarrassed publicly again, but on the other, I had come to love his antics and wouldn't miss them for anything. I made sure I went out the door last so I could keep a watch on them and at least for a few moments be forewarned of any tricks.

The clouds parted enough to let the sunlight through for a while. We were walking fast, straight into the crisp breeze as it came off the ocean. The air felt like life itself as I was breathing it in. Domano was right. The quick movement of my muscles seemed to shake out the last remnants of fear. It was wonderful to be out in the weather and walking again between my two old friends.

The bus was at the stop when we arrived. We took a seat near the back. Chea was next to the window and I was next to her. Domano sat sideways in front of us, with his feet on the seat. The rear half of the coach was empty except for three teenage girls in the last seat. Domano looked around, pointing with his chin, "What do your senses tell you about this place?"

I looked covertly through the bus. There were two old women with canes next to the driver and half a dozen college students, all self-absorbed, scattered through the front. The floor was dirty with ridges of sand and leaves that the wind had carried in. Advertisements covered the walls above the windows. They were selling radio programming, a boxing match, chewing gum, and a local ballet school. It was stuffy but not warm. The old women were talking to the driver and the girls in the back giggled over a rock and roll deejay on a portable radio. I described my observations in great detail and my teachers attentively listened to every word.

"You have not described your sense of touch," Domano said without expression.

"What?" I asked.

"You have not described your sense of touch." His response was unchanged.

I was sure I had covered all the senses with care. Now I was confused about what I had actually said or not said.

Chea added, "You left out your taste, too. And didn't get too far with your smelling either."

I looked at them both and laughed nervously. I assumed they were right as they had always been, and turned my concentration toward what my skin was feeling. There was an entire world of sensation there I had totally missed. It was hard for me to believe I could have left out so much, but there it was.

"Today you can blame your culture for that," Domano laughed. "But not after today. Then you have no excuses."

We laughed and I asked, "What did I do?"

They laughed at me. Domano tapped my leg, "This is what your culture has done to you. You can't even see the difference. First the church and now the state, too. They have robbed you of your senses. Your people have been taught with great cunning, for centuries now, to deny and ignore what your bodies are telling you.

"Our senses are a way our Song reaches out to find other Songs and messages. They tell us what is going on. This is how they interact in the world of livingness. If you are not paying attention to your senses then those people can do whatever they want to you and you don't even notice. They take your health away. They take your power away. They take your world away. They lock you in a world that they control. Do you see?"

"Uh..." I didn't agree with him at all. I wanted to say something but I found myself unable to contradict him and just babbled something noncommittal instead. "You'll have to explain that. I don't follow you."

"Yes, you do," Chea said. "It's OK, though. 'Cause now you have to change it for yourself."

"Just to be Human: *this is a sacred task*." Domano rubbed his chest. "To feel through your senses: *this is a sacred task*. Look around you here. These people, they use most of their energies to stop the world from touching them in any way."

He flashed his eyes over at the students in the front. I could see his point but I couldn't believe the condition was as severe as he was saying.

"Watch them," he said. "Look how they are very busy shutting out all the smells they can. They don't want to know about the smell of the people sitting nearby. Or the smell of the city. They are careful not to look around at everything that is here. They pretend they don't hear the sounds that are here.

"Look at how you answered what your senses observed. You didn't say a thing about what your skin and muscles felt. These people here would all answer the same. For most of your people, they hide from the sense of touch the most."

"What's so special about touch?" I asked.

"We are Humans," Domano said. "We live in this world as the animals do. Without our senses we would not be able to know the physical world we are in. When we lose smelling or tasting, hearing, sight, we have lost a piece of the world around us. In the jungle it means you cannot protect yourself as well or do your jobs. It can even mean your death. If you lose your ability to feel in the skin and muscles, you will die, and soon."

I had never considered the role or importance of the senses before. I couldn't comprehend why they put so much emphasis on them. I looked back and forth between them for a clue as to what was really going on, and Chea added, "When a child is taught to ignore, degrade and deny their senses from the time they come to this Earth, there is a great injury. A great hole is made. An emptiness. As this child grows to be an adult, instead of filling the hole with the senses, they turn away even more, because there is so much pain that surrounds the senses. Especially touch. Your people deny touch to each other. You even turn your attention away from all the different touch you feel through the whole day."

"You don't believe us?" Domano asked. "Just take smelling. Look at the way your people act about smelling. Go ahead. Smell what is on this bus. Find your center and turn all your attention to what you smell."

"Oh, come on," I objected. I really didn't want to smell what might be there—body odors, bad breath, the mess they stepped in and got all over the bottom of their shoes. It sounded like a revolting and unnecessary thing to do. "I get your point. Looking for the unpleasant seems kind of odd, don't you think?" Just the prospect of smelling everything made the odors on the bus stand out. The girls in the back had on a disgusting amount of a sickly sweet perfume and someone near the front had been eating garlic. I started to breathe through my mouth so I wouldn't have to endure those odors.

Domano thought that was funny. "Look how you hide from feeling the smell. I make my point. Right there at your open mouth. What is it you feel inside right now? What is this stress? Where does it come from? Hmmm? Look at all the thoughts and feelings you have about smelling this place your body is in. Why do you do this? Why is smelling the surrounding so hard and uncomfortable for you?"

"I would prefer to choose the things I want to smell," I answered. "That's all. I don't want them shoved down my nose, thank you." I was beginning to feel invaded, as though those people on the bus were assaulting me. I didn't want to share their space or know anything about their worlds and their problems. And I certainly didn't want them in the middle of mine. It wasn't that this environment or they themselves felt dangerous; it was rather that their odors felt somehow unclean, unsafe to bring into my body. To smell them seemed almost an intimate thing. I didn't want to have that degree of intimacy with strangers in an unkept public place, and especially not to have it forced on me.

I looked out the window. The clouds covered the Sun. It seemed oppressively dark outside. The midtown stop was coming up. I pointed to the street and we stood up to make our way to the door.

I was looking forward to a fresh breeze. As the door opened and I felt the rush of wind on my face I took a deep breath. Instead of clear unscented air it was full of the exhaust from the buses all stopped together in a row. Now I was becoming angry.

"Ah," Domano pulled his shoulders back and filled his lungs. "Yes. The American way of fresh air." And he slapped his chest as though he were very satisfied. "Ah!" Everyone near the door laughed.

Domano seemed quite pleased with himself and slowly led us away from the groups of people and over to one of the empty benches. "Let's sit here for this minute," he said pointing with his chin.

I started to sit on the end of the seat and he scooted me over to my left by bumping my hips with his. Chea sat on my other side and hummed. We watched the crowds as they got on and off the buses. Santa Cruz always provided such a remarkable variety of people. I could be entertained for hours on end.

Domano leaned over, "What do you think about the smells here?"

I hadn't noticed. I didn't realize it but I actually had still been breathing with my mouth open. "Well," I answered, not wanting him to notice my lack of attention. I thought I'd say something safe. "The exhaust kind of drowns out a lot of it."

SECRET LIAISONS

"Hmm," Chea looked at me with the corner of her eye. "But the buses have all gone away."

"Uh, yeah," I squirmed and laughed at being caught. "I...uh...guess they have. You don't really want me to keep sniffing at everything, do you? That's not what this is all about, is it?"

"What's wrong with a little sniffing?" A slight smirk came over her lips.

"This is a joke, isn't it? It's got to be. You guys are setting me up for a real doozer. Aren't you?"

They both turned their faces towards me. I looked back and forth between them. Domano started to giggle in spurts. "Boy," he said. "You really are in a predicament. You have to face how you receive your world. How this world makes you feel. And what you send back out into it. Geemaneeze! That makes me nervous just to think about it."

"Come on, guys," I complained.

Chea laughed and looked around me to Domano, "What kind of a word is that? 'Geemaneeze?'"

"I learned it from those three girls that were on that bus. They said this fine word a whole lot. It is a fine word." Chea didn't look convinced. "You will see. It is." He grinned at her with all his teeth showing. "It is."

She smiled at him with her eyes. "I bet I will see all right."

Her voice was soft and serious as she turned to me. "Listen to what we have said. This sacred link between all life is one of the most precious things to our people. To learn about this link is sacred. To learn how to perceive the links is a sacred task. To learn how to use these links is one of the greatest honors. It requires the seeker to be of the most worthy nature. This link is our Creator, the Oldest One, living and speaking through all the things in our world, as different as they are, tying them together. It is how we come to know the Creator and all the others in the Creation. It is wondrous and beautiful beyond all words, beyond all imagining. Remember your linking with the wind keeper and the Mother Earth. The feelings of being merged for a time with them. Of knowing them and sharing your very essence with one another. The giving. The love. This is the Human heritage.

"You are going to have to look at how you turn your senses off. At how you react inside yourself to whatever information comes or doesn't come to your senses. There is much denial and pain there. As you do this training you will have to work through all these hurts that are locked away. Some of it will be a great struggle, but you must put on your 'birthing paint,' like a man puts on his battle paint, and keep going. Your commitment must be to come out the other side in victory. Like the birth of a child, there is no turning around and changing your mind about it in the middle. Once you decide and make the commitment then you take the knocks, you take the difficulties, you continue. Even to your death. Because what you are battling for is worth it."

Domano stood up and gestured for us to walk to the center of town. He kept swelling his chest and breathing in loudly through his nose as he stepped. He said, "A Human must have something in their life worth dying for or life has an emptiness. You are very fortunate. You have many things in your life worth dying for."

I thought of my two children and the difficulties I had in carrying, delivering and raising them. I would do anything for them. I understood what Chea had meant about 'birthing paint.' No matter how hard it gets, you just keep going. I wondered if I had the ability to apply that degree of tenacity to something else.

The more I learned from the Hetakas the more I wanted to learn and the more I realized how much I actually didn't know. Everything they had to teach me just kept growing in intrigue and fulfillment. And now I was discovering that it also involved an increasing amount of responsibility. I didn't know if I had what it takes to complete such a training. But I wanted it. I knew I even wanted it enough to die for it and I was willing to paint my face and step forward.

I wanted to tell them how committed and determined I felt but I was afraid it might be the wrong time. Even though this seemed to be a real training I still had the feeling they were probably setting me up for a joke. "So this is actually the training." I looked at Chea. "This really is it. So I have to go around sniffing." I turned my eyes to the ground. "This seems somewhat undignified, you know."

"Poor dear." She shook her head and laughed.

I didn't dare look up at her. I was so nervous I would have just giggled.

Pointing sharply to the ground I was standing on she said, "We'll start here. And don't give me that look. It is a good time. No better time than this moment now. Nose up. Here we go." She lifted her chin and flared her nostrils. I had to laugh.

"Listen, now," she said grinning. "These are your instructions, for real."

I tried to flare my nostrils the way she did but I couldn't make them move. Chea shook her head. "Laugh and joke, but remember this. You must pay attention to all the emotions and thoughts you have while closing your attention in on each item. Notice what each smell has meant to you in the past. Take no expectations with you. Observe what is actually there on the outside and the inside. Always start with your Song and observe from your center. From the eyes of your heart."

I nodded.

We looked at each other for a few moments. "Go ahead," she said. "You can start any time."

I felt silly trying to sniff excessively in public. But we were walking in front of a favorite restaurant of mine on Pacific Street. It was too expensive for me to eat there but I always enjoyed spending time in front near the dining garden when they had a live jazz band. The people were great fun, the music was steamy, and the food smelled like a test of temptation. It was Saturday and just about brunch time. For this I was willing to open up and sniff.

I closed my eyes. It was easy to find my Song with such enjoyable music to lead me there. One by one I pulled each of the gifts of the directions that the Hetakas had so strongly impressed upon me into my attention until I had all four in my consciousness with equal strength. My center felt comfortable and familiar, Song filled and vibrantly alive. I thought perhaps that I would be able to hold it for a longer time than usual. In that state of mind it is hard to imagine thinking and feeling any other way. A sense of affection for myself and all else becomes the foundation that my experiencing rides on. It becomes the natural order of things.

While delighting in that inner atmosphere and not letting go of it, I aimed my center toward the sensations being offered my nose. I identified potatoes, pepper, sausage, the smoke from a mesquite fire, fish, lemon. The stimulation was not restricted to my nasal passages. It became a whole body experience. Awareness of my physical presence on this piece of Earth exaggerated. My aliveness began to push outward in my body like a balloon expanding.

Somebody shouted behind me and I dropped everything that had been in my focus. I opened my eyes and turned around. A vagrant, who seemed to be mentally disturbed, was walking down the street in our direction waving his arms and arguing loudly with the air. His anger and aggression seemed to push in front of him like waves. The smell of the black pepper stood out above the others. I became very uncomfortable. I wanted to take off around the corner and get away from the pepper smell and the anger. My chest began to feel tight and my neck and shoulders tensed. I started to step away.

Domano grabbed my hand tightly. "What do you feel right now? Where does this come from? It does not come from this man here. Search inside. Where did you feel this before?"

He was right. I remembered this feeling from long ago in my childhood. It was associated with food being prepared for dinner and there was arguing.

"Look where you are, Kay." Domano still held onto me. "That time is over with. You are here now. Look. It is long gone and yet that old time is still controlling you. You throw away your power to a ghost of the past. You don't have to do that anymore."

I took a deep breath. The memory faded and so did my reaction to it and the pepper. The exotic jazz from the band came back into my awareness. The breeze moved across my face and through my hair. I stretched my back.

"That was sure weird," I thought out loud.

Chea was expressionless. She glanced around the mall and said, "This is what I told you about. Concentrating on the senses brings what is attached to them to the surface. Some of these are nice and some are unpleasant. You need to know all of them as well as learn what your senses are telling you about the Songs and medicines of what is out there now."

"Yeah." I understood what she meant. I had felt both the good associations and the distressful ones, and I was just getting a hint of the existence of the medicines that were present in the smells when I allowed myself to be completely distracted and thrown off center. "Birthing paint," I said. "No matter what is happening. The seed has been accepted and the paint has been put on."

I had caught a glimpse of the gravity of the new awareness that I was about to step into. It was as though the world was opening up a whole new piece of itself to me.

63   SECRET LIAISONS

We moved slowly north down the street. Chea gestured to me with a single nod, "Try again."

I couldn't get my center while looking through the street and walking so I stopped and closed my eyes. Soon I was able to concentrate all my attention on the odors at hand. We were near a shop that sold candles and incense. The first thing to come to my awareness was the smell of patchouli. It reminded me of the Haight-Ashbury district of San Francisco in the first days of the flower children and how my sister-in-law would come visit us from there with all her crazy stories. It struck my curiosity and repulsed me at the same time. I didn't want it in my nose and turned to face the other direction.

"Observe with your Song," Chea said. "Start with the joy. Then the great passion of the Song can guide you. Give you the proper perspective. It is your protection."

I found my Song again and moved easily into my center. The strong physicalness of my presence returned. I pulled the air in slowly. It was slightly sweet and hung, shaking, in the roof of my mouth. I knew this smell. It was long walks by myself through the old neighborhoods on my way to the beach where I'd sit at the water's edge and talk to the sea. It was roses. It was moments of stolen freedom.

Chea whispered in my ear, "Let go of the memory that has that scent locked in it. And come back here. What is that smell telling you today?"

I did as she instructed. I felt the tiniest bits of rose throughout my body. Waves of energies and feelings came from them. It was as though I could actually smell its livingness. It had a quality, a vitality all its own. It was so generous by nature and there was compassion in this essence. I felt my cells taking it in as fast as it entered my lungs. The plant was giving and I was receiving.

My concentration wavered. I couldn't hold my mind steady. The sounds of passersby began to take my attention and I lost my center. I opened my eyes and Domano was grinning from ear to ear holding a small potted rose in front of my face. It was just as I had imagined it, pink with profuse blossoms.

"I did it," I smiled back. "But I can only seem to hold it for a minute or two. Why doesn't it last longer? Am I doing it wrong?"

A short, dark man came out of the store we were standing in front of and waved his finger in my face. "Hey! You! Are you going to buy that plant or what?"

Domano handed the man the rose and smiled, "Thanks, mister." As the man walked back into the store the three of us looked at each other and laughed.

Domano motioned us to walk on. "Each sense is a tool of our Song," he said. "It is how Song reaches out into the world to see what is there. We are not just spirit. We are flesh, too. We are animals here in this world. We are made to learn through our senses. The spirit learns in its other ways, too. Yes. But this is our special gift, this is what this means to be inside flesh, to know the worlds through a body. Why bother to keep a physical body if you spend all your time denying it? Or pretending and wishing you don't have one?" He laughed lightly.

"To our people that seems like a pretty silly thing to do. This place, these bodies, are so rich, so full with surprise and delight. It is a crazy thing to us to not grab the chance, to not live it and enjoy it as much as can be done."

We came up to a bench that was empty. "Can we sit here?" I asked. "I think I can concentrate better, to start collecting the gifts in my attention I mean, if I'm sitting. It just seems so hard for me to do all those things at once."

"Of course," he answered. "But grab it quick! Before we lose it." I plopped down on the bench with all my weight. Domano chuckled at me, "Don't break it. Then we won't have a place to sit."

The three of us laughed. Domano teased me often about gaining weight. He said that if the elements in our lives were balanced I wouldn't be so inclined to put on extra pounds, that I shouldn't be so quick to believe in the popular propoganda enforced by the powers that be about what one should or shouldn't get in one's body. I decided to not let those worries distract me and concentrated on the work of the moment.

"Try using your breath," Domano suggested. "Fill your whole self like it is an empty vessel. The breath is fuel. And what you take in on the breath is fuel as well. Try it now. Breathe in real slow. Feel your heartbeat. Let the two rhythms become one.

"Yes. Close your eyes. Watch just your breath and your heartbeat till that is all there is. Now add your Song. They are each a rhythm of your Song, coming together into one harmony, one thing.

"The breath goes to the center. It touches the Tree, the center of the wheel. Relax. Let it be. All things move around this point in the wheel. Around the breath. This is good. Now let the other gifts come. The life energy flow. The letting go of the words. Opening the mind to the beyond. Keep the breath the same. It will hold you. From your center let the smelling be noticed."

I did as he instructed me. It was a wonderful sensation. My breath mixed with my Song as it spun in my heart, reaching in and out of my body through my lungs. Everything moved according to it, around it. It was easy to feel my body and hold my center with this awareness.

The wind shifted, coming from the north. On it was the inviting smell of coffee beans being freshly roasted and then the odor of whiskey followed by the hint of garlic frying in a skillet. My reactions were mixed. I had to separate the smells one at a time and deal with each by itself.

I hadn't started to drink gourmet coffees until I decided to go back to school and to work with the Hetakas. For me coffee meant excitement, learning, freedom, exotic experiences, adventure. It was a joy and pleasure to feel this scent. I didn't want to let those feelings go to see what they were concealing, but I did.

A tingling pressure rose through my whole body. The smell was full and stimulating. It enticed me to breathe even more deeply. As I did I felt that the act of smelling by itself encouraged one to breathe more, and that there was something behind that, beyond that. It was as though the inspiration to breathe and smell was a trigger for something else, something vitally life sustaining. I could detect it but I didn't have time to investigate it before my attention again wavered.

I noticed three kinds of messages that came with the action of smelling. The first was the automatic unconscious reaction to the odor based on events from the past. The second was the purely physical, chemical information alerting one to the presence of things currently in the environment. The third was another kind of information. It was subtle and vast, something that was without words and had to be felt within the quiet of the self. It spoke of other things, secrets about the components or perhaps the interactions of the environment itself. I knew that I had only skimmed by this third kind of message and that an entire universe of experiencing was just waiting there for me to feel it, to live it. It was a revelation for me.

Even the idea of such a thing had never occurred to me before. The possibilities captured me like a moth to a flame.

As I opened my eyes Chea said, "You will pursue this whenever you can. Of course you do your exercises as usual, but this you must do as often as you can remember to do it. Wherever you are. Except driving until later. This is not an exercise. This is a training for a way of living and is more like a questing than an exercise. Can you see what I mean?"

"Yeah," I answered. "I can see what you're getting at. There's something else going on here, isn't there? I mean there's more to this than the smell receptors in my sinuses detecting particles in the air. This is what's behind the linking, isn't it?"

Domano looked around the street and back to me, "Yes. It is part of it—eyes of the heart. There is much in this. Much more.

"I think for a moment here, we should sit and enjoy this place and all it is offering. I will tell you a little story. Of course, it is a good story, because I am telling it. You relax here with your new knowledge and I will tell a story of the north for you."

I laughed and sat back against the bench. Everything was perfect—the quaintness of the mall, the marvelous variety of the people, flowers in the planter-boxes, good smells from the local businesses and, as long as it didn't rain, even the drama of the weather. I was with my dearest friends exploring hidden mysteries and listening to Domano's bountiful stories again. I thought about my mistake of having written on my experiences for my class and how incredibly lucky I was to be allowed to continue my studies with them in spite of my error. As I sat there I relished in the fruitfulness of my good fortune.

Domano put a foot up on the bench, resting his elbow on his knee and leaned against the bricks of the planter. "If the Sun rises in the east then the north is the night time. This is about this time and place.

"A long time ago the Two Leggeds, the Humans, all Lived in this one valley. There weren't so many of them then as there is now. So they all could fit in this pretty little valley together. They had everything they needed. The Deer, the Monkeys, the Birds, Snakes and Frogs, Turtles, Lizards, Fish. They had every kind of Tree and Plant. Food was everywhere. Medicines and Water everywhere.

67   SECRET LIAISONS

"They made circle houses for the Families as their Ancestor-Creator, Sun, had taught them. He was a good Father to them. He gave them Fire to cook, stories to tell, marriage and laws to Live by. And many, many more things. They rose from their beds in the morning when he called them with his bright Light. When he went to sleep at Night so did the People. They Loved their Father very much.

"There was this tiny Woman Child among the People. She asked questions all the time, all the time. They called her Tiny Turtle. She was a good Child, but she would not leave shoes on her feet. All the time she walked everywhere barefoot. One Day she was with her Mother and some of the Women when they went to find Nuts and Seeds in the Forest. She sniffed everything and wanted to Know about this Plant and that Plant. All the things they came across she wanted to Know about.

"She asks her Mother, 'Mama, why does this Tree make this red Seed? Is it just to feed us?'

"Her Mother says, 'No, Young One. This Tree Person makes many, many Seeds so that we can eat, but also, so some can become Baby Trees. That is why we only take a few and always leave the rest. Our Father the Sun has told us this.'

"Tiny Turtle says, 'Mama. Where do these little Seeds turn into Trees? I don't see anything here on this Tree but this Tree and these Seeds.'

"Mama looks close at the Tree and the Seeds and all around at the other Trees. 'I do not Know,' she says. The Women look at each other but no one Knows. 'Sun has never told us.'

"'But Mama, don't you want to Know?' little Tiny Turtle asks.

"Her Mother giggles with the other Women. 'What for, Child? If it was worth Knowing Sun would have told us.' The Women walk on with their gathering, going from one Tree and Bush to the next.

"Tiny Turtle was not Happy with her Mother's answer. But she didn't want to be giggled at again so she did not ask this of anyone else. She decided that she would watch the Seeds and Trees and maybe they would show her this Secret. Sun was much too busy to come down and talk to anybody these Days so she probably wouldn't get to talk to him.

"Each Day she watches and watches. She sees nothing. Months pass. One Day she is with the Women in the Forest and she sees a Nut fall by itself to the Ground. A little Squirrel runs from the top of the Tree to snatch up this Nut. Tiny Turtle looks all around the Dirt and sees several other Seeds and Nuts on the Ground.

"'Mama.' She pulls on her Mother's arm. 'There are Seeds on the Ground here. I think the Tree threw one down just now. Why don't we take these?'

"Her Mama says to her, 'Those are the Seeds and Nuts the Tree has given to the little Animal Brothers. That is for their Food. We are not to eat those. Father Sun has told us. This way everyone in the Forest has something to eat. You see?'

"Tiny Turtle's Days go by and she plays and helps her Mother. She is digging in the Dirt, playing that she is one of the Animal Brothers and she finds a strange sight. It looks like a Nut but there is a little branch sticking out of it. She digs some more. There are other Seeds with branches stuck inside them. And there are little bitty Animal Brothers that crawl all around down there. This is very curious to Tiny Turtle. She has never seen such things before. No one has ever talked about 'under the Ground' or things that look like this.

"She digs along until she finds a small Flower Plant that is just a Baby with its head stuck up above the Dirt. She uncovers its whole Body and there at its center under the Ground is a Seed. This Baby Plant was growing out of the Seed under the Earth. Now she Knows that these other Seeds are becoming Baby Plants and Trees while they are Living under the Ground in the Dark. She says she is sorry for bothering them and thanks them for teaching her this Secret. And she puts them carefully back where they were.

"This is so very, very Exciting for Tiny Turtle. She looks all through the Forest and sees that all the Plants go under the Dirt deep into Earth. She Knows they all started their Life in the Dark, under the Ground. And while they Lived among their relatives in the Light of Sun, part of them always stayed in that Dark place.

"She runs home to ask her Mother about this. 'Mama,' she calls out. 'Why do the Plants and Trees spend their whole Life with half of their Body in the Dark under the Ground?'

"'Oh, little Tiny Turtle,' her Mama says. 'You ask so many questions. The Trees and Plants are not in the Dark. They are where Father Sun has put them. That's where they belong.'

"'But why?' Tiny Turtle asks again. 'What is in the Dark of the Earth that they stay there?'

"Mama shakes her head. 'My Child. The Dark is no place to be. And no place for us. Father Sun has told us that he has made all things and put them in their place. He makes the Light that keeps us all Alive. We Live as he has told us. Things don't belong in the Dark. There is nothing in the Dark.'

"'But Mama...' Tiny Turtle tries to tell her Mother of all the Wonderful Things, a whole World, that she saw in the Dark under the Ground. Her Mother does not want to hear and sends her out to play in the Light of their Father Sun. Tiny Turtle decides that it is probably best not to talk about such things to anyone else.

"Time goes on and Tiny Turtle grows. She is becoming a young Woman soon and her Mother and the other Women teach her all the things she will need to Know to be a grown-up. She helps as the Women deliver Babies in the Village. She sees the Babies come from the Woman's Body with the very Blood of the Woman's Life. It reminds her of the little Plants that come from the Dark, underneath, up into the Light. The new Baby, she thinks, also comes from the Dark inside the Woman out into the Light. The Woman Mother is like the Soil and Ground of the Earth. And she sees that they are both Mothers.

"Tiny Turtle watches the Plants and the Animals in the Forest now very closely. And they let her see as they give Birth to their Young, and it is the same. They too, come from the Dark of their Mother's Body. She says to herself that the Human Baby has a Human Mother, the Animals each have Mothers, the Plants are Mothered by the Earth, and we are all Fathered by Sun. Everything has a Mother. So who is Sun's Mother? No one has ever mentioned this. She thought and thought but could not figure out who this Mother was.

"The Oldest Woman of the Village comes into the hut where a Birth has just happened. Tiny Turtle asks, 'Old One, you have had many Children. You have helped many others to be Born. You remember your own Mother. Everyone has a Mother.' The Old Woman nods. 'Do you Know who is Sun's Mother?'

"The Old Woman is surprised. No one has ever asked such a question before. She thinks for a time. This is a special question. She thinks of all the things she has learned through her long Life and she Wonders if Sun does indeed have a Mother. She tells Tiny Turtle,

'This I do not Know. Sun told the Old Ones before me, the First Humans, that he was their Father. He said he made all things. This is the Knowledge he gave to us.'

"Seasons pass by and pass by. Tiny Turtle Wonders still about the Mother of Sun. She has Children of her own now and many responsibilities. One Day the Oldest Woman in the Village is about to Die. And she calls for Tiny Turtle to be by her side. The Day is ending and all the People leave her hut to go to sleep except Tiny Turtle. The Old One does not want to Die alone and asks her if she will stay with her until she is Gone.

"Tiny Turtle is honored and agrees. The Old Woman says it will be Dark soon and she would understand if Tiny Turtle wants to follow the custom given by Sun and go to sleep. But Tiny Turtle says she wants to stay awake to be with her Friend the Old One. Besides, she had a question about the Dark of the Night. She has never seen it and Wondered what it was like.

"The Old One confesses that she too has always Wondered. Tiny Turtle says, 'Why don't I help you outside after everyone has gone to sleep. We can be together through the Night out in the Dark.' That way the Old One could find out what Night was before she Died. The Old One agrees and when all was quiet they snuck out into an open place in the Forest.

"As the Light left, so the sounds of the Forest changed. There were calls from Animals they never heard before. Bugs flew around them. And beautiful Lights appeared in the Sky. The Dark of the Night stretched out forever and it was full of Life and Wonder. They were Delighted and talked about what this might mean. Tiny Turtle told the Old One about the incredible World she discovered in the Dark of the Ground when she was a Child. She dug into the Dirt and brought up a sprouting Seed to show her. The Old One marveled at this Secret and told her of a time when she was a little Girl that a Snake had come to her. This Snake played with her many times and told her one Day that the Mother of All Things in the World was a Great Serpent. The two Women shared many Secrets through the Night. They had lots of Fun. And this was a good thing.

"Finally the Old One grew very weak and asked Tiny Turtle to hold her up a bit so she could see the Night Sky as she left this

World. Tiny Turtle stroked the hair from her face. Then the Old One pointed up into the Night and said with her last Breath, 'Why, there is the Great Serpent. That is Sun's Mother.'

"'What is?' asks Tiny Turtle. 'Who? Where?' But the Old One could only smile as the Airs left her Body.

"Tiny Turtle returned the Old One's Body to her hut and told no one of their adventure.

"Many seasons passed until Tiny Turtle herself was the Oldest Woman in the Village. She Wondered often of that Night she had spent out in the Dark and what the Old Woman had meant. Many times she snuck out into the Night to explore the Secrets there. She thought if Sun did have a Mother why did he not let us Know? It made no sense to her. But if the Old One was right, Sun's Mother was bound to be mad at him by now for this indiscretion.

"Then one Day this strange thing happened. Sun was high up in the Sky. All the sounds of the Forest stopped. And the Light of the great Father Sun started to disappear. Little by little a Black Mystery took away his brightness. Everyone was confused and horribly, horribly afraid except Tiny Turtle. She knew at last what the Old Woman had meant. The endless Dark and its specks of Light that stretch their way across the Sky at Night could be seen. That was the Great Serpent, his Mother. She was there all the time but he had been hiding her with all his blinding Light.

"Tiny Turtle told all the People of the Mysteries she and the Old Woman before her had discovered, and the Darkness passed on from Sun's face letting him shine another time."

I started to ask about the story but Chea interrupted me. "We have to go now. We can talk about this another time. Let's walk to your bus together. I want to remind you of the training a little bit."

"Yeah. Sure," I answered. "It looks like it's going to rain real soon anyway."

She nodded, "Yes. It is. Can you smell it? The smell of the wet in the air?"

I sniffed as we walked but all I could smell was restaurant food and perfumes.

Chea reassured me, "Just keep trying to notice the difference in the smell from before and after a rain and you will figure out what it is.

"Until we see you again we want you to pay attention to what your sense of smell is telling you as often as you can. Just the way you did today. Don't worry about any of the other senses. Just aim at the sense of smell. This is a long training, you know. You will be spending a long time on just this. So be persistent."

We rounded the corner to the transit center. A campus bound bus was there at the curb. I hugged them goodbye.

"Remember the birthing paint," Chea said as I turned toward the open door.

I flashed my head back to answer and stubbed my foot on the steps. The entrance was crowded by a cloud of cigarette smoke and pizza fumes. I was on my way.

Monday was the first day of the new semester. In the afternoon I went to a class on the primitive uses and techniques of pit fired clay. We were to combine the book research and lectures with the hands-on hunting, digging, modeling and pit firing of our local Santa Cruz clay. I was very excited about this opportunity and walked across the fields to the meeting site at the farm project before the class began to scout things out.

The weather was perfect. Flowers were blooming and I could see the bay from the herb beds. The setting had a primitive charm and seemed quite appropriate. One by one the students arrived and we all introduced ourselves.

The fresh aroma of barnyard animals hit my nose and it reminded me to pay attention to my sense of smell. The need to be socially present prevented me from attempting to reach my center and observe from there. In order to achieve that I needed complete concentration. So I decided to just be aware of as many smells as I could and observe how I reacted to them. This proved rather interesting. I would turn my head discreetly and sniff everything, trying not to look like I was sniffing everything. It was a covert and secret act. And sometimes it was quite amusing.

The air coming up from the south off the water was warm and had its characteristic edge of salt. Periodically, as the breeze ambled around us, there was the fragrance of a blooming plant or the rich organic soil. And when the air came through the north side of the farm it smelt of the animal pens.

SECRET LIAISONS

The professor arrived and we all gathered around a large bonfire pit not far from the farm buildings. He described the requirements to complete the class and handed out the necessary paperwork. At least half the time we would spend outside at the farm or hiking through the forest hunting clay deposits. We were not to use any modern tools or equipment in any of the steps. In fact, we had to personally collect dry cow dung patties by hand in our campus cow pastures to use as fuel for the primitive pit firing. Those not fulfilling their share of the gathering for the group firings would be severely docked in their grade evaluation. This put a whole new light on the meaning of "anthropological field studies."

I was fascinated at the range of information I gained by just paying attention to the smells that were present. There was a primal quality to the whole affair. The aliveness and expanding that I had felt before returned. It seemed to come into me through the very ground.

One by one I worked my way around the members of the group to see what I could find out about them from their scents. Some of the hippie dressed students used no deodorants and their natural body odors grew stronger the longer we stayed in the Sun. Then there were a few of the more socially conventional minded who used their deodorants and perfumes in excess. One young man smelt of cigarette smoke, another of marijuana, and yet another of medicines and vitamins.

I reacted to each one of them. I was repulsed, attracted, smothered, comforted, endangered, suspicious, disappointed and concerned— all simply by their smells. Some people, I discovered, I didn't want to have anything to do with ever again, while others provoked curiosity and a desire to get closer. With a few, their smell felt as though they were hiding away in an armored box. The process felt highly intimate and I found the odors of some people to be an invasion into my being, as though I were being robbed, while the presence of others was a gift. Why I had these particular reactions I didn't know, but I could sense the deeper layers of meaning underneath them.

For the next several weeks I went about my daily business directing my attention whenever possible to my sense of smell. Finally I got up enough nerve to go by myself to a public place and try to observe the scents from my center. I chose the coffee shop at Stevenson College.

It was crowded and noisy. I sat in the corner near the door. People had to pass by me to go in or out. I could smell the food and, as the door opened, the fresh air from outside. It seemed logical that this seat would provide me with the most variety of stimuli. I opened a book in front of me as my disguise, then proceeded to collect my attention in the gifts of the four directions and move into my center.

The smells were a disparate mass of information that somehow made an inviting atmosphere. As I singled them out one at a time I found my usual range of reactions from interest to displeasure. Memories poured to the surface of my mind. I was able to approach them from my center, feeling their dynamics but remaining full of the joy of my Song.

Just as I was reaching past them to find the subtle messages, a new group of students came in and the whole flavor of the room shifted. I felt disrupted and violated. It was as though the café had been besieged with an angry confusion and I began to feel the pressure of emotions that were alien to my present mood. I couldn't bear it and found myself back in my usual uncentered awareness.

I tried to get rid of the disruption by forcing my attention to something else. That wasn't enough so I got up and went outside. I had trouble shaking the feelings off. I didn't understand what was happening to me. I decided to walk down through the fields to the bus and go see if the Hetakas were home. I knew they could help.

My bus connections were fast. I arrived at their apartment still feeling the stress of the café experience. I was thankful to find them home, but somehow I knew they'd be there.

"Hello, hello," Domano said as he invited me in. "Chea. Come see what the cat drug to the door." We laughed and he gave me a big hug. "Yes. You sure look like you could enjoy a cup of coffee. Come. Tell us what you did while I fix a little potful."

We walked into the kitchen and Chea was washing the last of some dishes. We hugged hello and I proceeded to tell them about my smelling adventure in the coffee shop. They listened carefully and when the French roast was ready we all went out in the front yard and sat down with our cups. It felt good and safe to be with them again sitting in the Sun.

Domano sat with his back to the bay. He reminded me of the first time I saw him. He had on the same white peasant tie pants and pullover shirt. I had rarely seen him in it since then and it gave me a feeling of continuity with the heritage I was learning. The sunlight streaked around the only cloud in the sky and caught him down the left side of his face.

"By learning to observe," he said, "you take apart what used to be your shield. Your blindness is what kept the discord unnoticed...at bay. Now you must learn to live by your Song. When it's strong and you are always aware of it, then it becomes your shield. These people who came into the café with their disruption, they startled you and caught you between shields. This makes sense to you."

"Yes," I agreed. "Yes it does. I've felt that shield sometimes while I've been doing this practice. It doesn't block the world out or smother it. It actually made it quite clear. It's like I watched and felt everything, even intensely, but I didn't get swayed by it. I didn't get carried off in its storms, so to speak. And that awesome feeling of the Song is there. It's under it all, or in the middle of it. So what is happening here?"

Domano drew several little circles on the dirt with his finger and then pointed from one to the other. "There is energy given back and forth. Information, back and forth. With everything we contact. Often it happens that one side is giving more than the other. Exchange is not always equal. This is how some healings are done. So this giving and receiving serves many purposes. And energies we ignore, that the rest of our self feels is important, will come into your mind usually in dreams.

"This is the kind of information you are learning to catch as it comes at you. The more you learn to observe while awake, the more you will free up your sleeptime dreams for other experience. But that is another thing. For another time."

He looked over at the blooming flowers near the apartment and sniffed the air. "Smelling is similar to touching. It is like touching at a distance. And it is like tasting because we take it inside ourselves. But its secret is that it is a trigger for the fuel that sustains us—the winds, the airs, they are our breath of life. When one breathes in, one breathes life into the lungs, into the heart. And it pulls the breath of the Earth Fire Serpent into our body. When we breathe out, we breathe out a little life also." With one line he drew a continuous, unbroken series of figure eights that connected all the circles. "Giving and receiving. Giving and receiving. This is the way of things.

"It can be said that on the path of life one is always choosing between living in the pain of the blindness or in the joy of the Song. If you choose blindness you make a separation between you and all things, all your relatives. You re-act on the world in discord. The world is 'the other,' and you feel driven to control it. When you choose to dance with Song, you interlace with the world, you are intimate like lovers. And you make harmony with all the other parts."

He nodded to me. "This is dancing the web. This is what you are learning to do."

Chea had been sitting with her legs crossed and her skirt tucked over her knees, quietly observing everything. She pushed the loose hair back off her face. "When you are learning to live by your Song, each act you perform successfully from your center in this way, it is an act of equity. A show of honor to all your beloved world. Someday all your acts will be a show of honor.

"These ways of thinking are woven deep into our tribal culture. We have a custom for hello or good bye. We say, '*Manaole u manaole*' (mah-nah-ol). We touch our heart, then touch our hand toward the Earth, then touch the heart of the one we are speaking to. The words mean 'Song to Song,' and it wishes the blessing of the Song of our Mother Earth to live in our heart and in the heart of our friend. It asks that we always will be able to interact with each other from heart to heart and Song to Song."

Domano rolled over on the ground, "I want to tell you a little story. This would be good for right now."

"First," Chea interrupted him, "before you start with that, I want to tell her about this man she wants to date." She turned to me. "We've observed him. And I want to tell you to be careful about him. Don't get clouded by your desires. He has lots of charm. Yes, he sure does. But I'm warning you. Don't pick him for your mate.

"There," she added. "Just a word. Don't keep him around. Now we should hear your story."

"OK." Domano propped his head up with his hand, smirking. "Now we hear a story."

"No," Chea shook her head. "We hear a story. You tell a story."

"Ah!" Domano laughed. "I see this is a plot. Well. OK. I got a good story here for the women. This is about a young woman who was captured and then escaped. The war party after her was gone for a really long time. Such a long time that it was embarrassing for these men. She was to be their sacrifice and they would not give up. But this little woman, carrying her newborn infant, tricked them for many Moons. This is why they called her Many Feet the Beautiful One.

"Her captors were called People of the Round Water. Every nine years they made war on their neighbors to capture a young woman for their sacrifice to their gods. They would hold ceremonies to fertilize the Earth. She would be mated to a man from a strong warrior clan and before her child was to come into the world, she and the unborn would be offered to their gods in trade for another good nine years of corn and hunting.

"Many Feet's people did not believe in sacrificing of Humans or animals. Her people offered and shared grains and tobacco and other herbs with all the spirit nations. To them this Human killing was unthinkable.

"They lived a great distance from the People of the Round Water. Many Feet had been on a journey with a small group. They were going to the people who lived across the plains to share the knowledge of the storytellers and elders. Suddenly this war party is on them. The men fight to their death to let the women escape in different directions. The war party singles out the youngest and smallest of the women and lets the rest run off. She was hard to catch, and hides among the herds of animals for a long time. But the warriors were many in number and they finally bring her to their village.

"She's with them for many months. They treat her well. Anything she wants they give her, except her freedom. In ceremony they mated her as was their custom. And as her belly grows with her child she planned her escape. Then, in the dark of the Moon, she drugged her guards and snuck out into the night. A night and a day she ran.

"The most honored and worthy of the warriors in the village are sent on a war party to get her back, but she is very clever. Sometimes she would go for miles up a river or step just on rocks so she would not leave foot marks. But her child would wait no longer to come into the world and so she hunted for a hidden place among the river plants to have her little girl.

"Many Feet quickly buries all signs of the birth and rubs their bodies with mud and riverbank herbs. Then she straps her tiny baby to her bare breast, as was the way of the women. She did not dare to stay any longer and begins her hike again toward the mountains of her home.

"As she climbed up on the first of the plateaus before the great forest, she could see them on the horizon, still following. She does not have time to remove her tracks from the ground so she hid them among a herd of deer that were grazing across the grasses toward the sunset. Her Grandmothers before her had taught her the trick of leaving a foot mark that looked like the animals'. They are not afraid of her and she is able to move with them until she reaches the first line of trees.

"The men were good trackers. They followed even the tiniest signs she left on the land. And sometimes they could see her in the great distance. They knew she would tire soon and they would catch up to her. 'It is only a matter of time,' their leader told them.

"They came to the plateau where the herd grazed, and the clear tracks of Many Feet disappeared. There were only the hoof marks of the deer. They searched and searched but could not find any sign of her. This is very strange to them. But the leader said she has to be there somewhere. She could not have flown away. So they keep going in the direction she was heading in, to the west.

"The Sun was very low in the sky when Many Feet came to the forest edge. The deer would not go any farther. It was time for her to leave them and run for the cover of the trees. She tightens up the sling that holds her infant and runs as fast as she can. Once in the forest she could find things to help make her invisible.

"When the men reached the trees the herd was far off. With the last of the light they covered the ground for any signs but none could be found. They camped there through the night and with the first of the morning's light, searched again. Finally, a single pair of Human footmarks were found by the edge of the trees. They found her trail again and they were off.

"In the forest Many Feet walked on logs and tree trunks and up the beds of little creeks. She has a good start before them and could take branches and whisk away any prints. Her Grandmothers taught her how to move through the forest and not break branches and plants, so this is what she did. She makes a paste of leaves and painted her skin and tied vines to her body. She grew real hungry. So now food is plentiful in the forest and she ate the fruits and leaves as she ran.

"When the men entered the forest they are baffled. They could not find where she had been. They spread out and headed in the direction of the footprints they last found.

"Many Feet could hear them now. She needed to trick them again. She climbed up into the trees with her baby still tied to her breast. When they passed under her and out of sight she climbed down and walked back and forth on their foot prints working her way back toward the plains. Before she got to the edge of the trees, she climbs back up high into the branches and heads north.

"The little infant girl began to cry. Many Feet quieted her and fled fast through the branches. The men heard the sound and ran through the brush to where it was. They see the tracks she made and could not tell what direction she is headed in. One man says she is going this way. Another man says no, she went that way. And another man says they were both wrong, the sound came from over there. They began to fight among themselves and the leader is killed. Finally, they decided to spread out once more and cover the land with great care.

"Many Feet came to a place where she could no longer climb through the trees from branch to branch. She must walk on the ground once again. Digging by the roots of the trees are a family of peccaries. She could walk among them and make the footmarks of their kind. This could be good if she can get them to move fast enough. These peccaries are very interested in eating what they found in that little grove and are not going to be too interested in leaving.

"She dropped to the ground soft and quiet like. They looked at her but were not afraid. Then she let out the warning scream of the red haired monkey and they were all off and running. When they came to a stop to hunt for food she screamed again. Three times she did this and then the peccary family ignored her and would not run any more. So she thanked them and went on her way towards the north.

"The men found her tracks and lost them. Found them and lost them. They knew her homeland was in the mountains to the west.

And so they would not give up their sacred quest. For them, they would hunt her till their death. Nothing in their lives was more important. Bringing the gift to the gods back for the renewing of the generations was everything. But she is a worthy catch. Never before had they ever heard of a war party having so much trouble to bring the sacrifice.

"Many Feet walked among the different animals to hide her marks. The deer, the peccary, the monkeys, the wild cats. And the men could not read it. As the forest began to rise into the mountains she returned to the trees. And she saw in there, hanging up in the air, the dead trunk of a whole tree. She thought it would make a good trap for her enemies. First she dropped to the ground and made many tracks under the tree that looked like she had to leave in haste. Then she tied the trunk with vines so that someone walking near these tracks would make the trunk crash to the ground. With a little luck, more of her enemies will die. She left the spot, careful not to leave any signs of her real trail.

"The men came as planned. The vine was snapped and three died. Now there are five left.

"Many Feet was in her own country now. The lands she knew well. She dared not lead these men to her people in case they bring harm there too. So she stayed just out of sight of their war party tricking them day after day. They were shamed but they would not give up their sacred promise. And this she understood. She respected the strength of their commitment to their generations and to their gods.

"One by one she killed her enemies until there is just one left. He was the strongest of mind, spirit and will. His worthiness is unmovable. She decided she will honor him by letting him see her home and family. She will gift him with a meal offered to visitors of great status. An adversary of this quality was found only once in a life's time.

"She lured him up high into the mountains. He knew she was allowing him to follow and made no resistance. He figured his chance would show itself if he was alert and with patience.

"She comes to the end of a canyon near the top of the mountains. He could see her from far down the trail. She was boxed in. This is his chance. He starts to run toward her when suddenly she vanishes.

He can't believe it. He ran to the end of the canyon to where she was. But there is nothing. No sign at all. There is some kind of magic at work here, he thought, and he was going to figure it out. The Sun had long ago dropped beyond the mountain so he spent the night there and waited for the dawn.

"When the light of the day came he examined the cliffs foot by foot. Then he saw it. In a long crack, as he stood just right, a hole through the canyon wall can be seen. He moves into it. There, on the other side, the land drops a little and the small crest of the mountain is near the center of this hidden place. And on this knoll is a small hut of rocks and mud. She is there with her mother, her three Grandmothers and her baby slung at her breast. The six generations together. They are watching him.

"He raises his bow to shoot but can not bring himself to cause harm to her and throws his weapons to the ground. The women go into the hut and he follows. The oldest points for him to sit on the ground. Many Feet sits across from him. Hours pass and one by one the Grandmothers each bring a special food in his honor. The young warrior can't take his eyes off Many Feet. The longer they stare at each other the more his heart fills with his love for her. He no longer desires to return to his home. He feels that if he cannot stay his life near her, to love and care for her and her generations, then life will be too empty to be worth living.

"When the meal is done he cannot keep silent. He tells them of his love and what his only desire is. Many Feet consents. The Grandmothers can see the love she has in her heart for him and they are happy."

This story fascinated me. I enjoyed the character of Many Feet a great deal. I could identify with her instinct to protect her baby. I think if I were in her position I would feel the same. The rest of the story was a mystery to me and seemed to take odd twists. I knew I would be thinking about this one for a long time to come.

The Sun was low now, my clue to get back home to my own kids. I took the coffee cups back inside. We hugged goodbye and set our next meeting time.

For months I studied the sense of smell with all the concentration I was able to maintain. Every opportunity I could make I observed the scents around me and my responses to them. The Hetakas and I met many times, going to the beach, downtown, into the forest, all solely for the purpose of observing the sense of smell. I could see the difference in my attitude toward being touched by the outside. With each day the numbness that was my mask to hold back the world diminished. Observing the sense of smell was an easy and guaranteed way to find my Song. It made me feel intensely vibrant and agile. The environment outside my body was becoming my ally. I wondered what I had done all those years before, how I ever managed without this awareness.

It was the end of August, four days before I was to meet the Hetakas again. I went down through the meadow across from the student apartments into a favorite little rain gully to work on the training for the whole day. It was a secluded place that I always felt good in. I had no classes and my kids were spending the day with friends, so there was nothing to distract me.

I moved slowly around the grasses and wild flowers as I practiced walking while staying in my center. This usually eluded me when I was not with the Hetakas. I became distracted and tossed off my center by everything. So I decided to alternate the practice between sitting for a time and then walking. I found my feet becoming very sensitive and even buzzing. I wanted them to be bare, to touch the dirt. So I took my shoes and socks off. My knees felt a need to move and bend. I didn't want to keep still.

As I enjoyed the Song inside myself I sensed the Songs of all those around me. It never ceased to fill me with awe. Everything was so fiercely alive—the rocks, the dirt, the little plants, the bugs. They sang and played together as they have through the passage of time. A small squirrel ran up near where I was sitting. He stopped and sniffed the air in my direction. I sniffed in his direction too, but could not detect a scent that might have been his. He didn't seem to be bothered by my presence and went about the business of his games with his neighbors.

After I had been there a number of hours I was taking very slow steps up the gully, drifting in and out of my center, when something shifted. There were two pictures of the land around me, each transparent to the other. I recognized it. It was the effect of seeing different time layers simultaneously.

I glanced around at the two worlds. Then I stopped moving and held perfectly still. Not one yard from me was a huge mountain lion.

She was crouched low, scouting the area. Her eyes were exacting. She knew everything that came into her territory. Her natural state of alertness thoroughly impressed me. She was so independent and self-sufficient, perfectly wild and free, and yet interactive with the whole of her environment.

Something caught her attention. She began to sniff the air and tense her muscles. As she turned to catch the wind from my direction I started to shake. I knew logically that she wasn't in my world but I couldn't hold back the fear of her discovering me there and attacking. The breeze moved past my face. There was the smell of a fur bearing animal. We were face to face. Our eyes met. She had such a curious look about her I was sure that she could see me. I didn't even breathe.

We stared at each other for an eternity.

The memory of what happened next has gone. It was dark before I found myself in the field, cold and barefoot. My mind was disoriented. I slung my shoes over my shoulder, still shaking, and walked home to fix dinner for my kids.

FOUR

THE DEVIL STOLE THE APPLE

THE time layer experience with the mountain lion entered my thoughts less and less until I had forgotten it altogether. It's as though, in a day or two's time, it just drifted away out of my memory and I wasn't even aware that it had been there, let alone that I had lost it.

Fall classes at the college hadn't started yet and I had more free time than usual. I went to the beach cliffs on the west edge of town. The tide was low when I climbed down on the boulders to the bay's edge. The waves seemed almost asleep, barely rocking back and forth over the seaweed. It was hot in the Sun and a haze was rising from the surface of the bay. I could feel the water in the air as it evaporated and dispersed into the sky.

It made me think of the life providing cycles in which water has moved on our world. A few months ago I had gone to a science lecture on the origins of life on our Earth. It was said that some scientists believe a large portion of our planet's water came from meteors and comets, and in the explosions of their collisions with

Earth the oxygen and hydrogen they carried were released. In time the gasses condensed into water and with the developing atmosphere began the cycles of evaporation, cloud formation and rain.

Staring into the thin wisps of mist I wondered if the hypothesis was correct. How does water come to be on one planet and not another? Surely meteors and comets strike other celestial bodies as well. What is the component missing on those worlds that we have here? Are there keepers on other worlds? Is it the keepers who make the difference? The Hetakas said that without water life would not be here, that water was responsible for our life. I wondered what it was about water that the science of my culture had not been observing.

The air was full of the scent of salt and seaweed. I loved that smell. I had grown-up with it. The seaside was always there for me, always comforting, always showing me the perspective of time. I picked up shells, rocks and water plants to smell. There was a continuity through the passage of the millennia in their essence. Their lives with the sea were primary to their being. I could feel the great waters of the world in their bodies.

As I held a little empty shell I thought about the creature that must have lived there once. I wondered what happened to it, what it did in its life, where it had been, if it were dead. All these cycles reminded me of the cycles I had undergone. And my thoughts turned once again to the time I spent in the cave, the burning of my flesh, dying to what I had been before in order to begin a new kind of experience, a new kind of strength for a road of no return.

Thinking of the cave brought back its feeling. The quest Chea gave me to find whose Song it was I felt in that cave weighed heavily on me. Its identity always felt so close but I could never quite recognize it. My frustration was worse every time I thought about it. And now it almost seemed that the Song was coming at me from these cliffs, the sands, the waters. While the tide was low I decided to look for a cave I could enter and recreate some of the effect of the original experience. Maybe that's all it would take to jar my memory.

I felt the pull of that Song throughout my body. I climbed as fast as I could, clinging to the rocks and dirt. I ran the sequence of the cave passage through my mind. In recalling the midwife I felt reassured the Song I was questing was not hers. She was another thing, another being. Her Song and individuality were clear to me. She was my guide, my friend.

This other, the presence in the cave, was bigger, even older. She was deeply seduced with diversity of form and sensuality was an ember that drove her. We were linked, but why or how I couldn't say.

I clambered and slipped on the wet, broken ground and sea anemones. I knew I was close to something. A breeze was stirring and the waves were beginning to splash up onto the rocks. The tide appeared to be rising fast. If there was a cavern in these cliffs I would have to find it soon before it went under water.

I came to an impassable place. The wall jutted up and out over the water. I would have to wade through the waves or turn back. It didn't look very deep, maybe waist high. So I decided, what the heck—all or nothing, and stepped out into the surf.

As I came around the bend there was a little cove maybe forty feet in width. There were plenty of boulders to climb and sit on. I noticed coming out of the water was a massive piece of cliff that had the same kind of rock formations as were in the cave. It looked like a giant, undulating serpent. It reminded me of a story Domano had told me of the Great Dragon.

The story takes place in the days when the Sun, Moon and Stars were young. A number of small tribes of peoples lived then. There were tiny insect people, four-legged people, flying people, swimming people, green people, wind and water people, two-legged people, and one huge Dragon person.

One day the Sun stood still in the sky and large balls of fire began to fall from the heavens. The peoples were afraid and many died. Everyone ran to the Dragon for safety because they thought it was going to be the end of all things.

So the Dragon tucked them under her scales and feathers. She fed them with her own flesh, quenched their thirst with her blood, and blew on them so they would be cool and would have air to breathe. Then she danced and rocked her huge body back and forth until she made the land rock. Sun lost his grip and rolled across the sky. Then Night came and pushed Sun back where he belonged.

As I climbed up to the first flat of the formation I could feel a vibration almost like the low, inaudible hum of a motor. I reached out and touched the rock of the cliff. Perhaps it was coming from

THE DEVIL STOLE THE APPLE

cars that might be driving nearby. I listened carefully for the sounds of automobiles and realized I had walked far enough down the coast to be at least a half mile from the nearest road. I had never noticed feeling anything like this hum before. Maybe it was caused from the movements of the waves.

I stared up at the cliff trying to find a clue to the burning cave's secret. Both she and the Dragon were strongly feminine. Both gave of their own flesh and life for the well-being of another. If this was truly a quality of the female I wondered if I could or would ever be able to perform such an act. And I realized I already had. I had given of my own flesh and blood in the birthing of my children.

The waves began to splash up higher and higher with each crest now. I looked at the rock I was sitting on. It was easy to see that the tide usually came well above this spot and was now returning fast. Luckily there was a way to climb to the top along the side of the Dragon's back.

When I reached level ground I discovered that I was at the edge of somebody's artichoke field. I had walked a great deal farther than I realized. Now I was going to have a long hike through private property and down the highway to get to the bus stop. I was thankful there didn't seem to be anybody around. I didn't want to explain my presence to some annoyed farmer. I walked down the side of the field and into a grove of eucalyptus trees.

It was getting to be late in the day and the shadows were long and harsh. As I headed toward the highway I began to feel uncomfortable. There was a rustling noise behind me, like footsteps through the leaves and bark strips. I wondered if I had made a mistake to come all the way out here by myself. Women had been disappearing with little trace from places like this.

I picked up my pace. The sounds stayed close behind me. I whipped my head around fast to catch a glimpse of what was there. I could see nothing but the shedding eucalyptus and their shadows. Fear began to take little pieces of me. I didn't want to give in to it. I knew that if I did I would lose all clarity and that is no way to meet one's trouble or Death.

I tried to stay calm as I began to run toward the highway. At least there the road was crowded; an attacker would be seen by many. And if I had to I could actually run into the traffic.

I jogged down the bicycle lane of the highway toward the bus stop. It was several miles away. As the Sun set the feeling of being watched pressed on my stomach. I was becoming terrified that it might be a long, dangerous time before the bus arrived. Tears welled up in my eyes when I got to the covered waiting area and the bus was rolling up to the stop.

What an incredible relief to get inside a vehicle. I was an absolute wreck and shaking all over. My clothes were wet and cold. But I didn't care. I was grateful to be in a safe place and on my way to my own apartment. As I sat there looking out the window into the darkness I wondered if the sounds of the footsteps had been made by a dog or the wind, or even by some spirit being. Or perhaps it was another challenge of my strength by my adversary. I didn't know how to tell.

The next day I met the Hetakas as planned at the old clock in the downtown mall. We watched the people pass by as we caught up on details of the last several days. I was going on and on about all my experiences with smelling and my adventure on the beach cliffs.

Domano interrupted me, "Uh-huh. Great. Good. You are on a real talking roll, aren't you? Can I shove some words in here?"

I was so self-absorbed I didn't realize that I wasn't letting him say anything. Now I was embarrassed and had to laugh at myself.

"Don't worry," he said. "Your work has been strong. You find joy and learning in this way of life, and that is as it should be. So now it's time to move on, time for you to face the sense of taste. But you better prepare yourself. You can't judge the sense of taste by what you have learned from the smelling. It is a different thing, you see. You must approach tasting for itself, making no assumptions."

I sipped my espresso and nodded. My concentration was on the smell of the coffee that I was holding in front of my face. The sweet and bitter tang of the dark roasted flavor was carrying me off.

"Have you heard what I say?" Domano asked me with a big grin.

"Oh." My awareness drifted back to the mall. "Yes. Of course."

"Well," he continued. "What would you do if I didn't repeat what I say all the time? You would be up a creek. Huh?" He laughed and poked me with his elbow. Chea leaned over and smiled.

"I did hear," I defended myself. "Maybe my mind was busy sniffing a little, too. But not so much I didn't hear what you said."

He giggled again.

THE DEVIL STOLE THE APPLE

"Really. You said tasting is different and I shouldn't assume. See?"

"It's a good thing I repeat." He shook his head and patted my knee. "Oh. Geemaneeze!"

Chea turned her head around at him and laughed. He loved to tease her. He smiled with all his teeth showing and said, "That sure is your favorite word, isn't it?" Chea popped him on the head with a stack of napkins. The people walking by seemed surprised at their behavior.

"Look," Domano said holding his face in a very serious configuration. "You are embarrassing me in the public." Chea and I laughed. It was quite funny to hear him be the one complaining of embarrassment after all the absurd pranks he'd played. He stared at us with his expression of sternness slowly growing more exaggerated.

"That's remarkable," I said. "How do you make your face do that so gradually?"

Chea and I laughed. He stared back until finally a smile crept onto the corners of his mouth. "You two have no respect," he scowled.

We answered with him, "No respect. No respect."

"Now you two behave here," he shook his finger at us. "This is always such a good spot for a story that I think I'm going to tell a story of the west for you today. Before we start with the work on the tasting, I would like to tell you this little story. So you be nice."

"Oh, good," I answered. "Let me get real comfortable. OK. Shoot."

Chea and I looked at each other and giggled. He shook his head at us both and went into his story. "There was this farmer man. He was one who lived all alone. He was young and handsome but none of the women would have him because he was always angry and cruel. So, he lived all alone. His cabin was old and falling apart. And out behind the empty barn he threw all his garbage. He had some animals once but they all ran away because he was so unkind to them. Sometimes in his loneliness he had nightmares.

"One day he is throwing garbage into the heap. And he sees this wiggling in the pile. He stops and looks. In the garbage comes these scuffling sounds and grunting.

"'Come out from there!' he yells. But this intruder just keeps on digging around under all this mess.

"'Come out, I tell you!' And he grabs a stick and stabs hard into the pile.

"There is a huge squeal and out comes charging a really big ugly sow. He darts aside and hits at her with the stick. He is very repulsed. She is flabby and covered with all kinds of filth. The smell that comes from her makes him gag, she is that awful. He yells at her. She stops charging and looks at him with her big brown eyes. There was something strange about her stare. It startles him. He drops the stick and runs into his cabin and the sow runs into the woods.

"That night the farmer sleeps very restless. He tosses and tosses. He dreams that a beautiful woman comes to him and stands at his doorway. She wears a gown like moonlight. And sings to him. Calling him to come to her bed, that her heart he has stolen forever.

"The farmer wakes up with a start. He looks around and runs to the door. But no one is there. It is just another dream. He stomps around and goes back to sleep.

"The next day he is at the garbage pile again. He gets furious. That old sow is back digging around. He runs to the barn and gets a pitch fork and attacks her and screams at her, 'Get away! Get out of here! You are disgusting! I hate you! Don't ever come back again. You are not welcome here!'

"At first she won't come out from under the garbage. She shuffles around making foul noises. He pokes through the pile at her and yells obscenities. Finally she tosses her head and runs for the woods. When she reaches the trees she stops and turns to look at him. Again the farmer is scared by her eyes. He screams and throws the pitch fork at her. She steps to the side and it misses. But she does not leave just yet. She just stares at the farmer until he runs back into the safety of his cabin and bolts the door behind him.

"Weeks go by. The farmer sleeps poorly. His nightmares return. Then he dreams of the beautiful woman again. He sits up in his bed and she is inside the cabin. The door is open behind her. The Moon shines in her hair and outlines the shape of her body. Her gown blows in the midnight wind. She sings songs of love and desire, holding out her hands to him. She is everything. His heart and body long for her. And he starts to get up from his bed to go to her when a huge crash shakes him awake. He looks around. No one is there but the wind banging the door open and shut.

"He is very surprised. The feeling of the woman there was so clear and strong. How could it be only a dream? He believes she must be real somehow. He is deeply in love. His heart cries out in pain for the loss of her. He feels he would do anything, anything, to see her just once again.

"The time passes and he lives his life day by day. Always she is on his mind. He does not know what to do. One day he is taking care of his chores and goes to the back of the barn.

"The sow is there again. He thought he had gotten rid of her. But she is there groveling and rolling in the muck. He is so disgusted by her. 'You are wretched, you ugly sow. Go away and never come back here. I don't want you. I can't stand to see you.' And he picks up rocks and hits her with them until she flees to the woods. But just inside she stops as before to look at him. And this time she would not leave. She stays behind the trees where he can not hit her and watches him the rest of the day. Her eyes trouble him even more. There is something not the way they should be about her eyes.

"Days and weeks pass. He sees the ugly sow often just inside the woods, watching him. He yells and throws things but she remains. After a while he thinks maybe she isn't all bad. She makes his garbage pile smaller. Just so long as he does not have to see her groveling in it or smell her. Just as long as she stays out of his sight, maybe it isn't so bad that she comes around after all. But when he sees her he cusses her and says cruel and filthy things to her.

"The full of the autumn Moon comes. That night the farmer sits on his porch looking at the sky. His heart pines for the woman in his dream. Why wasn't she with him in his daytime? He wonders if he will ever see her again.

"Then, like floating on the wind, she comes from the woods at the side of the house. Her beauty is like a magic spell. He can say nothing but rises to embrace her. Her passion for him is as wild and delicate as an orchid in the deep of the forest. He picks her up and carries her to his bed. To please her and give his love to her is his only wish. Through the long night their love for each other fills the Earth and the Heavens. Not a word is spoken.

"As the Moon moves low in the sky she leaves his bed. He reaches for her but she says, 'No. No, you must not follow me. I am beautiful to you now because of your kindness tonight. But until you free your heart from the cruelty that buries it we can never be together.'

"'I can't live without you,' he cries. 'I can't let you go. Stop.'

"Her tears cover her face, 'Tomorrow in the sunlight you will see as you always see. And hurt as you always hurt.' And she ran out the door.

"He jumps up and runs after her. As he comes around the house there is no sight of her. Running towards the woods he hears a noise in the garbage pile. He looks over there and diving under the filth is the ugly sow. His anger explodes and he grabs the pitch fork and thrusts it at her screaming violent, horrible things.

"The sow crawls off under the muck towards the woods. She is desperate to escape his wrath. She scuffles into the trees and the farmer hears the crying of his lover in the mouth of the sow. She turns to look at him one last moment before running into the forest. Her face covered with tears and blood. Her eyes are the eyes of his love. He throws the fork down in horror. His cruelty has blinded him and even drove him to strike his beloved. He cannot believe what he has done. He calls to her to forgive him. But she is gone. He falls to the ground. The truth of his life is like a spear through his heart.

"The days that follow, he searches for her. But it is no good. He only sees the selfishness and cruelty he has inflicted on so many others in his life. He goes to them one at a time and makes amends. He helps his neighbors bring their crops and repair their farms. And they help him make his farm workable once again.

"Time goes on and he becomes a different man. He is thoughtful and kind. Everyone loves him. But his heart still dies every night for the loss of his beloved and the cruelty he inflicted on her. And sometimes he hunts for her through the woods. But there is never a sign.

"Many, many seasons pass and it is autumn again. One night the Moon, she is full, and there is a wild storm with thunder pounding across the sky. A great bolt of lightning strikes the farmer's cabin. He jolts straight up in his bed. The door blows open and there in the silver light stands his beloved. The room fills with the wind. She steps inside. He does not dare move but watches her as she comes closer. His heart soaring like the storm. She comes to his bed and stays with him till the end of his years."

Domano had never told me a story like that one before. I was so struck I could barely think. I wondered where this story could have come from. I looked around the mall and it felt strange to be there. My mind had been so completely occupied with seeing and feeling the little farm and woods of the story. I sipped my espresso. It was cold. I hadn't drunk any of it through the whole story. I think I actually had forgotten I had it in my hand.

"Well," said Chea. "It's about time for you to start tasting. We brought some things along with us just for this occasion."

"Already?" I asked.

Domano opened a small bag he had been wearing strapped over his shoulder and took out a piece of dried meat. As I reached for it he said, "Now don't sniff this. Don't be looking at it a lot either. You just close your eyes. Be in your center and then put it in your mouth to taste. Let it stay in there a long time. Feel it, chew it, suck on it. Put all your attention to what this taste is."

I took a breath and looked at it. "I don't think I'm back from that barnyard yet."

He gestured with his chin for me to start so I grinned back and did as he instructed. Taking myself from the effects of the story was hard at first. I couldn't help but wonder what it might have to do with the directions or the senses. I was in shock from the intensity of it. This story was going to haunt me for years.

I finally relaxed and let myself collect to my center. I tore off a piece of the meat. It was unusually dry and hard. I ran it over my tongue, back and forth. The taste was not immediately available but when I had worked the piece enough it began to get stronger and stronger. It had a smoky, salty flavor, almost resiny. I couldn't tell what kind of animal it was. There were no familiar meat or smoke tastes, yet I knew it was some kind of smoked meat. The flavors were very concentrated and rich. They felt sustaining and nourishing.

As I continued to chew it I could feel the fat of the meat being released into my mouth. It was a most unusual sensation. I wasn't accustomed to eating very much meat and usually avoided the animal fat altogether. The longer I chewed, the more fat came into my mouth. It was beginning to feel uncomfortable. It lined my palate and coated my gums and tongue. And although the flavor was agreeable the texture was becoming intolerable. I spit it out into the planter behind me.

Chea tossed her hand in the air. "You didn't give that very long."

"I couldn't help it," I answered. "I had to get rid of it. My mouth is still layered with that grease. What was that stuff? I've got to stop for a minute here and get that out of my mouth. I'm going to chew some gum. I just got to get that grease off my tongue." I dug through my purse and found some chewing gum and popped it in my mouth as fast as I could.

Domano tried to slow me down and reached for my hand but I jerked my body around and got it in my mouth before he could stop me. "Well for Pete's sake, close your eyes, get to your center," he said. "You just spit out your chance to learn something incredible. Maybe you can try it with this gum at least."

With my eyes closed I ran the gum all through my mouth using it like a tooth brush. Then I quickly took a swig of espresso to hopefully wash all the residue of the animal grease down my throat.

"Hey!" Domano said taking my cup away. "You are cheating very big! I'm going to take this away for a while. Now let's stick to this right. One flavor at a time. You choose the gum, so keep to the gum." I opened my eyes and dove for my coffee cup. He looked genuinely surprised. I had never done anything even in play with him before that was that bold.

"Hey!" He yelled and giggled in his delight. "No fair! You have to work now. Not bounce." And he held the cup in the air just out of my reach.

"OK." I sat back on the bricks and closed my eyes. I was chuckling too much inside myself to seriously find my center and work but I pretended to begin the process. The taste of the gum reminded me of eating candy as a child. And I thought of my sister, who when she was very tiny used to always make tasting sounds like num, num, num, when she was smelling or eating chocolate. I couldn't resist the temptation.

"Nummm. Num, num, num. Nummm."

I tried to keep a straight face but just couldn't. My broad smile quickly turned into laughter and I opened my eyes.

Domano laughed until I thought he would fall off the planter. "This is important for you? This sound?" he finally managed to say.

"Yeah," I answered. "It's the magical chocolate finding and eating sound."

"Oh!" he said as though it were a great revelation and cosmic truth. "A chocolate calling and honoring chant. This is good to know."

He made me coach him on exactly how to make the proper sound. Domano and Chea sat there practicing and joking until Domano laughed so hard he knocked over his and my espresso right down the front of his jeans. I gave him my hanky to try to wipe some of it off.

It was allergy season and I kept my pockets full of hankies and Kleenex. He rubbed his jeans a few times and then looked at the hanky as though shocked.

"I think this cloth was used before," he said. "Did you blow your nose on this cloth before you give it to me?"

"Well," I tried to talk over my giggling. "My nose runs a lot. I gave you the cleanest one."

"The cleanest one?" He held it out by the tips of his fingers. "Holy smokes! I will go get some napkins in the coffee shop. I think so." He pushed the hanky into my hand and laughed all the way into the coffee roasting shop.

Chea and I teased each other until Domano returned. He brought three fresh hot espressos with the napkins. Chea sipped her coffee and said, "Now, really, for serious. What you are learning now is how to live in beauty. In this moment. Like we have been right now. But if your mind was lost someplace else you would have missed it. Wasted it."

Chea paused then tapped my cup. "You need to figure out how you waste so much of the present moment. This is where you have to pay attention with the tasting."

"How on Earth does that figure in?" I interrupted.

"We Humans connect taste to our emotions," Chea went on. "To what we are not usually aware of deep inside ourselves. We take emotions inside us the way we take what we are tasting inside us. When we taste something we bring it into a sensitive, private part of our body. It is intimate. Deeply personal. Taste is for the self. An inner, inward experiencing. It is finding out about the world from *inside*.

"We can take apart our emotional addictions by what we do or do not put in our mouth."

"How?" I asked. "How can that possibly make any difference?"

"We don't know this world or our selves through the words in our minds, Kay," Chea answered. "We know them through our body and our feeling. Experiencing. We are many things, but we are made into flesh. Here. In this place. This is the only way we know our whole self. Eventually it always comes back to here." And she crossed her arms and patted her shoulders.

"You have to reclaim your knowledge of body. It's all locked up in there somewhere." She squeezed my wrist.

Domano's eyes met mine for a moment. They penetrated right through me. It was as though he could see parts of me that had always been hidden. A chill ran up my back. "Yes," he said. "Return to your body. To the garden. You have been gone from there a long, long time. Your people have lost this sacred thing. It is time to return."

The reference to the garden confused me. My knowledge of biblical details and symbology was embarrassingly limited. I decided I would look it up later in the library and see what I could find.

"Okey dokey. Give me another taster." I took a deep breath. "Let's get to it then."

Domano reached out and took my cup. It was almost empty. "I won't spill it this time for you. I'll trade you." He reached inside his bag and handed me a fresh, ripe fig. I knew from the expression on his face it was time to turn my attention and proceed to find the gifts of the directions one by one. When I was ready I bit into the fruit.

I was familiar with dried figs but not fresh ones. The texture was a surprise for me. It was soft and moist with a definite but flexible skin. The center was a myriad of tiny seeds that filled my mouth, I thought, like the stars fill the sky. There was a gentle sweetness. The taste was much lighter than the dried ones, almost like a different thing altogether. I held it on my tongue letting the taste be everything that was in my awareness. I waited for the physical sensations of tingling and expanding, the emotional impact of past memories followed by the subtle information that showed me the potential benefit or drain offered from the thing in question.

Nothing came. I kept swallowing my saliva and retaining the mass of the fig in my mouth and, even though the flavor was pleasing, holding it that long became almost nauseating. It distracted me and I lost my center. I gagged and spit it out into the planter.

"What did I do wrong?" I asked as Domano handed me my coffee.

"Just sip it," he said. "Run it around your mouth real quick. You are taking all your expectations with you. You are expecting it to be like the smelling. It is not. It is another thing. Do it again only don't plan on anything. Just...just let it happen."

I took another bite, and another, and another still. Each was as unsuccessful as the first. I didn't know what I was looking for. I couldn't imagine what would be different about the nature of the experience.

"I must be doing something wrong. What is it?" I was practically whining. "I don't know what's supposed to be there. What am I waiting for?"

Chea would never cater to my self-pity. She looked at me with her face expressionless. It always seemed such a hard and stern appearance and it unnerved me a little even after coming to know her so well. When she was sure she had gotten her point across about feeling sorry for myself she said, "When we taste we connect to a knowing of our self."

I just stared at her. I didn't understand what she was trying to get at.

Touching her belly almost as a gesture of a sign language she continued to try to find a way for me to grasp her ideas. "A way we know our self, our medicines, what we need or want. It can be a way we pamper our selves. In your culture maybe even self-abuse, or punishing, or especially a way of hiding and trying to numb the feelings and memories. Our masks are held together with emotions. What we put in our mouths can show us these emotions or hide them. We touch how we relate to our self or how we relate to the others around us. It has to do with how we know the self and other through our self—inside."

She looked at me hard. I was having trouble trying to catch up with what she had said. I started to ask a question but she interrupted me, speaking very softly. "Oh well. You will find it for yourself."

She handed me a maple bar wrapped in plastic from Domano's bag. "Here. Try with this."

I loved maple bars. But I didn't want to eat all that sugar and grease.

"You don't have to eat the whole thing." A tiny smile cracked over the edge of her lips.

"Oh!" I grinned back at her. "But I want to. That's just it. They make me all hyper and fat and kind of sick to my stomach. But god! I love eating them! They are so much pleasure. For a while at least.

Till it hits my blood. Then I wish I had never seen it. Well, here it goes. I'll treasure a bite or two, but then you guys better take it away from me so I don't hurt myself."

"You mean you don't trust yourself?" Domano teased me.

"No. I sure don't," I answered. "Not when I'm hungry and there's a whole maple bar sitting under my nose. I'm afraid I'm just a weenie." They laughed.

I took a deep breath to set myself to my center.

The maple bar in my mouth was all the pleasure I remembered it to be. It reminded me of warm little bakeries with a few good companions and talking late into the night. Or bright and early breakfasts with a friend or two, on our way to do something special.

I waited for something to change, some kind of insight or sensations in my body or emotions, and again nothing happened. The flavors and textures were familiar and pleasing, even comforting, but it was just food in my mouth as I had had food in my mouth countless times before. I felt aimless, lost. I took one last little bite and handed the rest of the maple bar to Domano.

"That's a pretty big pout you got there," Domano said as he studied my face with an exaggerated seriousness.

Chea handed me my coffee. "Here. Charge up. You need it," she said. "You're going to be communicating with the world inside of you. The world that is so very private and guarded it doesn't even want *you* looking in. You're going to see how the medicine of that place is shaped and kept."

"Now I know when it..." I tried to ask about the psychological impact of smelling and what the relationship might be to tasting but Chea stopped me.

"It has a different purpose than smelling. Forget the smelling for this moment. If you can allow yourself to see into tasting then you can find how you keep yourself from seeing with the eyes of your heart."

I must have had a very stressed look on my face. I followed what she was saying, I just couldn't find any way that it possibly related to the act of tasting. I felt like a first grade flunk out.

"Let me put it this way," she said. "If you can't communicate for real with your self how much do you think you are going to communicate with another being?"

THE DEVIL STOLE THE APPLE

I nodded, "Let me have the rest of that maple bar. I think I want to try to drown my sorrows and frustrations." I reached around Domano to his bag.

"No you don't!" He laughed at me and secured his bag. "First you make me take it away from you, and now you want me to feed your self-pity with this? Oh no, I don't think so. I don't think so." He held it to his stomach, shaking his head and laughing.

"My friend, you know," he continued, "Humans have the job of being idea makers. That is their place, their power. They make all kinds, you wouldn't believe. And all their emotions they pour into them. Sometimes they pick up somebody else's. And they don't let go of any of them, not for nothing.

"They drown out the here and now. Then keep themselves company by talking and feeling these ideas over and over and over inside themselves. They got pieces of their attention thrown to hell and back with these ideas. Scattered. Wasting.

"The white culture wastes huge attention this way—at all costs. That is how this system keeps control over so many. Your people have been without their power so long that when they got it in their hands it is frightening to them. Now the shifting has begun. And it is for each person to see what they have made their self and their world into. To face their addictions. That's what they are constantly talking and feeling to themselves about. They better collect their attention. And fast. Before Earth shakes it loose for them."

Staring into my coffee cup I asked, "And what you put into your mouth keys you into these ideas, these addictions?"

"Or what you don't put into your mouth," he answered. "Yes. Yes, indeed. Just try to go without food. For four days. Water only. And see what your mind and feelings keep repeating to you. You will surprise yourself."

"Are you telling me to try this now?" I asked. "Is this part of this practice?"

Domano set his bag down and looked me in the eye. "If you choose. If you have the determination."

"Oh," I mumbled. His response caught me off guard. It was almost a challenge. I couldn't think straight for a moment.

He held his stare as though to say, "Well? I dare you!"

I was curious about it. This would be my first real fast. I wondered what it would present me with, if I would be able to last the four days or fizzle out before the finish line. If I agreed, was I going to be taking on too much? I couldn't tell. I had no sense of my limits in this regard. There were no events in my background that could even give me a clue as to what experiences I might be in store for.

His eyes on me were unchanged. I felt an energy creeping up my legs and through my body. Here I was again at a door just partially open and I wanted to see what was on the other side. I couldn't resist my curiosity or the challenge.

"OK." I stared him back. "I will try it. Starting tomorrow morning. For four days. Water only. Is there anything I need to do to prepare?"

Domano gave one nod of his head. "To prepare, no. Drink lots and lots of water through your fasting. And watch your mind and feelings. Remember everything. Watch for patterns. Search deep into the things that come up. Follow them wherever they go. No matter what. Remember, this is your power you are trying to recapture. This is your prayer. This is not to be taken lightly. Find your center. You ask your mother the Earth, and your friends the Wind and River, to help. You ask Creation to take care of you in a good way. These are the things that are done."

"OK." I didn't flinch. It didn't sound so difficult. I thought that this excursion into the unknown would be much simpler and milder than the others. I could handle this one.

"OK." He slapped his knee and stood up. Chea handed me all the coffee cups to throw away. "We will see you two days after you finish. At our place."

"That'll be good. Yeah. I can get there probably around two o'clock. Will that work?"

"This works good," he said. "Until then." I hugged them goodbye and they walked off down Pacific Street toward the beach.

When I began the fast the next morning I wasn't really hungry but I had a nervousness that made me want to eat. I had never paid much attention before to the difference. Wanting to eat was wanting to eat and warranted filling my mouth with something. I stood at the sink and drank water until my stomach felt stuffed.

THE DEVIL STOLE THE APPLE

Dinner time rolled around and I had the kids fix something for themselves. I thought a lot about food through the day but I had not become desperate to eat. Going without was uncomfortable but certainly not unbearable. My mind drew my attention to eating by repeating the thoughts of food, as well as other concerns, at regular intervals like a tape stuck on replay. By the end of the day I was sick to death of listening to myself repeat the same, now annoying, words and sentences. The addictions I held for all my mental habits became disgustingly clear. They were still there late at night chattering away to me as I drifted off to sleep.

Day two began with more difficulty. I woke up with a furious headache from lack of coffee and food. My blood sugar level felt stable enough but I was on extreme edge. I had to hold back from exploding in anger at the kids. My mind was now in serious league with my emotions and I didn't just have mental thoughts about how it was time to eat—they came charging up through my body like a stampede of wild pigs. I kept thinking how ridiculous and useless this fast was, how it was teaching me nothing of any value and how much I deserved to take care of myself by being comforted and nourished.

As time and circumstances would allow I investigated how I was reacting to my oral desires and thoughts in general as well as to specific foods and what they really represented to me. By bedtime I was feeling a little shaky in my body from the lack of calories. I considered the effect the fast might really be having on my physical well-being and came to the conclusion that it was going to be for too short a time to be damaging. I would go for the duration of another forty-eight hours.

I awoke on day three with no sensations of hunger. My classes were very demanding at the college. I was on my feet and required to interact with others through their difficulties for hour after hour.

When I arrived at home in the evening I was exhausted. I hurt all over. My stomach was highly aggravated. Now hunger had not just returned but had reached a state of panic. The only thing that kept me from quitting was remembering Domano's eyes and his dare. I wasn't about to lose this challenge for anything. No matter how bad I felt I had put on my birthing paint and was completely determined that I could see it to the end.

I practically fell onto the couch. As I lay there feeling sorry for myself I remembered the maple bar that the Hetakas had given me those few days before. I could see it clearly in my mind, feel the texture in my mouth. I could actually taste its sweet, gentle flavor on my tongue. At that moment I wanted a maple bar more than anything else in the world. Just the thought of it in my mouth was comforting. I remembered the bakeries I had gone to and the friends that I had shared those times and delights with. The maple bar was reward and hope. It felt like all the potential of the friendships coming into the moment. There seemed to be a chance for some kind of fulfillment that was touched on with the maple in my mouth, like a sweet glimpse, a little sample, of the possibilities that might be coming.

Underneath this image there was only what I could describe as a pull for the different people involved to come together, close enough to be able to trust and accept each other, to fill the gaps of separateness between us. It seemed that the maple bar was both the need for close social interaction and the substitute and appeasement for its absence. It either stimulated the desire toward developing relationships or it placated the need and covered it up.

I had no current framework in which to place these realizations. Even though the Hetakas had been talking about the concept of food being so deeply connected to my subconscious nature and contents, it was in reality very peculiar to me. All at once things I put in my mouth took on a critical impact in terms of what I was feeling or trying not to feel. There was so much locked up in there it alarmed me, the implications were just too big. It was as though I had opened an intrusive secret door that I couldn't get closed again. And now I would never be able to look at anything oral in the same way.

The night seemed long. I slept sporadically, tossing and sweating. After a while I gave up trying to sleep and watched the first light rising in the east from the terrace of the apartment. I wished I had a cup of hot, dark coffee to sip. It almost seemed lonely without it.

On day four I had to spend the entire afternoon in classes again. I was not looking forward to it. My energy level was very low, my emotions were an open wound and my tolerance was like a shattered glass. All my mental habits were running amuck, pulling me every which way. I didn't want to go but I couldn't afford to miss classes.

I got dressed and took the trolley over to the seminar rooms at Stevenson College.

The people seemed annoying and immature to me. All I could see was their insecurity as they each tried to outdo the other. The abdominal region below my waist ached. I became inundated with impulses and fears that were not native to me but that I was experiencing and responding to inside myself. I didn't understand why I was feeling things so strongly that I had never felt before. It seemed reasonable to question if the stress of the fast might produce such effects.

Everyone was in the front of the room so I slipped off into the back and tried to collect my center. I had to get calm. I felt like I was losing myself in a sticky swarming infestation of mental and emotional debris.

As I sat there and got closer to my center I recognized the same quality of "something not belonging" that I had experienced in the coffee shop a few weeks back while I practiced observing the sense of smell. It was a result of being momentarily without anything shielding me and consequently vulnerable to every stray thought and emotion in the area. It was happening again. The only thing I could think of to do was to try to stay as close to my Song and center as possible.

I had walked into this realm of these still teenaged college students that I didn't fit into. I could feel now what Domano and Chea had often said, that when we live without our Song we create a world that we become trapped in. These young people were stuck in a world of their games with each other and blind to it. At the moment I was harassed by their mental refuse but I was neither blind nor stuck. I could choose to interact inside their realm with their rules or not. Or I could observe, detached, from the outside. Or I could leave.

I left. The idea of going back to my apartment and standing under the hot shower until it turned cold was very appealing. I almost felt as though I wanted to wash off the effect of those students.

When I got home I couldn't get into the tub fast enough. I was exhausted, weak and light headed. The water felt incredible. All the thoughts that were plaguing my mind seemed to dissolve away and I noticed my Song as though it were dancing gently there inside me. I leaned my head back and drank and drank. I could feel the water spreading throughout my body, saturating every cell, lulling me to my center. The water felt cleansing, sustaining. It felt alive. Even long after it ran cold I let it pour over my face and body and it held me in a kind of tingling quietness.

By nighttime I was not concerned with hunger at all, but I was shaky and easily irritated again. In the morning I would be ending the fast. I had bought fruit juices and herb teas just for the big event. Domano had told me that once my stomach felt comfortable I was to eat fresh fruits then breads. Now that the cravings were gone I felt I could continue longer without much trouble if I needed to. But I was glad it was almost over.

I went and sat on the terrace by myself and thought about the hidden aspects of tasting I had learned. It was unsettling to think of the inevitable responsibility of facing all my mental and emotional habits. It didn't seem to me that any of the senses should have so much to do with the workings of our internal psychology. I had always assumed that the senses were only a means of informing us about the details of the physical world outside. I couldn't even guess how this knowledge might affect me in the months and years to come.

When I got up on the fifth day I didn't even want any food or juice. My stomach felt fine but the thought of food was very unappealing. I followed Domano's instructions anyway and began drinking the tea and juice. Within a few hours I became ravenously hungry and I wanted to eat everything in sight. It took a lot of control to begin with only one piece of fruit. I picked a nectarine.

I decided that since I was alone I would take the opportunity to pull myself to my center and taste it in the way of the training. So I sat in the Sun, breathed deeply for a time, and began. The effect was so outstanding that without having lived it I would never have believed that food could produce such an experience.

I took into my mouth a piece of heaven. Fruit from the Tree at the Center. I couldn't help feeling like Eve. I took to my tongue a knowledge I did not have before. My world and the world for those near me would be irrefutably changed. To taste at the foot of the Tree gave an ability for focus and growth that was new to my being. It seemed to me at that moment that we were never kicked out of the biblical garden, we just quit eating the fruit and wandered aimlessly

THE DEVIL STOLE THE APPLE

off by ourselves—lost. And if there were a devil in the garden, he didn't ruin everything by starting the eating of the fruit. He did his damage by *stopping* the eating of the fruit.

When I drifted from my center I couldn't help feeling as though history had developed a kink in it somewhere. How on this Earth did we ever come to be as we are? The discrepancy surprised me. I wanted to be around something old, something that had a perspective of the time before we wandered off lost, if there ever was such a time.

I thought of the keepers and decided to take a walk down through the forest gullies and creeks. Perhaps I'd go all the way to the waterfall. I wondered whether they would come to me if I called them and if I would understand what they might show me of the history of our species.

I ran, put my shoes on and left. The weather was perfect. As I walked through the pasture I could see the Monterey Peninsula all the way past Lover's Point. In the trees the air was sweet like bay leaves and heavy with moisture. Ripples of sunlight came on the forest floor as though they had been painted there. It felt like home. Every rock and branch, the drops of dew still hanging on the ferns, they all seemed to be dancing to the morning.

The trail up the first ridge was easy. Standing there on the top I called silently for my friend the wind keeper to come and visit. I wasn't sure if I was doing it correctly. I remained perfectly still and listened for her in the trees. There was nothing. I called again and still I couldn't hear or feel her so I decided to keep hiking. Maybe she would show herself later.

The sound of the waterfall came over the next hill as I approached it. In the trees above me was a large woodpecker with red feathers at his head. He yelled out when I first walked near before hopping on a lower branch to watch me. He would turn his head one way then the other, flashing his bright red colors.

There was a noise in the distance. I held perfectly still, not even breathing, trying to make out what it was. I hoped it was my wind keeper friend. It was so faint against the sound of the waterfall it was hard to tell what it could be. I moved my head to the side and picked my hair up off my ears. It was difficult even to tell what direction it was coming from.

I was just catching enough of it to be sure it was wind when the woodpecker screeched again. His big voice drowned out the little one. When his echo died out the wind was gone. I said goodbye to him and slid my way down to the waterfall. As I reached the bottom of the path my ears felt funny, a little like they do when the pressure changes in an airplane.

"Grandmother!" I yelled out. "Grandmother water keeper. I'm here to visit. It's been a long time, I know. But I would like to just be with you today. I need your company. I'd like to just sit here and talk with you for a while with my feet in your water if I could." I stood waiting for something to change, something in the forest or perhaps a feeling, that would indicate her consent. There was nothing but the atmosphere of welcome that I had felt since I arrived.

I took my shoes off and sat on a rock in the middle of the stream at the top of the falls. The water was cold and fresh. I could feel the sound of the waterfall clear into my bones. It was like a litany that the water keeper sang. I looked around me. Everything drank from here. This place was like a hub and she was the incredible individual that kept it turning. I could feel her near by.

Sitting here like this restored energies that I had lost from the fast. I splashed my feet around. A wind came and blew the branches apart in the tree tops letting sunlight reach the water and me. Her breeze touched the side of my face. It seemed as though the two keepers and I were sitting there together on the rocks at the top of the waterfall like old, old friends who savor each other's company though no words are spoken.

The hours passed unnoticed until a fog rolled up the creek from the bay. The cold was uncomfortable. I started to think of laundry that needed to be done and dinner to fix. I gave the keepers my thanks and hiked on back to the apartment. I fell asleep early that night and dreamed of the water keeper.

In my dream I was in the forest at the edge of the keeper's waterfall and climbed down its west side. The cave that I had seen in a dream before was in the cliff. She was there in the form of the same graceful woman standing at the opening. She invited me to come and sit with her behind the fall of the water where the sunlight was shining through.

Although the image she portrayed was an attractive woman of thirty-five or forty, the feeling of her was incredibly ancient. It seemed there was much of her that was unseen. The way she cared for the world poured out of her in every movement she made.

"I'm glad to see you have returned," she said. "You know you are always welcome here. What is it you seek that you come to search for me?"

"My Grandparents have been guiding me on the secrets of the senses," I answered. "I've been working with the mouth, with tasting. Grandmother, I don't understand what happened to me. I don't understand what happened to my people. I think I wanted to come to you, I wanted to be with you, because you're so old and comforting. And maybe too, I thought you might know these things."

She smiled at me and answered, "For Humans the sense of taste can show you what's obstructing your path to the Mountain at the Center of the World. It is an individual decision. Understand: what is done with your mouth and tongue is medicine."

Medicine, I thought to myself. The word echoed inside of me. *Centuries of medicine.* My god...

I looked out at the forest through the curtain of falling water. The sunlight on the droplets shone like falling rainbows full of diamonds. I knew then that I was in an unusual dream. To my left was the water keeper's spring bubbling up inside the cave. It was all as I had remembered it.

"Please," she gestured with a nod and movement of her hand. "The cup is there next to the fountain for you. Drink."

I scooted over on my knees and dipped the cup into the water. It was cool and fresh on my hand. I wondered if I would react any differently to it now that I had been working with the training.

I swallowed and it was as before, as though I had been dying of thirst in a desert and this was my life given back to me. It went in deep, striking every cell as a finger to a lyre string.

"All the waters are sacred, Kay." She spoke very gently but there was a sense of urgency and sadness to her voice. "Every drink, every bath—these are very sacred things. Give this message to your people for me. Tell them they have broken their covenant with the waters. They have broken the sacred web."

FIVE

TOUCH THE CLAY: TOUCH THE ALTAR

My work with the Hetakas focused solely on taste for the next five months. The growing awareness of the subtle harmonics of this sense gave me a new perspective on how I related to what they called the spiral path. Instead of it being something abstract that I kept only in my head with words it was becoming what I was standing on and my senses were what made it feasible to walk it.

Chea had told me my path would get narrower the farther I went and in that respect it would be harder to stay on. But it would also become second nature to walk in the way required because it is with the natural movement of Humankind. Things always want to move with nature, she would say, and it takes a huge amount of energy to continually push against it.

In the past I wasn't quite sure when I was going with the flow or against it. One way felt to have more energy and the other was familiar clear to my bones. Sometimes it seemed to be easier to follow the old and familiar. It was a path of habit with well worn and predictable footsteps. But in comparison to the other course it was guaranteed to be an uphill climb dragging a cart load of useless but treasured possessions.

The underlying currents of the sense of taste now brought me face to face with how I internalized the elements of my life, with how and why I walked the way I did. It brought each step into realness for me, not just theory or movements that are made as though from inside a cellophane bag. Each moment took on a greater intensity, depth and meaning. I felt more alive with a richness of being that I hadn't imagined before.

My role as mother pulled more than ever for my attention against the time necessary for my studies with the college, selling my art and working with the Hetakas. I wanted desperately to do justice to each. Somehow there was never quite enough time, and no matter which one I was momentarily involved in, I felt guilty that the others were going unattended.

Juggling the supermom routine was always stressful but now the heightened sensitivity of my emotions, especially concerning my children, made everything even more difficult. Chea would tell me to feel it, walk it, understand it and then let the pieces that hinder go. Walking and feeling it I could do with little difficulty. It was the discerning of which elements were hindering and letting them go that eluded me.

February was here already and it was cold and dark. I was to meet the Hetakas at their home. I brought them some sliced deli pastrami. When we had had some in town Domano seemed indifferent but Chea had reacted like the Sun rose and set when she tasted it. I thought it would be a nice treat.

I arrived a little late. When I knocked at the door they yelled for me to let myself in and come to the kitchen. They were laying out a variety of things across the counter. Domano had strings of a stinky, bulby seaweed he was rinsing in the sink. Chea was sifting pebbles out of a bowl of beach sand. Across the cutting board was a pile of small thorny seeds, a piece of black and white fur, and the dried and slightly shriveled head of a little reptile.

I could feel anxiety racing up my legs and chest and catching right in the back of my mouth. "Oh! My god! You guys don't think you're going to get me to taste any of this stuff do you?"

They looked at each other and chuckled. "No," Domano said. "This is for you to touch. No tasting. I think you got a tasting addiction now. Everything is tasting. Tasting." He turned to Chea and said, "She puts everything into her mouth now. You have to watch her real close-like any more."

I laughed. "It's your fault."

"Now there you go again." He shook a hunk of dripping seaweed at me. "Always trying to put blame off on me. What kind of respect is this? This is how you treat your elders? Shame. I say shame." He puckered up his mouth and forehead until I could hardly see anything but the wrinkles.

"Whoa!" I said. "Come back. I can't see you. I won't be rude any more. Honest."

He lifted one eye and peered out at me. Chea smiled. Her great affection for him was written across her whole being. I looked back and forth between them and wondered how they have managed to stay in love all these years. I tried to think of people I knew that had been together for a long time and how they interacted. I could think of no other couple that seemed to still have such feelings toward each other. That awareness made me feel uneasy. There was something very wrong with how my people interrelated. Why can't they find and hold that kind of enduring affection and love for each other? Where did they lose it?

"OK." Domano let his face settle into a soft grin. "I believe you. I let you off the hook."

"Off the hook?" That seemed funny to me. Now that I had been learning from them all this time I doubted that I'd ever be "off the hook."

Domano laughed and plopped the seaweed back into the sink. "Tell me now," he said, "how do you go with your exercises? Those regular ones, not the tasting."

I had to stop and think for a minute. I had been so involved, so preoccupied, in the process of observing the senses these last months that I had completely forgotten about the other practices. "Oh. You mean the concentration ones, the ones to make pictures in my mind?"

"The leaf-on-the-water and the remembering-the-rock and the gathering-the-gifts," he answered.

"Yeah." I nodded. I had been doing the gifts of the directions to shift my consciousness toward my center as part of the sensory training but it never even occurred to me to also work on it by itself or to work on the other two exercises. "Oops."

"Oops." Domano imitated me. "I see. Well, how *did* you do on them? With the leaf, did you feel water touch your skin? The heaviness from your body on the bottoms of your feet?"

"Oh, yeah," I answered. "It was hard at first but I could do that."

"And the rock, you remember its feeling, can you remember all its colors?" He leaned against the counter tilting his head back slightly.

"When I concentrated on just that I could. I could make all the colors come into my mind. Even though they were usually a little different each day."

"Can you hold the patterns of lines without them changing?" he continued.

"That's the easiest part," I said.

They both smiled and nodded with approval. Domano shook his finger at me. "You keep doing them now. Okey dokey? Even when we do not remind you. Yes?"

"OK." I looked down at the floor and laughed to myself. My mind wandered off to the time when I found the little study rock on the beach.

Domano cleared his throat to get my attention. "With the rock now. Oh, yoo-hoo. I say with the rock, it is time you look at a second face." I swung my head back up trying not to laugh. He opened his eyes a little bigger as if he were saying, "Are you here yet?"

"Pick a side that touches the first face," he said. "Start by doing with the second side as you did with the first. Stare at it a little bit, then close your eyes, remembering what you saw. When this is coming easy for you return to the first side and look at it for a bit. Keep careful watch as you turn it to the second. Study the second. Then close your eyes and remember the first face, the turning and the second face. You understand? Yes?"

"Yes." I didn't want to ask how many times a day I should be doing these. I was afraid he'd say several and I was wondering how I was going to manage time for just once a day. I turned my eyes away and he never mentioned it.

Chea handed me a bowl to put away in the cupboard. "So," she said. "That leaves the gifts of the directions. These things here on the counter can wait for us. Let's sit down in the big room. We're going to talk about this now."

I walked to the bench by the front window and looked out at the graying sky. It started to rain. The water was slow and silent. Domano brought out the little heater and set it in the middle of the room. We all crowded around it on the floor close to the warmth.

The front of the heater had a grill that was in the pattern of a circle divided by a cross. Chea said that was like the symbol for the Medicine Wheel of Life, which for us is situated on our Mother Earth. The spokes described the four directions and the four elements, and the space beyond described the fifth direction, the above. She said that all things here were made from the four elements and the five directions, each in proportions unique to themselves.

Chea pointed to the lines of the cross. "Every direction has its own nature, its own part of life that it regulates. Part of your long journey is to figure out just what that is. You have your mind, your senses, your heart and you have the gifts of the directions to guide you.

"Look at the south, the gift of knowing your own Song. Have you ever learned how to do something really well?"

"Yes," I answered. "My music. My art."

"What did you feel when you did this thing really good? What was in that feeling?" She grabbed her arms around her knees and rolled back and forth.

I thought about times I had been playing an instrument years back when everything was coming out easefully and well. I had felt at those moments as though the only thing in the world was the beauty that I was making and myself. I was full of affection for it. Somehow this action was a portrait from deep inside me. They were moments when I was truly being and expressing me and not living out the traits and expectations of some mask. They were my most precious times in those days. I hadn't thought of them in years.

"I recognize it," I said. "How could I have forgotten feeling like that? It was my Song. The sensation of my Song! How could I possibly have turned around and ignored something that important to me?" There was pain high in my stomach for the loss of it all these years. "What's wrong with me? How could I do that to myself? It's like I spit on the best part of me and threw it away." Tears started to run down my face.

Chea wiped them off with her sleeve. "And you have never felt this again with other things? Hmm?"

I thought for a few seconds, "Well, yeah. But how could I just ignore that time from before? Sure I've felt my Song with my painting, watching my kids. But back then, each time I felt my Song that way, that clear and strong, not even knowing anything about what it was, just that it was the time I felt like I didn't have a cavern of pain inside me. I felt whole and so, so full of love. Those were the best moments in my life when I was a kid.

"Oh god. I felt it when I was real little too, playing outside by myself in the woods. I don't think I've thought of how that felt since I was still that little. That was my sanctuary, the woods way out where nobody else was. It was like the trees and bushes and the dirt were my true friends. It was so satisfying. I always felt special, like I had been given a gift from those visits.

"Chea, how could I forget such a thing?"

I was so shocked and upset. I was rediscovering a vital piece of my life I had literally lost. For reasons I didn't understand I had allowed myself to give it up and not remember it anymore.

She put her hand on my shoulder and answered, "When we are very small we sense that to feel our Song in what we do is natural, it is the way of things. We think everybody feels this. But as you grow bigger, in your culture, you see that the older people do not have a knowing about their Song. So you come to believe that in order to grow into a real adult, in order to be accepted, you must stop this feeling inside yourself. This is terrifying. Much too painful to remember. That is why it becomes forgotten.

"But it is yours again, now, to feel whenever you want to. The Song of your childhood will show you wonders you set aside long ago."

"Wait," I interrupted. "Is it different than my Song is now?"

She looked me clearly in the eyes, her face softened gently. I could feel her gaze reaching down inside me. "It is the same. But all things through their movement in life develop new harmonies within their Song. They become part of it. And through the years we explore different medicines that dance within our Song. These different harmonies and medicines are now yours to know again.

"Your Song is your piece of the Creator, Kay. It is how you experience your aliveness and the Creator and the world you are in. In this way it is a prayer. It is your constant prayer to all of Creation whether you are aware of it or not. When you consciously feel your Song you are in the act of knowing Creation and it knows you. Unconditionally. You are touching Creator with your gloves off and your eyes open."

This concept of "prayer" that the Hetakas would sometimes refer to had been unknown to me before I met them. My whole reference for that word came from the modest Christian background I had. "Prayer" meant to me a memorized statement of archaic words, empty of meaning within my daily life, that were spoken to a temperamental and fear provoking deity who was beyond my reach and, all too possibly, not listening to the likes of me anyway. It was a word that had brought stress and suspicion.

As I came to understand the Hetakas' meaning, the contrast between these two ways of living and feeling became greater and greater. In the beginning of my studies with them just the idea that one could be living in a constant state of open and loving communication with the Great Mystery seemed like something only a rare saint or guru or medicine person could accomplish.

But now I have experienced my Song many thousands of times with only a moderate effort spent. Each day it gets easier and the moments last longer. I can see the likelihood that to stay on this path one would eventually come to the state of experiencing one's Song all the time no matter what the event at hand might be. For me the Hetakas' belief was livable, beautiful and health giving, where the Christian concept was not.

Domano stood up and patted his chest, "Who is wanting some coffee? And maybe that fancy meat? You want bread too? Both of you?" Chea and I nodded. He stepped toward the kitchen and said, "Ah, good. I'm starving. When I bring it back I will tell you a story. OK?"

He clanked and banged around in the kitchen so loudly it sounded as though he was having one accident after another. Chea and I looked at each other and said, "Cookies." And broke out in waves of laughter. It wasn't long before he returned with a wonderful tray of treats.

"Now," he said. "Here you go, you two gigglers. Don't you be laughing. I am to make the meal for tonight. You see? I am a great cook."

Chea opened her eyes wide and nodded at me. I wasn't sure if she was agreeing with him or not. Then picking up a little sandwich she said, "My chef. What kind of a story do you have?"

"Oh," he answered. "Today the south calls my attention. I think I will tell about the two tribes of Ecununda Valley. The Red Painted People and the Grass Chewers.

"There was among these people a sacred carving that stood on the end of a staff. Each tribe believed that it belonged to them. They fight over this for centuries. The Red Painted People would have it for some years. Then their neighbors the Grass Chewers would mark victory in battle and steal it back to their tribe. And then some years later the Red Painted People would make war again and steal it back. Over and over this goes on. Nobody knows how many lives back into their ancestors.

"It was summertime and the Sun was high in the midday. The carving is in the care of the Red Painted People. They had it for nearly the whole life of one of the old chiefs. Only a few elders were left who could remember the war party that brought it to their people the last time.

"In the village where this carving is kept, the women and the children are by the river washing roots for the meal. Some of the men are far off hunting. Not too many were there that day. These people knew only quiet and peace.

"Then, when the Sun is high, the warriors of the Grass Chewers' village sneak into the camp. They were good hunters. They moved and made no sounds. They could keep themselves from being seen. They had been preparing for many years to make this victory on their enemies. In and out of each hut they went until they find the one that hides the sacred carving. And they take the whole bundle it's wrapped in.

"In the way of their tradition this was a war battle of honor. No blood was to be shed. Only three people could not be tricked in-to going away, so they were tied and strapping was stuffed in their mouths. Hides and baskets and tools were also taken. This is good. This is the way of war. To take other things like their food, or medicines, or to take a life through death or theft is the greatest dishonor. The whole tribe of the war party would be in dishonor for years to come.

"The Grass Chewers were clever. They had listened to the talk and plan of their elders. They stalked in and out with their prize before anyone could make a try to stop them.

"So then all the Grass Chewers' villages came together to have a real good party. Everyone would feast. Gifts given. And the elders would decide in which village the sacred carving hides. And which family earned the right to be the watchers and keepers.

"Back at the Red Painted People's camp the Sun moves far before the tied up people got found. Everyone went running and screaming all around the camp. The sacred carving was gone. And many other things too, they found gone. They did not expect such a strike to ever happen again. It was so many years since any raids were made between them and their enemy.

"Now they are in the place of dishonor. They got soft. They got careless. They no longer earned the right to be keepers of the sacred bundle. Bad things now are sure to fall on all the tribe.

"They sent runners to all their camps and villages. The news touched hard on the ears of all. And mostly on the elders. They counseled for the whole cycle of the Moon. It was decided that a small band would scout to each camp of the enemy. They would spy on them and find where the sacred carving hides. Then they would return with a full war party to attack and regain their honor.

"The Red Painted warriors were worthy hunters. But none ever saw battle or even learned the ways of battle from their fathers. Everyone thought for certain the days of the great wars were long ago. The oldest man in the tribe saw years ago the last battle when he was still a boy. He knew from the way their enemy attacked that they trained and planned for longer than a generation. It will not be likely that his people will succeed without training also. But the younger men will not listen. They want their revenge. They want their glory. Now.

"The scouting parties of Red Painted men set out for the camps of their enemy. The first band came on a camp where the huts were put in a circle inside a circle. And a single hut in the center. This was not the usual way for their enemy to build a village. They are pretty sure that this means the sacred carving must be inside the center hut.

"They watch for a while and always someone is in this center hut. Always a warrior is nearby. Clearly they guarded this middle hut with great care. The people entered and left with much respect. This is not the hut of a family or even an elder. They have no doubt. They have found the keeping place of their stolen prize.

"The five scouting parties came back to their main village close to the same day. Each is sure they found the hiding place. They all describe the villages made in these circles with a center hut. Two of the parties returned in shame. They had been caught by their enemy. Their clothes and weapons all taken from them. They were blindfolded, their red paint removed from their bodies. And then the enemy released them only minutes walk to their own camp.

"The scouting warriors and the elders counseled on the many details of the hunts. The old ones can see that they had been tricked well. The Grass Chewers knew what the Red Painted ones would do and had made a good plan. They were watchful and patient. They made their bodies and their minds strong. The Grass Chewers are worthy.

"The council decided someone must get inside the center huts of each of the enemy's camps. This would be difficult. Many ideas were spoken. One warrior said he would set fire to an outer edge of the village and drive all the people out. Then they could go into each hut until they found the sacred carving.

"But the oldest warrior says this would have no honor. People can find their death in those flames. The tiny ones and the old and the sick would have little chance. There is no honor in spilling blood. Only disgrace.

"They all agreed in this.

"Many times they gathered to make a plan worthy of the sacred carving. After the Moons came back to spring it was said that the best five warriors would go to their enemy's camps at the same time. All disguised as friendly wanderers taken sick. Then when trust was earned they would uncover the place of the sacred carving.

"The warriors went. Each was taken in by their enemy and cared for. And when the time came each found a way to the center hut and one saw the bundle that kept the carving. He would have stolen it by himself, but he was only one. And his enemies at the hut were many.

"The Moon came around again and the warriors met. They told all that they had seen. Now a full war party could be led to this camp. They prepared and painted themselves and were off.

"When they came to their enemy's camp it was deserted. All the huts are gone. There is no one in sight, not even a dog. They searched the ground in all directions for signs of where the people went. Tracks were heading out on all trails. It looked like these people all left to go and live in the other four camps. The Red Painted men were outsmarted again.

"The war party split into four groups to follow the signs left behind. Mile after mile they followed until they were close in to the other camps. Then the signs stop. The people it seems just disappeared. Not a print on the ground or a twig broken. There was just nothing. They crept up silently to watch the camp, to see for signs of the new-comers. There was no such things going on. No new huts, no extra animals.

"This is very strange. Their enemy is too cunning. The people of the missing village are nowhere to be found. They must have hidden their tracks and gathered again somewhere else. Each scouting band knew it was time to accept defeat and return to their village. They were disgraced again.

"This time the old men of the council decided to send each warrior out into the forest alone. Each to a different part of the valley to hunt for the new camp of the missing people. And then, with cunning and cleverness, reclaim the sacred carving bundle by himself alone. The warriors want to go in groups and follow the known hunting and gathering courses. But the elders say no. Groups are easier seen and heard and tricked. Only a single worthy man by himself can take the enemy by surprise.

"So each warrior sets out into the wild alone. Each to find his own way.

"The first warrior to leave comes to a little hot spring. There was a young woman there. She was kneeling by the water washing her body. He could tell she was of the Grass Chewer People. But he was far away from any of the four villages. She must be of the missing camp. He thinks maybe this new camp is very close.

"He was dressed in all his battle finest. He stood tall and proud and beautiful. She knows he is a Red Painted warrior but she is not afraid. They stare at each other for a long time the way a young man and woman sometimes do.

"Finally she motioned for him to come to her and sit at the edge of the water. He set his bow and blade aside and went to be near her. They smiled at each other and touched for a while. Then she motioned for him to stay where he was. She has to go to the bushes and then she would be right back to lay with him.

"But as soon as she was out of sight a big net fell from the trees covering him. And many women ran out to tie the warrior up in the net. They took his loin cloth and the feather ring he tied to his hair. It was the sign of his family's place among the tribe. And they put women's garments on the ropes so his people would know that it was women who tricked and captured this warrior. Then they dragged him to the outer edge of the forest by his village and left him there all tied and tangled in the net for his people to find him.

"The best of the hunters in the tribe chose to be with no clothes or paint or decorations. As all were preparing he stood in the middle of his village cutting his hair and rubbing his body with mud and leaves. And he took the signs of his tribe off his weapons. Then he left to sleep by day and stalk by night.

"Weeks passed and he finds the location of a new camp. He waits for dark and then slips in among the huts. Nobody even suspects that he is hiding there. He watches the people come and go from that center hut until no one is left inside. It is his chance. He crawls low to the ground, never making a sound, and enters the center hut.

"On the other side of the room sits a very old man, laughing. The warrior looks around quickly. His foot catches on a rope on the ground. And from the roof the rope pulls a basket of stinky root sap that spills all over the warrior's body. He chokes and gasps for air. This stuff is pretty bad smelling and hard to wash off too. The only folks who like this root are the little blue beetle people. They don't bite Humans any but they sure like this root.

"Grass Chewer men rush in and tie him up good. They put an arm flag of the Grass Chewer warriors on the rope. And they too, leave this warrior at the edge of the forest by his home for his people to find. Only by that time he is covered with blue beetles trying to eat this free meal of their favorite food.

"One after the other the warriors of the Red Painted people are tricked and defeated. They are no match for the warriors who spent their lives training to win and whose fathers spent their lives training to win. The old ones in the council tell the people that now there is only one thing they can do. They must learn to live as the best of warriors once again."

I was perplexed as to what this story had to do with anything, especially the direction of the south. And as so many of Domano's stories, it took unexpected turns. I was rooting for and expecting the Red Painted People to rise to the call and champion the day. When they didn't it was as though it started a war council of my own inside my head. I didn't want to deal with this story but I knew it would continue sneaking back into my thoughts and demand my attention.

"So there!" Domano chuckled.

I stacked everything on the tray and carried it to the kitchen. I had forgotten there was no room on the counters to put anything. I stood there looking around wondering where I might set it down when Domano came in and took it.

"We've talked about the south and the Song," he said. "Do you question this?"

"Not at the moment," I answered. "I can't think of anything I want to ask."

"Good." He put the tray on the floor and motioned for me to return to the front room. "Then we will talk about the north. It has to do with the gift of life from our Mother Earth that makes this body here. The substance of life and health. And she always keeps giving, giving. This we come to know from what we call the Earth Fire Serpent. It's always present, young one, in all things. This is the way the Mother gives, with her love and her life energy. This feeds us. Heals us. Teaches us. You yourself know her this way."

I nodded. "The ceremony on the beach cliff," I said. "And in the exercises to get to my center."

He pointed to the spoke at the top of the heater circle. "It helps you find the ways of nature. It is what draws one living thing to another. Pulls. It is what makes all things equal and yet pushes them to be as different as can happen. The gift of the north.

"Put your attention on it. It has always been and always will be present in you and in all things. Now use this gift the way she taught and let it grow very full inside you and move through you like a great river of fire. A great rushing, surging river of life. Through all your body. Your bones. Your skin. Your breath."

It had been a long time since I had put my attention to that gift all by itself. It felt a little strange to focus on just this and not have the other gifts come into play also. I closed my eyes and remembered the ceremony on the cliff. As soon as I turned my mind to it I could feel the great force of energy from the heart of the Mother Earth as it rushed up through my being.

Domano's voice became smooth and rhythmic. "What does it feel like as it moves into each of your parts? Watch it. Listen. What does it say? What does it do? Don't stop it anywhere. Let it go. Let it move. Even out your hands. Good."

I observed it as it filled my form and pushed outward through every pore into the air around me. All these parts of me became more vibrant, more alive, and saturated with the heart of the Mother. I felt accepted, appreciated, befriended. In the presence of her energy troubled areas in my body eased. I felt connected to the source.

Then Chea's voice whispered in the same pattern, "When she comes strong, when the Earth Fire Serpent comes to you, she unties the patterns you have made that hold your mind and body in their grip. She heals. We live in a changing Earth. And you too must change. These are the days of the heart now. The time mentioned in the prophecies of hatred and warring is passing, Kay. Let it go. Let her heal you."

I focused my attention to follow the Earth Fire Serpent as it went from one part of my body to the next. Old stress that I carried in my tissues faded away in the brightness. My muscles were poised but held no tension. My skin was pleasantly attentive, even alert for anything that might contact it. I wondered if this was some sort of preparation for the work to come on the sense of touch.

After several moments Chea continued to direct me. Her voice was so faint it was difficult to hear. "Now add in the first gift. Bring your Song into your attention with the Earth Fire Serpent. Let it be full.

Let it ride the power of the Serpent and send the words in your head away. Use the gift of the west and remember your Death. Remember your Destiny. Remember what the world was like for you when they stared you face to face." She paused until all the words crowding my mind were gone and there with my Song and the flowing energy was the awareness of my Death and Destiny.

"Now look at the gift of the east. At your whole mind—the simple part that analyzes with words and the greater part that reaches out to all Creation. I want to show you your attention."

As she continued to speak a picture was taking shape in my mind. It was similar to a drawing she had made a long time ago in the sand, but now the image was colorfully forming inside me in three dimensions. I saw a brilliant, transparent sphere that represented my consciousness, my true identity or Song, as it radiates into the world. Going out of the sphere were dozens of lines with arrows on the ends all pointing outward. They indicated my attention.

During my average state of mind each arrow was touching a separate box and each box represented one of my thoughts, feelings, beliefs, fears or mental habits. These were the things that described the limitations I had given myself. All my attention—all my power— was scattered to them in every direction.

The beliefs in some of the boxes were completely opposite of the beliefs in other boxes. The energy I poured out to them not only cancelled out what effectiveness they might have had in the world, it created conflict and stress within my self.

When I was strongly in my Song and center the picture altered. Instead of dozens of boxes surrounding the sphere there was only one large box—the subject I had chosen and was directing. All the arrows went into the big box. All my attention was clearly collected and focused on one purpose of honorable intent. I understood now. This is what the Hetakas called one mindedness. This is what's required to experience the Tree at the Center of the Wheel of Life. In this state one lives in beauty from the heart. True balance and health radiate from it.

When I looked at the first image the only thing that was up front and clearly visible were the boxes that were closest. They became the controlling portrait of the moment.

As I looked at the second image I saw beyond where the many boxes would have been obstructing the view. The true central identity became observable. There is a power and a presence, a Self there, far vaster than generally conceived, deep with compassion and understanding, and wondrous beyond all fairy tales. Chea said that this is the heritage of our species and of all beings.

"Stay in your center, Kay," she continued. "You just sit and listen. There's another little story I want you to hear."

Domano picked up the same soft rhythmic pace again that Chea's voice had carried. "A very long time past there was this place with many small and beautiful valleys. There was lots of little villages there. These people were simple. They were farming kind of people. They walked with their Creator and his helpers in the forests and in the fields and in their homes.

"The people loved the Creator and his helpers. And they loved the people. They did much together. Sometimes one of the helpers would even take one of the people as their mate. And this was good.

"There was a woman among the people who was a favorite of everyone. Her name was Lealu. She does much to help her people and she gives them great joy and laughter all the time. She cares for many children, some of them are hers. Sometimes crops fail in the village. But her harvests are always rich and full, so every year she gives much away to make sure her people have food and do not go without.

"There are many many men she shares her love and pleasure with but she chooses not to marry. To spend her life in that kind of partnership was not her way. Being always open to share her passions and sorrows with whoever she chooses was the way of many women. And their lovers thought this is a beautiful life for a person to make. This is how it always has been for generations. And this is how it always will be.

"One day though, she sees one of Creator's helpers talking to a young man. They glance over at her again and again. She doesn't understand about this. The young man did not smile. She began to feel troubled.

"The next day there was other people, talking quiet like by themselves. Some of them look at her funny. She would say hi to them and they were uncomfortable. Sadness came to her heart. She could not imagine what the matter is that people should be like that to her. It was strange, she thought, that nobody came to her to say why they felt bad.

"Day after day went like this. Finally she is disgusted. She is angry. She goes to her close friend, a man who is a leader among the people, and she asks him what is this that is happening. He tells her that the Creator's helper, Cuza, has said to many of the village that she has stolen from his house.

"She is so shocked. Never in her life has she ever even thought to steal a thing that belongs to another. It is a terrible thing to steal. Now she understands. The pain in her heart is great. It is wrong to steal but it is worse to call someone a thief falsely. Why would a person do this thing to her? She has done nothing to hurt anyone.

"The days pass and Cuza goes to the council of the people. He demands justice. He says she has wronged him. She has stolen from him. And now she must be driven from all the villages of the land, never to return. This was the proper way of things. This is what should come to be.

"The council has heard these stories passed in the village. They listen to Cuza. They listen to others, and they listen to Lealu. They find no proof that she is guilty. But the claim is told by a great helper himself of the Creator. They can't imagine that such a being would speak falsely of another. They are in a very bad place. They don't believe Lealu is guilty. There is no proof. But they are sworn to honor the helpers of Creator.

"The oldest of the council stands up and says the talking is finished for now. No decision can be made. Lealu is free to be as she chooses until something new is brought to them. All the council quickly agrees and gets up and leaves.

"Cuza is furious. He gathers his friends around him and tries to talk others to join them. They make a plan to run Lealu off. He took to calling her thief in the streets of the village. He taunts her every chance he gets. Sometimes he would throw rocks at her.

"Most of the people do not believe Cuza's lies. They love and respect Lealu. And they help her any way they can. No one could ever remember trouble like this before. They want to see it end, but no one knew how to stop it.

"One night Cuza sneaks through the village to Lealu's house. He has a knife. If he can not drive her out for the fear of her life then he thought maybe he would kill her. He'd hide the body way off in the forest and no one would know. He wants the people to say she must be guilty and fled out of her shame.

"Cuza gets into Lealu's home but he is clumsy and makes noise. She sees from the light of her fire that it is Cuza. He waves the knife in the air and comes towards her. She picks up her sewing work and throws it at him. He stumbles and she runs out the door.

"He runs after her yelling, 'Thief! Thief! Stop her this time.' But she disappears. The men come out of their houses. They are friends of Lealu's. They ask Cuza to tell them what happened. Cuza holds up the knife and said Lealu stole it from him and tried to stab him. He says that the people must now carry out the law and banish Lealu forever.

"The council meets but no one can agree. Still no decision can be made. Now Cuza and his friends openly try to find where she was hiding. They will carry out the law by themselves if they have to. But the people of these villages love her and honor her too much to let harm come. Each one takes turns to hide her.

"How could such trouble ever start? The people did not understand. Creator has been away from them too long. They sent out messengers to find him, to tell him they need him.

"And no matter what Cuza and his friends did, the people protected Lealu. He threatened them. And they still protect her.

"The day comes and Creator returns. He calls the people all together. And he asks, 'Cuza, what is it you say about this woman?' And Cuza tells his lies.

"Then he asks, 'Lealu. You must answer to this.' And she says in front of all, she did no wrong. Creator says to her, 'How did you know this helper of mine, Lealu?'

"Lealu says, 'I did not. When he came to be with us he did not spend time with me. He followed me with his eyes everywhere. One night, late, he came to my home. He asked me to bed with him. I refused. He says he is bedding me no matter what I say and he is taking me for his wife. I told him I marry no one. And I did not feel to him the way I feel with the men I choose to bed. This is a woman's choice. This is the way of things. No one can tell a woman how she must decide such things. He acted strangely. There was anger and jealousy in his eyes. I told him not to come to my house again.'

"Creator nods. All the people turn and look at Cuza. He said no more and left the talk.

"Some of the people said they saw him walking out of the village. He was never heard from again."

I opened my eyes and Domano was sitting there grinning at me. I had to laugh. I didn't know why he was smiling like that and it made me a little nervous. Perhaps there was something about the story that had escaped me. I was hoping he would give me some indication but he said nothing about it.

Chea stood up. "It is getting late. You need to be going back now."

"Yeah," I answered. "The kids will be home before me."

She grabbed my coat and helped me on with it. "Don't do anymore tasting for now," she said. "We want you to do what you did today. Go through the gifts over and over again. Especially the Earth Fire Serpent. Let it run and run and run. When it moves through your skin and muscles put your attention on what that feels like. Let it make them sensitive. Ready to feel the world. Do this till our next meeting."

"Yes," I answered. We agreed that I would try to send the kids to their aunt for the coming weekend so that I could stay with the Hetakas. It would be a good break for the kids and I would have my first chance at an overnight experience with my elders. I was so happy about this opportunity I was practically jumping up and down. I said my goodbyes and was off for the bus.

I had no problems making the weekend arrangements for the kids. They were glad to be able to go visiting and even though I would miss them I was becoming more excited with every day about this rare session.

I arrived at the Hetakas ready for the stay. I brought a bag of food and coffee and took it into the kitchen to put away.

"Shall I put a pot of coffee on?" I yelled into the bedroom at them.

Chea came out with several leather and cotton bags. "No," she answered. "We need to start work right away." She motioned me to the living room. "You brought a little shirt and shorts?"

"Yeah, sure. Just what you said."

"Good," she replied. "I'll get the heater out here. You change into them."

The air in the house was cold. When I returned from the bathroom I crouched down in front of the heater to get warm. Domano came out of the bedroom and sat on the bench. He nodded hello.

Chea opened one of her bags and told me to get comfortable and find my center. "I'm going to give you a chance to get to know your sense of touch," she said. "Keep your eyes closed. Try to stay in your center. And just feel. Feel with your skin and feel with your flesh. See if you can feel with your medicine. Don't make something out of it that it is not. Just let it be."

"OK," I answered and closed my eyes.

I relaxed peacefully into my center focusing all my attention on the sensations my skin was experiencing. Then I felt a firm pressure on a small section of my upper right arm. My first reaction was to brush it away but I remained motionless and allowed myself to continue to feel it.

The pressure varied from strong to light and went up and down my arm. As it moved it scratched my skin slightly and I thought perhaps it was a stick. I found it to be irritating and had to struggle to stay in my center. I became very aware of the hot air from the heater and the hardness of the wood floor underneath me. A cool current of air moved through the room from the kitchen.

Again I was gently poked and scratched. Now the manipulations resembled strongly that of a large bug crawling and digging on my skin. This I couldn't bear. I lost my center, opened my eyes and swung at the offending intruder.

Chea yanked her arms behind her before I could see what she had been touching me with.

"Hey! You cheat already!" Domano yelled at me and laughed. "How can you do this? You don't give yourself a chance to learn. Come now. Back to your center. Be good, you. You have a whole weekend."

I rubbed my bottom and said, "I know. I'm just a weenie. This end is real weak—the floor hurts already. Was that a bug you had?"

They both laughed. Domano shook a finger at me, "This is work time. You have hardly started and look at what you do. You used to be so serious. I think somebody has contaminated your mind. All you think now is play and play." Chea looked at him accusingly. He turned his hands palm up and did his best innocent look.

I had to laugh, he delighted me so much. Then taking in a deep breath I began again and turned my attention toward my skin. On my left knee there was a light scratchy tickling. It must have been the "bug" again. This time I resisted the temptation of my imagination and tried to understand what was stimulating my skin by observing the actual data of the sensations produced.

The proddings of the "bug" continued for several hours. Often I felt the need to verify my sense of touch with a quick glimpse to reassure myself that I was in no danger. But I remained still with my eyes closed drifting in and out of my center. I realized how much I trusted the Hetakas. If it weren't for that trust I would not have been able to give up my control and subject myself to such a procedure.

One at a time I tried to detect the exact nature of the item being used as the "bug," the memories it stirred, my emotional reactions to it and then to see if I could sense the medicine of the object as it made contact with the cells of my body.

The exact physical nature eluded me. Sometimes it was firm and other times its resistance gave way. It would scratch, tickle and dig. Every now and again it had a cold moistness that dragged itself up my skin. I kept catching myself wanting to sniff it or get my ear closer and especially to open my eyes to see it. The only thing I could guess it to be was a large bug. But this was unacceptable to me and I had to trust completely that the Hetakas concocted the sensations out of something else.

The longer I examined the sensations the more inquisitive I became. I had only one inconsequential memory that surfaced. My mind seemed primarily involved with the present moment creating emotions of intense curiosity and repeating alarms of possible danger. The subtle medicines seemed to be beyond my reach. I suspected that my own emotional and mental activity was drowning them out.

The rest of the evening and most of the night passed while I continued to tolerate the "bug." Domano would interrupt periodically offering us sandwiches and coffee. I'd get up and stretch or trot around the room. They instructed me to observe and to observe myself observing. Everything was important and worthy of being aware of. I was to discern my environment, hunt for the hidden aspects of the sense of touch and become familiar with how my mind accepted, denied or insisted on altering the information available to it. The process was captivating and vitalizing but still I noticed nothing extraordinary.

The next morning we began again. I wore the tank top with the shorts and sat on the wood floor in front of the heater as before. This time, though, they put a blindfold over my eyes so that I would not be tempted to open them and they tied my hands behind my back with a soft cotton scarf. My instructions were the same as the night before. They cautioned me to not make any sounds whatsoever, no matter what I felt on my skin. I was to remain seated, silent and observing from my center.

The sensations began with something soft moving very slowly on my leg. It was moist and felt as though it was leaving a trail of a thick liquidy substance behind it. My first reaction was to assume it was one of those large yellow banana slugs that are found in the redwood forest. My revulsion almost caused me to break my silence. I couldn't imagine what the Hetakas might have put together that would duplicate such sensations. I just hoped it wasn't a real slug.

I realized that as with the "bug" I was stuck in a position that required me to trust even more in the kindness and caring of the Hetakas. There were no memories of events from the past that came to my mind. My emotions became fully preoccupied with warnings of how inappropriate and possibly dangerous it was to have the slimy thing in question remain on my skin. It was extremely distasteful to relinquish that much control over my body. Sometimes the muscles on my belly would twitch violently and tingle. Under these conditions I found it increasingly difficult to hold to my center and at times even to find my Song. But I remained silent and seated.

I relished every rest period that came. I tried to get them to explain some of my experiences or their techniques but they would only joke around about completely unrelated topics. It felt good to laugh, though, like a shot of vitamins.

The rest of the day the sensations varied from prickly and poking to the tickling of a feather to extremes of temperature. Each was a challenge to my awareness. I felt my attention dropping from other worries and collecting together at one place on my skin. With every change my mind would question the safety of the experience and automatically develop a course of action suitable to the stimulus.

I could feel my muscles full of the instructions for action, ready to move to take control.

At one point they untied my hands and told me to stand up and walk around. With the blindfold still on I was to feel everything I could with my entire body.

I headed for the bench by the window and thought I would go around the room along the wall first. With my hands reaching out I found the front door then moved to my left. I swung my arms and legs around to find the bench but it didn't seem to be there. My hand slapped into the window instead.

For a moment I was disoriented. I had expected the items in the room to be as they always had been. Now that I knew I could not count on them to be so, my whole psychology changed. I was in an unknown space with unknown obstacles. I had to rely almost entirely on my sense of touch. I could hear no sounds coming from inside the room. There were no smells I could detect and no way to know how long this part of the process would last. Every moment was an unknown. I became very excited. I was in the adventure again.

I stood there and breathed deeply for a moment. My Song was as strong as my anticipation. Feeling from my center I stepped out into the room. I lived each movement as though it were my very first. I was in love with the ability to feel the action of each muscle, to feel the pressures and sensations on my skin as I stepped and reached. The dominion of my body was mine and with careful attention I could interact and manage my environment as well.

I moved into what must have been the middle of the room. Something was in front of me. Whatever it was had to have been recently placed there. I examined it all over with my hands. It was taller than I was and was constructed out of a variety of materials. Portions seemed as though they might not be entirely stable so I was extra cautious to insure it didn't fall. I wondered how the Hetakas got it into place so silently and with such speed.

At no time did old memories and their emotions rise to my attention. The moment had me captured completely. I was so involved with collecting physical information and the maintaining of my bodily and environmental control that if there was any other more subtle data it certainly escaped my notice.

It seemed as if I searched the room in this way for hours. I went from one place to another and each contained unexpected objects. At one point when I moved to the center of the room again to re-examine the tall structure it was gone and something else was in its place. I was continually forced to focus all my attention on my sense of touch and to stay present in the here and now. I could not make assumptions or hold any expectations.

A small hard object was set into my hand. I touched it lightly over its surface. It had many wrinkles and even a few sharp places. It didn't feel heavy or hard enough to be a rock. I thought it was more likely a piece of wood or dried root. The temptation to put it up to my nose to collect more data was almost irresistible. At that moment one of the Hetakas took it out of my hand, directed me to sit on the floor again and tied my wrists back behind me.

So far the experiences had been almost continuous. But now many minutes passed and I felt nothing, not even the rush of the hot air from the heater. I wondered if they were scrambling to find something appropriate to prod me with next.

At first my curiosity had pulled me out of my center. I wanted more of their stimulations. There wasn't even a sound. I began to feel anxious. I wanted to scoot through the room to see if I could tell what and who was there. Perhaps the Hetakas were gone and no one was there.

More time passed...and more still. Hours maybe. It seemed that there was nothing there at all, that I had become separated. Alone. I couldn't accurately define anything any longer. I wanted to maintain myself and manipulate my environment as I saw fit for my needs and safety. But I could do neither. I was losing contact with my own body and my surroundings. Horror came in the form of devouring emptiness. A vacant death seeped into the room. I began to sweat and shake involuntarily.

A hand patted me softy and securely on my shoulder. I knew it was all right now. The hand stayed there making a comforting contact. I tried to look at what I had just experienced and make some sense out of it but I was unable to. Chea's voice reminded me to find my Song and hold to my center. I was to be putting all my attention on my sense of touch.

As I sat there I could feel the warmth of the heater coming closer to me. The hand patted and gently rubbed my shoulder. It was soothing. There was a sense of closeness and belonging. Another hand touched my other shoulder. It rested there firmly and with caring. I felt surrounded with attention and affection.

Over and over into the night one hand would lift from my body and another would touch it some place else.

I remembered times as a child when my mother would hug me and she was so big it seemed as though she surrounded me. Or I'd be sick in bed and my parents would rub my legs or back or sometimes my chest to comfort me. In these actions of my childhood there was a fulfillment of a bonding. My environment was complete and I had faith in my world.

My mind ran through my life examining different times and ways I had experienced being touched. I remembered my first date, holding hands and the young gentleman leaning over to give me my first kiss. I had wanted to feel his touch more than anything else at that moment. Looking back on it now I could see I felt that until he touched me there would be a giant chasm between us. Somehow that chasm also extended between me and the rest of my environment and his touch seemed necessary to close that as well. He could not mend the world but for the moment of that gentle young kiss, I think, it became whole again.

I realized that as I got older touch decreased to almost nothing between the members of my family and between me and society as a whole. This was the cultural standard. It had never occurred to me to question it but now I saw a grating separation around each person that was a product in common of our way of life. It carried with it a sense of nagging aloneness and a kind of fear or distrust.

As an adult those brief times of security from my early childhood were recaptured with the loving caress of a man. The touch of the lover not only appeared to momentarily patch over the gaps, it precariously patched together my image of myself. If the lover denied his attention to me it brought desperate confusion and distrust. My feelings of safety would crumble painfully and I would feel abandoned to my separateness.

I thought to myself how pleasant and solid it was to feel the Hetakas' hands on me. It helped me see that through my culture, although I intensely needed and wanted touch, I had developed a suspicion and even a fear of it. What would a society look like that believed in a great deal of caring physical contact? For certain it would be radically different from ours.

One hand lifted off of me. Nothing replaced it. The other one patted the upper right half of my back. My attention was drawn to the tense muscles around my shoulders. It must have been very late and I was beginning to feel how tired I was. I bent and stretched my spine and then the other hand left.

I waited for a new stimulus of some kind to replace the old and challenge my detecting abilities. It was as though my entire body reached out beyond its boundaries to catch new data, to perceive the new sensation before it arrived on my skin. But I could sense nothing. Nothing was there.

The anxiety I felt before when the sensations had stopped returned. My tiredness was overwhelming me. I couldn't face another experience of emptiness. I wanted someone to touch me, to say something to me. I didn't want to be left there alone with my thoughts and memories of the cutting pain that comes when nobody wants to touch you.

My mind became crowded with all the countless times in my life that someone refused me that kind of closeness. It hurt so badly I bent over and cried hysterically. My body was extremely uncomfortable with my hands tied behind me. I refused to remain in that position and pulled my arms around under my legs and up in front of me. Then I just sat curled up holding my knees to my chest and rocked on the floor. The tears poured down my legs. I couldn't even feel the comfort of the heater.

The denial of physical contact throughout my years had created an outrage in me that I was unaware of until now. It came full to the surface. The denial was an assault on my being, a condemnation of my Song. My innocence had been robbed. My trust defiled. A wrenching separation between me and all else had been demanded. An unnecessary separation. I felt invaded, manipulated, betrayed.

Before I was twelve years old touch had been delegated to the realm of sexual behaviors and was tainted with Puritan ideologies of evil actions. To be physical with another was to, at the least, border on this sexual context. Touching for the pure and unconditional sake of experiencing, learning, closeness and giving had been plundered—raped by a culture that seeks to diminish and control the minds, hearts and property of all its peoples.

One after the other I had thought of those who had been close to me in my life. I forced myself to look at how we did or didn't touch within our interactions. The pain was excruciating. I thought my heart was being torn right out of my body. I hurt for my loss and theirs and for the loss of what might have been.

What injuries, what horrors, does one endure that result in a person's need to deny touch to another, even one's own babies or most beloved or to themselves? When my son was born he was perfectly healthy but the hospital staff refused to let me hold him or touch him for at least twenty-four hours. It was standard procedure. I was devastated. I can only imagine what my tiny infant felt. The horror of it engulfed me like a demon from the depths of hell. I could hear this children's doctor instructing me not to pick him up too often or run to him every time he cried. How could anybody even think up such debilitating treachery?

I remembered approaching lovers with the desire for simple contact and being rejected over and over again with the attitude that what I sought was somehow very peculiar or unnatural. Sometimes their denials seemed tinged with a need to control or with a revenge against something that wasn't even there anymore.

I cried until I thought I could cry no more. I felt abandoned and guilty. Fear took me as though I was being sucked down a trap door. I was terrified of that kind of cruelty being inflicted on me again. And I was even more afraid of never having a chance to truly be accepted by and close to someone. I felt horribly inadequate. I drew my knees even tighter to my chest and rolled over on my side sobbing.

The next thing I knew was waking up on the floor in front of the heater with a blanket around me. My blindfold and hand ties were gone. The Sun was well through the sky. It must have been at least three in the afternoon.

I felt awful. My head ached and my eyes were swollen. Domano brought me a hot cup of coffee. He smiled at me and patted my arm.

"Hello there," he said as he squatted on the floor next to me.

"Hello," I answered. There was so much I wanted to say to him and to ask but I couldn't make any of it come out of my mouth. It was as though there was a short circuit from my brain to my tongue.

"You need some time to put your pieces back together," he said to me. "You just sit here. Be comfortable. Enjoy this coffee and the Sun we have today. I think your Song waits for you in the light of this window here." He smiled at me and got up and went into the kitchen.

I scooted myself and the heater over into the light as it came through the window. It was warm and soothing. I wrapped the blanket around me and looked at the sunlight as it fell onto my arm. It occurred to me that it was actually touching my body. I wondered what it meant to be touched by such elusive things as photons or a foggy mist. There is something peculiar about things that do not involve all the senses in their detection.

Sitting in the sunlight sipping my coffee I reflected back on the night before. I felt as if a giant weight had been taken off of me. It seemed so obvious to me now that to touch our world in as many ways and as often as possible is a Human need.

When we are in the wombs of our mothers our entire bodies are being touched. At birth we lose that and touch becomes area specific and sporadic. To be deprived of touch is to be deprived of a primal Human necessity. I remembered reading a recent science article which said infant chimps that are denied touch, even though they are given proper nutrition and environment, become retarded in their development and die. And Human adults have been known to do amazing things concerning the prospect of being touched.

It was clear that to take in information through your body boundaries is an intimate event. To touch and be touched is a matter of trust, an issue I found to be very explosive. Can we as a race ever choose to give this experience to others in a good way, to share lavishly in this mutual exchange?

Domano came back into the room and sat down beside me.

"What is this thing about trust and touch?" I asked. "I don't trust someone when they touch me and I don't trust them if they don't touch me."

"Yeah?" He looked up at me. "You aren't alone. Your culture hides from things truly intimate. Especially Human to Human intimate. I want to show you something.

"Find your Song. Let it come into your attention real strong. The only thing in your mind. Yes. Look inside this Song. Can you identify it? Can you feel it? The center of your Song stands on trust; trust in Song, Creator, Creation, because they live the sacred connection—they *experience* it—they *know* it—they *are* it. This is the innocence that you lost in those early years. When people are very tiny they are all innocence and trust and growth. They are learning to control, to master. When touch they need is taken away from them and the trust and innocence is smashed..."

"The only thing left is to control," I interrupted him. "Oh my god! To control one thing after another. People. Things. Events. Possessions."

He raised an eyebrow and nodded. "And then they start to scatter their attention into doubts and fears and what-ifs. They don't understand what it is to have faith or trust in anything anymore. They forget what it means to focus their attention.

"*Power.*" He held his hand up in the air as though holding something large and heavy. "You hear folks all the time saying these days how they want *power*. How they are going to get themselves *power*. The real *power* is to always come from your heart. It is from your Song and the Songs of the billions. From our heart, from innocence, from attention..."

"'Whosoever shall not receive the kingdom of God as a little child, he shall not enter therein,'" I interrupted him again. I didn't mean to, but I got so excited with my revelations. It always embarrassed me a bit when I did it.

He looked at me blankly. I wasn't sure if I had bothered him with my interrupting or if he just didn't understand me.

"You know," I said. "Jesus was supposed to say that. I don't know much Bible stuff but when I was little they made us memorize things like that. I think it was in a play I was in or something. It's what you said. You enter into the kingdom of heaven as a child. Right?"

He grinned from ear to ear. "Right! To go back to what you were given in the beginning." He stood up and took the coffee cups.

I thought out loud, "So does that mean that if you control how much people touch and why and when, if you control their curiosity and affection, then you control their access to their trust and innocence and Song? You control their *power*?"

"Yes," he answered. "Do you like more coffee?"

"Holy nunneries!" I slapped the floor.

"Holy governments!" He mimicked me, slapping his hand on his leg.

"Oh yeah." The overwhelming amount of control that has been executed upon us through the centuries by the manipulation of our senses, particularly the sense of touch, was now really sinking in. "But what can I do to change it?"

"Don't live for them. Live for you."

Domano leaned over, "Take back what is yours. A person's Song can never get cut away from them. They tricked you into turning away from it. To blind yourselves. Make yourselves numb. But you do not have to be. You can fight. Only this war is inside you.

"The battle here is to find yourself and the path you stand on. It's knowing your own Song and feeling this life inside you and all things; living a life that gives as much as it takes from all the relatives and meet them, know them, share love with them, learn the wonders of the world from them; to meeting with your own species in harmony and giving; being able to respect yourself among the generations. This is dancing the web. This is wanowa ka ta see. It is a choice to walk this beauty or to give up and walk as one of the living dead.

"Coffee? Real cream?"

"Mmm. You bet," I answered, trying to catch up in my head with what he had said.

He was gone just a minute. The coffee must have been hot and ready. "Here you go," he said as he handed me the cup.

"Ah! Thanks. You've said this 'generations' before. Why do you say this? What do you mean, exactly?"

"'Generations.' For the many generations before," he said as he sat back down on the floor. "That means the generations of all the relatives, all things before, that you do so in your life as to make them honored, listen to their wisdom, take care of what they left you. And for all the many generations to come, it asks you to make them a beautiful world, so you leave them a knowledge worth having, a way of life worth living. For your own generation it means living all together in equity and harmony and beauty. It challenges you to live to your fullest, Kay. Humans have a special gift for great intensity and variety. It is an offense to waste it. This is what it means."

I looked down into my cup at how the light played on the surface of the coffee. "I really lost it last night, didn't I?"

"Yes." He made no expression on his face. "You had a right to. It is a horror to have such loss. Your people are even numb to the unspeakable horror of it. To be Human is sacred. A body is an altar. If that sacredness is not respected then there is great pain. Great pain. It is our right as Humans to find pleasure in giving and getting this sacredness. To touch is an honoring. It is a sacrament, a thanksgiving. A prayer. A prayer at an altar.

"Now you heal. You relax and let your mind think on these things as it will. Don't push it."

"But I sent out into the world all that anger and resentment and hurt," I said. "I put out there the very things that I don't want to see in the world anymore. So what do I do? I pollute the environment with it."

"You are Human, Kay." He set his coffee cup down and looked at me sternly. "Humans have anger sometimes. And fear, hate, revenge. It is part of what we are capable of. This is the possible way of things, but you judge yourself criminal. When those feelings come...you must go inside them. Live it. Understand it. Do not hide from it. Maybe you can remember their beginning time. Accept them."

I looked at him with surprise and disgust. I couldn't imagine him saying that.

He shook his head at me. "That does not mean you say OK to, you approve, abuse or wrong doing. It means you agree, yes, this did happen, and right now you do have this feeling from it.

"What you are doing with it *right now* is the key.

"Then ask your Mother Earth to take it away so it won't cause hurt anymore. You don't want it anymore, you want to forgive. And just let it go. Don't dwell on it. Don't hang on it to dredge it up and wallow in it again and again and again. It's in your way, Kay. Just do it and let go of it. Yes?"

"OK," I answered. "But aren't I sending out that pollution?"

"What do you want? Going through it when it is there, when it is young and fresh? And the energy is small? And then let it go with the Mother? Or to stash it away. Maybe you pretend it is not there? And have it fester and grow like a time bomb and always sending out its grimy medicine that gets uglier and bigger year to year?"

"Oh...yeah." After all this time of working with the Hetakas I finally understood what that was all about. I felt that now I was able to let go.

His eyes smiled at me. "The Mother knows how to take care of those things. We don't do so good at it. Let her do her job for you."

I lowered my cup from my mouth and nodded.

Chea came in and joined us. The subject was dropped. We ate the end of the deli food I had brought and talked and joked about nothing in particular through the rest of the afternoon.

For the next six months I was to observe touch in the same fashion I had observed smell and taste. It was seldom easy and not always pleasant but the rewards were uncountable.

I met with the Hetakas frequently and because of the intense emotional trauma surrounding the sense of touch we always worked on it in the privacy of their apartment until this last week of July. It was a Saturday morning when I arrived at their place. The kids were taken care of through the night so I had the whole time free. The Hetakas were all packed and ready for a day with a barbecue dinner on the beach. They had asked me to bring hot dogs and now I knew why. We lay in the Sun, played in the sand and waves, and intermittently worked on the training.

Through touch I could understand information from my world in terms of controlling my body and environment and satisfying my Human need for curiosity and sharing affection. I was now being directed in aiming my attention toward perceiving the subtle energies, or medicines, that are available through touching.

I was to observe from my center, leaving my mind blank of words and ideas, so that the quiet impressions could be caught. Sometimes they just appear in your mind, she would say, or try to get your attention through your body with little sensations. All too often I couldn't tell the difference between what was coming from outside and what was being generated from me inside.

I stood at the edge of the waves as they lapped up onto my feet, with my eyes closed.

"Don't just feel the touching with your skin," Domano said. "The experience you are looking for, it's like you are reaching out and looking out through your skin along with feeling the touch."

I did as he said and it almost seemed as though there was something there to be viewed. "Oh, I don't know, Domano," I whined. "It looks awfully dark."

"Well," he answered, "turn the lights on."

When he said that it was as though the surrounding area close to my skin lit up. I could "see" the waves as they moved back and forth from the perspective of my feet. Floating in the water was a little transparent blue form. As it rolled around over the sand I recognized it as a stinging jellyfish. I jumped back and opened my eyes. And at my feet was a small clear jellyfish with tiny blue fibers in its center.

My heart began to beat fast and I had to catch my breath. "That was it. That was it. I did it."

"Yes." Domano smiled and laughed. "Now come. Let's warm up and relax."

As the Sun set we built a little fire out of the wood we brought and stuck the hot dogs on the sticks. The few scattered clouds seemed to collect in the west just to make a painted show for us. We talked long about the hidden aspects of touching.

The darkness came while I stared into the fire. The waves rumbled and rolled in the distance behind us. Domano added wood from time to time and poked at the coals. They were deep red with small yellow and blue flames that climbed up into the cold salt air. It reminded me of the fires in the spirit cave that lit my way and consumed my boundaries.

In thinking on my death I hoped I would be ready, so that on that day my obituary would be able to say I was a strong individual; that I nurtured my uniqueness; that I always stood up for equity and diversity to their fullest among all things; that the ordinariness of the white culture is a crime of boredom and a waste of sacred potential. I hoped it would say that I was never ordinary.

SIX

SOUNDS TO ANOTHER WORLD

AUGUST was hot and dry. It was a Saturday and the Hetakas decided we should go to the Boardwalk. Hundreds and hundreds of people were there all trying to escape the heat. There wasn't a single spot of sand left to sit on. We walked slowly through the edge of the water dodging children, beach balls and yipping dogs.

I thought we were going to go to the mall to shop so I wore cotton pants and a blouse. I would much rather have had a bathing suit on and be splashing in the waves. Domano had on cutoff jeans, a thin peasant shirt and no shoes. Chea was also barefoot with an old skirt and sleeveless top. I felt overdressed, hot and out of place. I got tired of holding my shoes and wished I had left them back at the Hetakas' apartment.

Domano thought it would be fun to go down the pier and see how the fishermen were doing. So we turned around and headed back toward the west end of the beach.

Instead of walking through the water as before Domano led us into the middle of the crowded sunbathers. It was difficult to maneuver around them. I inadvertently stepped on towels, toys or toes. There was noise everywhere. I couldn't hear Chea talking to me as she walked in front. People were screaming and laughing and some were probably cussing at me. Every new burst of sound took my attention. I wanted to be polite to people but I couldn't focus well on anything, especially what Chea was saying.

Domano stepped in front of someone's rocketing volleyball and made it look like he caught it by accident. I was quite sure he did it on purpose. He convinced the young men who looked like college students to volley it back and forth with him a few rounds. Each time he caught the ball he stumbled closer to me as if he were thrown off balance. He was really quite artful at this kind of deception. But I knew better.

I became so involved in watching him it never occurred to me that maybe I should move. It didn't take him long and when he was only a couple of feet away he pretended to let the ball get out of control and had to stretch way back for it. In his reach he let himself fall backwards into me.

I wasn't expecting him to do anything like that at all. I completely lost my balance and fell back onto somebody's blanket spread with a beautiful lunch. When they saw the two of us headed for them they jumped out of the way. But I managed to land in a plastic bowl full of bright red salsa. It was a very good salsa too, homemade with lots of fresh cilantro.

Domano was on top of me laughing. He pulled himself up, managing not to disturb anything else. "Hey," he said. "You better close your mouth before you catch all these flies." His laugh was so contagious everyone around joined him.

I was so taken by surprise I didn't notice that my mouth was as wide open as I could get it. I looked around at the incredible mess I had made. The salsa was all over me, the blanket and was splashed into every dish. I could do nothing but lie there and laugh.

A woman's voice said, "If you don't wash it out of your clothes now you'll never get it out."

She was right. My nice pants were probably going to be ruined forever with tomato stains. If I was going to try to save them I had better do it fast before the heat baked it in. I looked around at the kids running and playing in the waves.

"Oh, what the hell!" I waved Domano over. "Come on, you old fart. Last one in the water eats ugly toads for dinner." I jumped up and ran as fast as I could through the people and splashed into the waves. I was expecting Domano to give me a true contest but I turned to see him gasp for air and doddle along as one his age would be expected to do. Everyone looked at me as though I was being a bit unfair and unkind to the sweet little old man I had been escorting down the beach.

"Well," I giggled at him when he got close. "You've done it to me again. Honestly. I can't take you anywhere." And I splashed him with an armful of water. He was delighted. He laughed so hard he could hardly splash back. Chea got the woman whose salsa I ruined to look after my shoes and she joined us. We had a wonderful little battle and the spots even came out of my pants.

After a while we walked up on the pier to find a place to sit down and dry off. There were mostly boys lining the east side doing their best to get a good catch. We walked slowly among them until we found an empty log used to mark off the parking area and sat down there.

"Ahh," Chea sighed. "This is a good day. The ocean goes like it never ends. So much water. What an incredible thing. This air, too, I think it's wetter down here at the pier. Not as wet as home, though."

"Do you miss home?" I asked.

"Sometimes," she said with a slight expression of longing as she looked around. "But there is always so much that is new to see, and to feel, to listen to. I just can't seem to find the time anymore to do moping."

I laughed. She had such a quiet sense of humor. "Just can't seem to find any time to squeeze it in, huh?" She nodded as though it was a legitimate concern.

Her eyes caught mine for a moment as she turned her head. It made my stomach roll all the way up to my throat. She said without warning, "This is a good time here to start work on the next sense. I want you to stop working on the touching for now. We will go to the sense of hearing today. Get yourself ready. Breathe deep and filling now."

145   SOUNDS TO ANOTHER WORLD

"But there's so much noise here." I was surprised at the abruptness of the change of subject. Even after all this time working with them they still frequently caught me off guard. This also seemed to be a strange choice of locations for listening practices. The noise level on the whole Boardwalk area was nerve shattering. "Is this really such a good spot?"

Her expression was unchanged. "It's good to be ready for any sudden challenge, don't you think? You can't afford to let something throw you off. If you are ready to move in any direction on the inside, you know, then you will be ready to move on the outside. Come on, breathe. It's time now."

Without letting myself argue about it any longer in my head I did as she asked and settled myself into my center. The chaos of the pier rose in my ears. There must have been every conceivable noise— shopkeepers and sea gulls screaming, boys laughing and cussing, cars sputtering, seals barking, waves crashing. The Sun became over- bearing and my hunger for lunch aimed me at every whiff of fish and French fries that all seemed to blow our way. This was a very distracting place.

"Oh, yoo-hoo." Domano's voice whispered up out the masses of data assaulting my senses. "We're here to listen, remember? Listening? I say. Are you in there?"

I opened one eye and peeked out at him. "Not anymore. I got stampeded. This place is unbelievable. How can there possibly be so much stimulus in one spot at one time?"

"Hey," he smiled at me. "Settle down. This is a good spot. It will force you to focus all you got to one goal. To aim yourself."

"Oh boy..." I whined.

Chea motioned all around her as she spoke, "You have all these messages coming into your body. Your job is to acknowledge them and let them be there to warn you if it is needed. But not to distract you. You can't let them take your attention and scatter it." Then as though scooping the air up with her arms and hands she pulled it to her mouth and ears. "You choose which you want to focus on and hold to it."

"Oh god." I was starting to feel tired already. In their apartment I was able to put all my available attention toward observing my sense of touch. It was almost an automatic response. But I had no other distractions. Touching was the only stimulus offered. Now in order to focus like that I would have to continually sort through huge quantities of irrelevant data to home in on one small range of information.

To a degree we do it all the time, but this would be a forced conscious effort. And one thing I had discovered, as soon as you tell your mind, "You can't pay attention to *that*," it immediately decides *that* is the only thing in the world it will pay attention to.

"Again." Chea pointed at me with her chin.

I closed my eyes and began to listen. The barrage of audio chaos returned. I tried to identify every individual sound in order to preoccupy my mind enough to help it ignore the extra information.

I had worked my way through much of the noise on the pier when Chea's voice instructed me to distinguish the sound of metal ringing as it repeatedly hit another object. I couldn't find it. I strained and even held my breath but it still escaped my hearing.

Then a larger wave rolled up the beach and on its ebbing I heard the faint haunting ring. What a remarkable sound. My mood changed instantly. It's as if I were back in the middle of an old movie about mysterious and unexplainable happenings. The only thing missing was a little fog and Bela Lugosi.

It rang again and then again. It seemed to be coming from under the pier and continued with the rolling of the water. It made me curious and even a little apprehensive. A sound such as this didn't rest well here. It belonged on the old docks of London or in some timeworn castle of Romania.

Domano's voice came into my reflections. "Remember this. Remember all about this sound. And then turn your attention, not your body, to hear the two talking in the car at the left."

As I moved my point of observation I found the voices of young love. How delightful. She said she loved him so much more than she loved Ronny. He told her that he respected her, loved her and wanted to know how far Ronny got. She admitted to making out but insisted she didn't go all the way with Ronny. He mumbled something about how much he was overtaken by his love and attraction for her and couldn't bear waiting to make her sexually satisfied. She squeaked and giggled. He told her again he loved her. There were lots of kissing sounds and then he said, "But this is in the daylight, it's a public place." They giggled some more and moaned a bit. And then their car motor started and they pulled out.

In listening to them my mood changed again. I felt the enticements of being in love with love and lust. The humor and tension of the wooing games filled my belly. My whole interior speed had altered. With the ringing I felt slow, as though caught in a century long past. With the voices and words of the lovers, I sped up. There was a feeling similar to heading for the drag scene down Main Street when I was a teenager. These were not direct emotions from memories of specific events, but more precisely, they were an interior climate.

The shifting was fast and complete. I was amazed that it resulted from only a few sounds and words. The feeling of it fascinated me. I wondered how often our state of mind darted from one momentum to the next in our average daily experience.

Domano whispered to me again, instructing me to listen for the little girl and woman who were walking to my right. I turned my head slightly in order to better catch their sounds. I could hear their steps across the pavement. Perhaps they were on their way to their car. The girl seemed happy and was humming "Pop Goes The Weasel." Her voice was not even, though, as if she was being bumped or yanked along as she sang. Then there was a faint crashing noise.

The woman said, "Oh god! Stupid! You'll never be able to do that. Who do you think you are, some kind of genius or something?" And the child became silent as they walked on.

My interior speed and inward reality shifted yet again. It was as though the ground had been knocked out from underneath me. There was an atmosphere of disapproval and personal failure, as if I could never live up to my responsibilities. I felt insecure about my own innate abilities. My inner rhythm was off. I was feeling so tired of trying to succeed at something I just wanted to give up. In a state like this I would never be able to accomplish anything, not even finish a simple school paper.

The power of those words that had been spoken could change the course of events for generations. Something about it was far more potent than my emotional reaction by itself. Those words were symbols that had a life far older and greater than all of us there.

The Hetakas had talked before on the ability of thoughts to collect together in like kind. They exist on their own for a period of time and will continue as long as they are sustained with more of the same type of thoughts and especially emotions. They said these ranged from helpful to harmful in accord with the nature of what had created them. And we connect to them by what we are thinking or feeling and by what rhythms or frequencies our awareness is operating at.

For a brief moment I had tapped into something that I could only describe in this way. I was awestruck at the potential impact of the continued cultural use of even a single word. Just what are we leaving to our generations? What will be the fruit of our speech?

Chea's voice broke softly into my thoughts. "Let your Song take your attention now. Remember these things clearly that happened today. And let your mind empty itself...so there's just the passion of your own living."

The awareness of my Song filled my mind. I relaxed and opened my eyes. As I looked around all the chaos of the pier returned.

"Let's go eat," Chea said. "I'm starving."

"Me too." Domano stood up and turned to me. "Aren't you hungry yet?"

I had to think about it for a moment. I had been so involved in my process that I had forgotten how hungry I was.

"Now that you mention it," I answered, "I am. Very. Thanks for pointing it out to me. Now my stomach almost hurts it's so empty. You're a real pal, there. Are we going to eat at the apartment?"

"Yes," Domano nodded eagerly. "I'm going to cook the roots. Yams and potatoes and other things."

Chea and I glanced at each other.

"Come on," he said. "Don't fiddle-faddle." He waved us on down the pier.

As we walked back through the water's edge beyond all the people Domano sang a variety of songs from his home about the birds and sky. They were light and playful yet filled with reverence.

When we arrived Domano popped all his vegetables in the oven and came into the living room. He said he had an old, secret tribal method for fixing them. Now all we had to do was wait a little. We talked about my kids and the classes at college. Chea asked me if I was still seeing that man she warned me not to see. I didn't want to have to tell her that I was. I hemmed and hawed until she shook her head in disapproval.

"I thought so." She almost sounded angry. "I tell you he is not what you should be after. You should listen to your elders. The Indian peoples in some of the north here, the elders arrange who you will marry. They see to the whole thing. This is not so bad an idea, I think."

"You don't really believe that, do you?" I couldn't tell if she meant it or not. I hoped she didn't. The whole issue raised many uncomfortable questions for me. I had not been very successful in picking the men in my life but I wasn't so sure anybody else could do any better for me—and I certainly did not like the idea of relinquishing my right of choice.

The oven timer went off and Domano jumped up and got his treasured roots. They were all wrapped in leaves of different kinds. The aromas were fantastic. I took some of each kind and proceeded to taste them. They were every bit as good as they smelled. We relished every last crumb on the platter.

"See?" Domano smiled at me. "Old Indian secret."

I eagerly nodded. "Incredible!"

The front and kitchen doors were both open to let what little breeze there was come through. Chea leaned over and closed the front door most of the way so we would have more privacy. I took the dishes into the kitchen and noticed that Domano was bringing a leather wrapped bundle to the living room.

As I came back in he began to open it carefully. "You remember these," he said. "Here are the whistles of the Andes." He spread them out on the leather wrapping in a circle before me. "Sit down here. Clear your mind from everything. And let your body feel this sound. Watch. Don't make something that is not there. You listen, now." He picked up the deer and blew into it.

I closed my eyes and followed his instructions. The tones were remarkably low in pitch for a whistle of small size. My ears felt very sensitive inside as if they were anticipating something that I was un-aware of. I could feel the inner part of my ear vibrating almost like a rapid twitching sensation.

I realized I had my tongue tensed so I let it fall loose and relaxed. The sensations didn't disappear, they increased in intensity and expanded down my throat and up into the roof of my mouth. I think the bones of the interior of my skull were actually vibrating with the sounds. As he changed notes the exact quality and placement of the vibrations altered slightly, and suddenly I needed to suck in a great deal of air.

I felt observant, calm and ready for whatever challenge came. There was an unutterable abundance unfolding in my mind; I had the passion of life pulsing through my body and the opened fertility of ideas all as one inseparable identity within me.

Chea spoke while Domano continued to play. "Remember exactly how it feels. How it sounds. How it is different from the way the other sounds felt today. Each has its own way of being known inside us. Remember it all."

Domano stopped playing and set the deer whistle down. There was silence. I opened my eyes. They were both looking at me without any expression. The feeling of the sound lingered. I was full of information, sensations, questions, but there was nothing to say.

"Come," said Domano. "Handle the whistles. Try them. Make yourself familiar."

I picked up and examined them one at a time. They encouraged me to blow into each piece and study the changes that occurred in my body and my interior environment.

As I played every whistle again and again I felt physical sensations moving from one location to another. My mood and quality of awareness shifted also. The experiences always remained consistent with individual whistles. It reminded me of the last time I was shown and allowed to handle them. They had told me then that each one was attuned to a different energy spiral, or center, in the body and was designed to stimulate it.

I loved to look at their forms from every angle. The delicate artistry impressed me as much as it had before. I hoped that someday I would be able to create things as visually beautiful and balanced.

"Can you remember what the deer sounded like?" Domano asked as he took the turtle whistle from me and set it down.

I tried to recall the main pitch and subtle undertones, but I was not quite sure if I was correct. "I think I do," I answered. "But I'm not certain it's exact."

He nodded. "Can you remember the feeling of it? Can you bring the feeling back into yourself?"

I leaned back against the bench. "I don't know." It had never occurred to me to try to re-create a thing so subtle within myself. My mind raced with the possibilities of what the reasons for such a process would be. "I'll try."

I relaxed my tongue and focused on my inner ears. The sensations did not return. I tried to recapture the clarity of the expanded mind and the alertness but that didn't help. Then it occurred to me to recreate the sounds of the deer whistle in my mind and hold them there until the feeling they produced returned. Only intermittently did I get a result.

Chea whispered, "The Earth Fire Serpent. Let her come to your ears."

As she said it I could feel the Mother's presence and energy coming up through my heart and into my throat, mouth and ears. Now the memory of the sound was clearer and the sensations were more consistent.

Domano picked up the deer whistle and said, "Remember this sound exactly as it is. Remember the actions it makes on your body." He blew the notes just once.

He waited a few moments and added, "Now bring it back."

This time I was able to re-create the sounds and the feelings of the inner atmosphere with accuracy and hold them for many minutes. My mind began to expand and open. I longed to explore the vastness it laid before me. So many things were there, the connection to the spirit worlds, to the ancestors, to information on the unseen workings of our world and ourselves.

My clarity began to fade. I opened my eyes and looked at them both. They seemed pleased for me even though they said nothing about my success.

Domano stood up to stretch and patted his chest. "Who is for coffee? I really would like some coffee right now. Both of you? OK."

He returned shortly with a wonderful dark roasted brew. Chea pulled the whistles out of the way and we sat facing each other on the floor. I was beginning to feel a little tired but the coffee perked me right up.

Chea leaned against the bench holding her cup in front of her. "Do you think you can bring back the sounds and feelings of the metal ringing on the pier?"

"Well," I answered. "I managed the whistle. I guess I can. Let's see." I set my coffee down and closed my eyes. Copying what I had done before I called up the memory of the eerie clanging. I had a little difficulty until I thought of the things the sound had reminded me of and then it was all there.

"Now the smooching lovers," Domano said just as I was becoming involved in the mysteriousness of the ringing.

I took a few deep breaths and followed the same course to the couple in the car. I could clearly recall the young woman's squeaky voice and the atmosphere that had been generated. I was surprised at how accurately I could reproduce the different moods in their entirety.

When I remembered the voices of the mother and little girl that came next I began to fall from my center. "Please don't ask me to bring back the last ones," I said. "I don't want to feel that one again. OK?"

"OK," Domano replied softy. "If you want."

"Yes. I definitely do."

"Well then." Chea put her arms behind her and leaned back. "Can you find the sounds and feeling, the Song, of the cave your body was burned in?"

I jumped involuntarily. It had been a long time since I thought about it. Sometimes that presence haunted me in my dreams. I could recall the feeling of it easily but I had still been unable to identify it.

"Go ahead to your center and remember the sounds in the cave. Bring it back," she instructed me.

I thought of the crackling and sputtering noises that the fire from the brush had made and the steps of the midwife echoing down the stone walls. It didn't take long. The entire atmosphere was mine again. The signature of the cave stood out above all the rest.

Who was this familiar being? I tried to relate her to all the presences I had encountered. I could find no match. I didn't want to let her go but my concentration jolted back to the Hetakas' living room with the racket of a backfiring motor out front.

This mystery being had me captured by my heart. I longed to be close to her somehow. At times while in the everyday working world I felt terrifyingly separated from her, as if I had lost something precious and essential, but I didn't even know what it was.

I re-created the sounds of the fire again in my mind and brought back the intensity of the cave. She seemed to surround me. It was as if she was breathing and I could feel her rhythm as she moved. I'd swear she was trying to communicate. From this feeling of her presence came waves of comfort and support as strong as those I had perceived originally. She wanted to offer something, to speak to me. But I could hear no words.

I felt Chea drifting into my concentration. "You have reached her. Now let yourself talk with her. Sense her. Listen. Listen hard."

Chea's words confused me. Even though I felt as if I were in touch with the being I still had trouble believing that it was so, especially to be actually communicating with her at such a long distance. I questioned what all this had to do with the sense of hearing. The feeling that such things couldn't possibly be filled my attention and I was out of my center.

"So who is she?" Chea asked as I opened my eyes. "She told you who she was. You searched her out and she responded to you. So what do you say? Who is she?"

I still had no idea of the being's identity. Chea's confirmation that I was indeed in contact with her made me nervous clear to my bones.

"I don't know, Chea," I said scooting backwards on the floor. "I don't know about who that is or if I can talk to it. I don't know anything about it but the feeling. Realistically, I don't know where it is, what it is, who it is, or why I'm associated to it. How can I be talking with it?"

"Her." Chea corrected me, "You know her by her Song. And that is the most important. If you know the Song of a thing you can always contact it. From your Song to their Song. Heart to heart. It is as simple as that."

I leaned back against the wall and started to fidget with my fingernails. I was afraid they were going to ask me to go on a quest for befriending another spirit and I didn't feel capable of the task. "But guys, what does that have to do with hearing?"

Chea pushed the front door closed and then leaned over near me. "We recall the Songs by recalling what our senses and emotions felt around a thing. We can re-create that inner atmosphere, the rhythm our attention was in at the time. That's how we record things in ourselves. The Songs and medicines come to us through our senses as well as other ways. When we put our experience to memory these all get recorded together. Your people rely mostly on their hearing and seeing. If you remembered all the images and sounds that you connected to the feeling of this one you seek, you could remember who she is."

"Why can't I do that? Even when I was in the cave I knew there was something else about her. Something from before. But it's like I can't reach it. Why can't I grasp onto those associations?"

"Trust yourself," she said. "You will. When you are ready."

I nodded.

Domano reached over and patted me on my knee. "It is late now. You need to get home. We'll get together in two Saturdays from now. Up by your place. Yes?"

"Yes," I answered. "What do I do till then?"

"You listen and remember," he said. "Watch how you change inside to each thing you hear. Think of the sounds of things and wait for what follows. Watch what your body does. Maybe it reacts too. It's simple. Just go to your center and listen."

"Got ya." I hugged them goodbye and made my way to the bus stop.

In the next two weeks I made it my habit to pay attention to the sounds around me and, when circumstances allowed, I listened from my center. My responses were similar to those I had had in the Hetakas' apartment with the addition of some interesting body sensations. They ranged from a tickling that I felt in my ears, elbows, hands and feet to feelings of pressure on the roof of my mouth and tongue.

It was still morning when we met in the parking lot by my apartment and hiked up into the redwoods north of the campus to a little meadow. We sat in the grass and talked about the way the old ones who lived here before set camp around the edge of the field.

SOUNDS TO ANOTHER WORLD

"They are still here in a certain way," Domano said as he ran his hand across the top of the grass. "Those people knew those trees. The trees still talk of them. And the stone people, too.

"What do you hear, Kay, when you listen in this place?"

I looked around. The spot was beautiful. I could see why a village would be set up here. As I began to concentrate my eyes closed automatically and the noise of the forest birds and squirrels rose up like a crescendo. The breeze shook the leaves of the trees and rattled the seeds of the wild grasses. The sounds were very relaxing and filling. I described everything I heard one at a time.

When I opened my eyes Domano pointed to a large redwood. "You see this tree here? This tree here has a tune it is singing just as the bluebirds there have theirs. Sit very quiet and still and listen for this."

I wanted to ask how I was supposed to be able to hear such a thing, but he only put his finger up to his lips for silence. I got as comfortable as I could and began to breathe long and deep. I suspected we would be here for a long while.

I stared at the tree and tried to imagine what it would sound like if it could speak. After a while Domano told me to go up and touch it, send my Song out to it. With my Song I could detect its Song. He said the sounds I was looking for were a form of, or a way of perceiving, its Song.

From my center I stood and leaned on the trunk with my hands on the bark. I concentrated on my Song as I moved it outside myself reaching and feeling into the middle of the wood. The tree was magnificent and strong. Its Song was deep and old. It filled the ground below me and the sky above. I narrowed my perception in on just that.

I came to know this tree like an old friend. It gifted me with images about the ecology of the forest. I saw the thousands upon thousands of huge old trees that had been cut down all at once. All the elders of the trees of the forest had been killed and it will take two to three thousand years for there to be any of these tree elders in their forest again. The knowledge of those ancient ones was beyond count and value. It reached across centuries and was the total of millennia of experience and sharing. And now all that is lost to us.

My attention shifted slightly, making my ears a second focal point. I can't say that I heard tones from the tree through the outside of my ears as a common audio wave would be perceived, although my ears did feel stimulated as if they were vibrating inside from just such an interaction. Somewhere within my awareness I heard the tree's voice, not words, but an expression of moving harmonics—huge, multileveled, a world unto itself. A sound never to be forgotten.

I eased myself to the ground leaning my head and hands against the trunk. I don't know how long I sat listening. After a time I heard Domano walking over. I lifted my head and opened my eyes.

He squatted next to me and nodded. "Move your attention to cover the whole of the meadow again. Say nothing. The bird over there on that branch. After a little moment I want you to hear his music from your center. There are sounds inside his sound. Find them."

I didn't understand what he meant by a sound inside a sound. I wanted to ask him to clarify what this was but he turned and walked back to where he had been sitting. I watched the bird hopping on his branch, calling to his neighbors and then I closed my eyes.

His melody was specific. He repeated it after a five second pause like clockwork. In the distance I could hear another of his species answering him. I concentrated from my center until his voice was the only thing I noticed.

The more I listened the more I was sure that his music was an expression of his Song. I could feel a special intensity for life reaching out of him on every note. And with it came waves of feeling that I would describe as boundary setting and mate calling. I listened to the tones he produced with great care and felt into his medicines and Song, but I could sense no other sounds.

I lay back on the grass and opened my eyes. Domano and Chea were talking quietly. It was getting hot in the sunlight and I wanted to move into the shade with them.

"I felt things from him when he sang," I said as I scooted across the grass. "But I didn't hear anything else. What did I miss? What is it I'm not aiming at?"

"You were aimed fine." A little smirk grew on the edges of Domano's mouth. "You just did not take the information into your ears. You felt it. You knew a little something he was talking about. Only you

SOUNDS TO ANOTHER WORLD

kept it there. With the tree you felt it and then you let yourself feel and know it in your ears. You see?"

"I think so. Yeah." When he described it I realized the difference. "Will I be able to control that?"

Chea raised an eyebrow and cocked her head. "In time. Don't expect to hear words and sentences now. Your mind can translate it to that if that is what you really want. But what is communicated this other way is far bigger than what words can hold.

"Everything talks in these ways. The medicines come in through the smelling, tasting, touching, hearing, seeing. They come in through the fibers and on waves of energy currents that the webs float on. There are many to talk with out there, all those beings we share our world with, and even our ancestors. They have so much they want to give to us, to tell us."

Domano stood up and pointed with his chin toward the campus. It was time to go back. We walked slowly through the grass and brush.

He reached over and touched his hand to my mouth, throat and ear. "These are connected. Making sounds and hearing sounds. People in primitive cultures sing a great deal. Your people, I think, do not sing enough. They don't make sounds to their relatives and they don't listen to them. They don't bond themselves together in making harmonies. So you study this. Sing and listen."

I nodded. "I think you're right. My people don't sing too much."

As we passed through the oaks to the old dirt logging road I heard a wind moving in the branches of the trees. As I turned my attention toward it I recognized my old friend the wind keeper. She circled around us.

The inner channels of my ears felt as though the air pressure was changing. I looked at Domano and Chea. They glanced up at the trees and then looked at me without expression. I heard my name clearly spoken. I could not tell what direction the voice came from. It was not being produced through my ears in the usual way. As before, they seemed to vibrate in sympathy to the stimulation. I knew it was the wind keeper calling me.

Chea and Domano indicated that they were leaving and for me to stay in the forest with the keeper for a while. I nodded and turned away toward the tall trees as the Hetakas walked on.

I collected myself into my center and held my arms up to greet the wind keeper. There were no expectations in my mind, only the knowing of our desire to communicate. She circled in the trees above and then raced toward me, face to face.

I was surrounded. She blew her power straight through me. It was so much like the first meeting on the mountain ridge. I was in the middle of astounding beauty and terrifying potential. She knew me and I knew her. Her visions crowded into my mind. We walked back into the forest toward the meadow and I stayed with her the rest of the day.

SEVEN

THEIR EYES SEE ONLY DEATH

ALL through these fall months I had been meeting the Hetakas every five or six days at a different place. They worked me on the sense of hearing like a team of drill sergeants.

I would study the sounds available, observe any memories or emotional changes, attempt to perceive identifying Songs or medicines involved and memorize the exact qualities and rhythm that my interior climate, or state of mind, was in. Then, at a later date, I would be asked to reproduce any or all of these things inside myself.

I came to discover that the subtle harmonics of the sense of hearing were concerned with collecting data on the environment in terms of one's state of mind and ability to aim and finely focus one's attention. By being able to recall pieces of a chosen memory pattern one could, at will, alter one's state of consciousness or proceed to contact another entity no matter how distant. I found these tasks far easier than attempting to hear what an entity's Song and medicines were like or the sounds that can be found inside other sounds.

To take such a detailed conscious account of, and be this responsible for, the frequencies and qualities of the inner environment and output of my mind was a revelation for me. The Hetakas had always stressed the importance of being responsible for one's own thoughts and emotions because of their ability to impress themselves on all we come into contact with. But this was something additional. This was quickly altering the entire state, or frequencies, that one was existing at to facilitate a specific purpose. By taking this action I could re-create the almost celestial states of mind produced by the bird man and jaguar man whistles, or be in a state required to make contact with an entity such as the wind keeper or a tree, or even create a vibratory state required for spirit journeys.

Sounds became a whole body experience for me, a treasured piece of living, a stimulator of mind, a guaranteed bringer of the awareness of my Song. Sound had become a door now open. And this forced me to realized that the only truth I really had in this life was what I have actually experienced myself. It didn't matter what I had been taught in school or by my parents or even what the Hetakas had said to me. There was only one thing that could possibly be real within my existence, and that was my own experiencing.

On this mid-December day I met with the Hetakas on the bench in the mall not far from the Logos Bookstore. The weather had still been unseasonably warm and dry. The smell of fresh coffee drifted down the street. It had been almost two weeks since we had been together last and it was good to see them again. A wind came up from the north with a cold bite. I put the sweatshirt on that I had brought with me.

We talked about the kids and how my son was adjusting to junior high school. My daughter, the younger of the two, was more than content to run around with all the kids from the student apartments and play in the forest. She tended to lose track of time now and come home late. As with most parents and their children discipline was becoming more of a challenge with every year. Chea reassured me that this was good, a sign of their own free will being intact and explored. I just nodded, hoping she was right.

"It is not realistic," Chea continued, "to expect your people to know true freedom. Your people are not free, no matter what they're taught to believe. They are not. They're slaves to the culture of the church and state, to the masks that this culture resorted to putting on their lives. The best thing you can do for your children is let them see this and explore it for themselves.

"A gift of the above. The ability to make the patterns that come from their heart."

I turned to look at her. "You never mentioned a gift from the above before. What did you say it was? How does it work?"

Domano gave me that knowing grin of his, as though they had just hooked a big fish for dinner. "Let's talk of this with some coffee. We can go just over there. Then we'll be out of the cold wind, too. Come on."

Out of the corner of my eye I caught Chea winking at him as we got up to go. There was a fluttering low in my gut and I was afraid they might be plotting something. I wasn't sure if I should concentrate on what she was saying or on what jokes or tricks they might have planned.

"The above," she said, "gifts us with an understanding and a way to let go of the old and build something new and better that comes from our heart. It helps us find what we can be doing and making to live from the heart. You see?"

"Ah..." I didn't know what to think or say. She was so direct with her answer I was sure there must be something hidden in her meaning. They had never given me such a clear, concise piece of information about a direction before.

Domano chuckled. "You think on this. Give it a chance to settle. Let's get some coffee and sit down over there. Today, you know, we go on to the last sense—sight. You have been waiting for this. So let's get good and comfy and really enjoy it."

"Yeah," I nodded with excitement at the prospect of something new and for the completion of such a long and intense project. It occurred to me how much I had learned from them and the incredible amount I had changed in these few years. The depth of my gratefulness could not be expressed.

We waited for a minute for the table in the far corner to become available. Domano spoke as we sat down, "This is the most difficult of the senses because we are in the habit to tie our words and thoughts around the things that come to our eyes. You cannot find the hidden aspects of seeing if you have your old patterns in your mind. The

THEIR EYES SEE ONLY DEATH

opinions you grew up with will blind you to hidden aspects. You need to be empty of words. Expecting nothing. Prepared for anything. The medicines that come to the eyes are very subtle.

"You will do better if we trade places. You be in the corner here where you can see this whole room."

We shuffled everything around and I arranged the chair to have the best advantage of viewing the room, counter and window to the outside. Domano and Chea scooted their chairs back against the wall on either side of me. We looked as if we were ready to watch the next show.

Facing forward Chea instructed me to collect the gifts of the four directions and be in my center. Without thinking I proceeded and automatically closed my eyes.

"Hey. You in the center here," Domano laughed softly. "You can't be closing your eyes. That is kind of hard to work on seeing that way."

I opened them with a start. I couldn't believe I did that and had a great laugh on myself.

"OK you," Domano said. "We'll try again. This is going to be rough for a while. It is your habit now to close your eyes to go to your center. You will have to be aware of this. So, are you OK to work now? Let's work."

Still smiling I nodded and looked around the room to see if anyone was watching.

Domano shook his head. "Don't be thinking of them. They don't care what we do. Now! This time for sure!" He giggled and nodded his head up and down in an exaggerated motion imitating me. "Yes?"

I copied him back. "I'm doing it. See?"

"Oh yes," he said. "Yes. This is progress."

I laughed until my nervousness eased and I was able to approach my center with the attention it required.

Chea leaned a little closer to my left ear. "Focus on everything and let your eyes slowly cover the room. Be aware even of what you see from the corners of your eyes. Don't let the thoughts come into your mind. Don't let the other senses distract you. Go back and forth. Then next, keep the field of vision as broad, but don't let your eyes focus on anything. Scan back and forth. After a time focus your eyes again. Do this over and over."

I complied with her instructions and ran my eyes through the room again and again. After many rounds of this an incredibly attractive young gentleman with a charming disposition came into the shop with his buddies. I was instantly distracted. He was as beautiful as a Greek statue. I couldn't stop looking at him and followed him with my eyes across the room. He kept glancing over at me. I wondered if there was some way I could get to meet him. Maybe he was a student.

Chea jabbed me with her elbow. I realized I had been caught letting my mind be completely pulled away.

"Uh, yeah?" I turned to Chea with a sheepish grin and whispered to her, "Kind of nice, huh?"

"Nicer than that creep you keep seeing like you shouldn't," she answered with a straight face.

I was so surprised to hear such a thing come out of her mouth I laughed out loud.

The corners of her lips turned up a little bit as she glanced over at Domano. "Maybe you'll get a chance to meet Mr. Beautiful here after a while," she said.

Domano began to smile slowly and looked over at the young man. He had that same look as when he had pulled pranks on me that were horribly embarrassing. I could see terrible things brewing in his mind. I knew that I would be very lucky to get through today without alienating the young man forever.

"Oh god!" I whispered. "Chea, don't let him do anything. Come on you guys. Chea, you said yourself he's not so bad. Don't you want to see me dating somebody you approve of?"

Chea's expression didn't change. "Who said approved? I said nicer than the creep." And a truly devilish grin came over her face.

I knew I was in trouble. I wanted to hide anywhere, but there wasn't even room under the table. The young man kept looking my way and smiling. Anxiety swelled up through my body.

"Look at him." Chea directed, "From your center. Don't take any other information with you. Glance for a moment and look away. Unfocus and glance again. What do these things tell your eyes?"

I did as she had said. He was wonderful to look at. There was something very appealing about catching information from him with my eyes. I didn't understand what it was. I had never noticed anything like it before.

Chea whispered, "What does this information hitting your eyes feel like?"

"Chea," I answered. "I have no words for this. He's...delightful."

"Keep going," Chea replied. "Look at just him for now."

I repeated the scan many times. It was as though there was a field that was part of him and extended outward about two feet from his skin. This was not something that I saw as one sees a physical thing. In those terms it was invisible, but there was something there that impressed upon my eyes. It wavered and fluctuated and moved as he moved. And at times the surface of it reached outward to me. It was gentle, warm and inviting.

Domano spoke without turning his head toward me, "That's it. Keep your attention exactly as it is. Now look in this way at the older man who sits at the window."

Changing as little as I could I shifted my view to the other man. There was nothing out of the ordinary. I closed my eyes for a moment to regain my center and tried again. I glanced at Chea and Domano and then to others who were sitting in the room. I could detect only the normal physical objects.

"What is it?" I asked Chea. "Why don't I see it with them? Why isn't there anything else?"

"Because your heart and gonads have a special liking to the young handsome fellow." Chea smiled at me, "It makes you open to him. And he has the same interest in you. That makes him stronger toward you than the others here. He's your good fortune today. Give it lots of time. These things aren't easy. You go ahead and watch him all you want."

She gave me a girlish giggle and nudged me with her elbow. I didn't argue. We sat there for another hour or so making googly eyes at each other until his buddies dragged him off. I studied what my eyes were able to perceive from him while I had the opportunity. Our exchanges of energies were delicate and stimulating. I wanted a chance to get close but perhaps that just wasn't to be.

"We need to sit out on the mall now," Domano said as he collected our cups. "Let's go up in front of the little restaurant. The one near the coffee bean place. There's lots of people moving around there. Are you ready?"

We left the shop and worked our way up the street. This part of the mall was just as Domano wanted it—crowded. As soon as we got there, like a little piece of magic, the bench became vacant.

"Ah good," he said as we sat down. "Now I have a fun thing for you to do. This is a good one. You're going to like it."

I must have had an expression of suspicion on my face. I had not been sure of his intentions all day. He just laughed at me and told me I was getting soft, that I needed to be kept on my toes.

"See," he went on to say. "All you have to do is watch people and remember. You don't even have to be in your center. But for today try not to be listening or smelling and all that. Just look. I will tell you when. OK?"

"Sounds easy enough to me." I scooted back against the planter. "Shoot, boss."

We watched the people shuffling back and forth doing their Christmas shopping. Domano spotted an older woman down the street making her way slowly to where we were. He indicated her by slightly pointing his chin. I watched carefully as she passed trying to keep all the thoughts out of my head that might lend to prejudging her.

After she had passed Domano had me close my eyes and recall every detail about the woman that I could. Then he asked me to remember the field of energy around her. I opened my eyes and stared at him.

"But I didn't look for that." I started to feel anxious and inadequate. He had never asked before about something he knew I was completely unprepared for.

"Untangle your arms from in front of you and relax. Close your eyes." He gently smiled at me. "You will see a most remarkable thing. Your body and mind are always recording all the details. We might not be looking for them. But they are still there anyway. So now, you will find this hidden memory of what was around the Gramma.

"Watch her in your mind how she walks down the street here. You see her clearly?"

"Yeah. Yeah I do. Her funny little limp like walk." I jiggled my head.

"Good," he added. "What is around her as she walks? What does the space around her do as she moves with it and moves through it? Remember exactly what she did. Don't watch her make movements she didn't do. Be exact in the remembering. Now what do you see there?"

"I see, well, it's not something I can see, exactly." It was difficult for me to describe. I could find no words or phrases adequate in our language. "It's just there. There's something there like what was around that nice guy. Only not as big and it's different somehow. It's not full all the way around her body like his was. Something is missing at the leg she limps on. And there's other little places where it seems to be missing. His was like it was the same dynamic strength all over. But hers isn't. It's like it almost struggles at times. What does that mean? Is she OK?

I looked over at Chea as she said, "She is old. And had many injuries. She has always believed in oldness. And so now she lives it out, her way. Look at her again. Look at the colors she carries around her. Remember as they touched you. Let yourself feel the memory of what that was like."

"But I saw no colors," I answered.

"Move to your center and remember from there. Keep watching her over and over. Just expect to see colors. You have to allow yourself to remember these things."

I watched her walk past me in my mind repeatedly but still there were no colors that I could detect.

Chea touched my arm to get my attention. "It's not very practical to limit yourself in how you think the world runs or what you think the world is."

"But..." I started to make an excuse.

She interrupted me, pointing with her chin, "Let's try a little trick on your memory to see this woman's medicines. Don't think on this. Only answer me quickly with no chatter in your mind. Be from your heart. Now, if you were painting her, but not to look like a photograph, and you wanted to put all kinds of colors around her, what would they be?"

Approaching the old Grandmother on those terms I saw her, frozen in motion as in a portrait, surrounded in lights of greens and pinks with streaks of yellow and rosy orange by her legs and a wonderful pale blue with white above her head.

"These touched you as she passed," she said. "Can you remember what they felt like?"

This time I watched the memory of her as she walked by with her bouquet of colors. I saw them in their activity, flowing out of her like delicate fingers of flames into the crowds of people. She looked at all those she passed and the colors followed after her eyes. When they touched me I knew she had profound concern for everyone there. She was filled with old time Christmas. Her gentle caring was all she had left and this is what she gave without exception.

"You see," Chea said. "She is OK."

"Yeah," I agreed. "She certainly is. Chea, how does seeing her relate to what you've told me about the Tree and going up the Tree?"

"These are things of the first branches as are spirit journeys, seeing time layers, singing fibers," she answered.

I nodded and was about to ask her to explain the interconnectedness between those things when Domano nudged me. I glanced over at him and he indicated for me to observe a businessman who was standing almost in front of us. I put my questions aside and turned my concentration on watching him.

The field this man carried was completely different from the last two I observed. His was held close in to his skin and was very intense with what acted as a hard edge covering its whole surface. His body language made me so uncomfortable I found it impossible to search for his colors. His energies didn't leave his field often but when they did they were tightly organized and shot off rapidly in precise directions. He didn't remain long and I was glad to see him go.

We sat working on the sense of sight for several more hours until it was time for me to be home with the kids. The Hetakas walked me to the bus stop and said to continue watching people in the way they had instructed. We would meet again in one week at their apartment.

I quickly became fascinated with this way of looking at the world but without the Hetakas present it was considerably more difficult. I spent all my spare time in the library and coffee shops on campus in order to observe as many people as possible.

The week went by fast and I met the Hetakas as planned. The kids were spending a few days with relatives so my time was completely mine. The weather was still dry and comfortable. We went over to the cliffs above the beach and walked along through the sand and ice plant.

"You guys told me to pay attention to everything that happens when I'm working on the senses, right?" I asked. They agreed. "Well, I've been noticing something with the hearing and now with the seeing. Not so much with the others, but a little. I've been having some pretty strange body sensations and reactions."

Domano grinned at me. "Like what? Does your hand fly up and poke you in the eye?"

"No." I clearly saw the image he described in my mind. I had to laugh.

"Then you have nothing to worry about." And he threw both his hands into the air and opened his eyes as wide as he could.

Chea and I glanced at each other and laughed. She said, "And he cooks, too."

"Now you two," Domano said through his laughter, "you are always picking on me."

Chea nodded and smiled at him. His eyes twinkled back at her for a moment before he continued to speak to me. "Just what has your body been talking to you about?"

"Well," I said, "sometimes I feel a tickling. Usually it's in my elbows, or the roof of my mouth and tongue, or sometimes it feels like it's actually in my skull. And then other times my muscles start twitching in my belly or my arms near my elbows. There's been whirling sensations. Tingling. Why are these happening? Why are they important?"

He closed one eye and with exaggerated actions pretended to examine me like a scientist. "Ah ha! I discover the cause. The cure is no more looking at pretty men."

"What?" My voice rose in pitch. That was a very peculiar thing for Domano to say. I laughed so hard I needed to sit down on the sand. "That's no cure. That's cruel and unusual punishment."

He was very pleased with himself at how he caught me off guard. As he stopped laughing and sat down on his knees he answered, "That's just your body trying to get you to listen to it. It doesn't babble uselessly like folks make their mouth do. It needs you to pay attention to it. Sometimes it's saying the energy and even the blood is pushing frantically to get through a blocked up path. And so that is what you will feel.

"But many times such things are felt because the energies are coming from another being or another place and are touching you with a story to tell. They want to be noticed. You will see, as you do the work on the senses you will catch this more and more. It will become like a language to you between you and your relatives. It is the way things are. It is the sacrament."

"Wow." I had no idea they were so important. I thought maybe it was just a sign of aging or deterioration or something. "I'm going to have to pay a lot better attention to this. Huh?"

He smiled and nodded.

Chea sat down with us. "Are you ready to try some seeing? Let's admire this little plant here."

"OK." I rearranged myself to fully face the individual ice plant she had picked.

"Be in your center and watch it," she said. "Don't bring anything to this from before. Don't expect. Don't prejudge. Just let it be."

The sand was comfortable to sit on and the sunlight felt warm between the breezes. I emptied my mind and pulled my awareness to my center. The little ice plant was in a colony of its own species. Their energy fields bonded together and covered the ground like a blanket. They almost looked as if they were trying to hold the sand down around them with their medicines.

I closed my attention in on the one single plant. Its field was completely intact and far more consistent around its body than the fields of the Humans I had observed. Within itself it was intensely active, everything seeming to move at a great pace. It reminded me of a roaring fire in miniature, only it remained well organized.

The succulent leaves appeared to be precariously vulnerable and delicate but the energy field was tenacious, adaptable and unyielding to defeat. Although I clearly observed these things with my eyes I could distinguish none of the hidden colors.

As I sat motionless I moved my attention onto the sand. There was something very familiar about viewing the sand from this perspective. I followed this feeling until I touched upon a memory from my early childhood. I must have been around one-and-a-half years old and sitting in the sandy dirt behind the house my family was living in. I was picking up the soil, running it through my fingers and arranging it carefully on the ground.

It was as though I were having a love affair with the soil. I was impassioned with it. It glowed an extraordinary light blue into the air around it with every color of the rainbow sparkling off each grain. This energy field was incredibly alive and active. Thousands of Songs made up its essence. It had scent, taste and sound. I spoke to it and it gave of its energy to me.

At the time I assumed everyone could see the dirt as I did. I couldn't understand why they didn't seem to like such a beautiful, living, understanding thing and continued to want me away from it. As I scanned the memories occurring after that I could see that social pressure forced me to drop that way of viewing the world and not remember it.

A gentle little whirlwind came up the shoreline and stirred the surface of the beach. I knew in time I would be able to regain that complete sight I once had. I reached down and picked up a handful of sand. A colorless field around it was plainly visible. I felt like a child again, examining everything with the excitement of seeing it for the first time. Each grain of sand had its own radiation that reached out and connected to its neighbors. Their community interaction was uncoupled and I couldn't help but compare it to the soil particles from my childhood whose bonding was tightly interwoven and interdependent but still flexible.

The cloud that had hidden the Sun moved southward. The warmth and brightness was more than welcome. Without thinking about my work at hand I looked up into the sky in gratitude.

"You need sunlight. Lots of it," Domano interjected.

When he spoke I realized that I had drifted from my concentration. I looked over at him wondering if I would be scolded.

"You need more Sun when you start to live this way," he assured me. "And times of real darkness too. You have to make sure you get enough of both on your whole body. Maybe even put a heavy shade on your bedroom window."

I thought about that for a moment and then said, "That lamp from the path outside is awful bright. That'd be really refreshing to have it dark."

Domano turned up toward the Sun and made a gesture as though he were fanning something onto himself. "Especially let the Sun on your face and into your eyes. I don't mean stare into the Sun. You don't want to burn your eyes. Just move them to it from time to time letting the sunlight fall in. You could say, like your eyes are the opening to an empty cavern that needs to be filled.

"Now don't be looking at me like that. I'm not telling you you need a Hollywood tan. Anyway your people burn too easy in the Sun. This is not a thing to toy with. So you be careful. You are better to leave your clothes on and just be around where the light is. Yes?"

That struck me funny and I laughed. "OK, boss. But that doesn't sound like much fun."

"Ahh." He chuckled. "You are still trying to find that pretty young man. So you think he would be lots of 'fun in the Sun.'" He raised his eyebrows up and down at me.

Even though my comment might have provoked it, somehow I just didn't expect such a suggestive joke about my sexuality to be coming from an elderly gentleman, especially Domano. This was something that was not done where I came from. It made me feel as though I had somehow been doing something indecent. I had no idea what to think or do next.

"Hey there. This is a fun thing." He looked at me as though he were hunting for something. "What mask is dragging you off? Hmmm? You just remember—living from your heart is living from your body. A woman's dance for her desire is to be admired, honored. This is an unfolding of great beauty. It is the way of things."

Domano openly held a reverence for women that was not common within my modern culture. His attitude and concepts were almost opposite to those I had grown-up with. I couldn't ignore the conflict between the two any longer. It forced me to question what it really meant to me to be a woman.

That was too uncomfortable. I looked away to the ground and my mind darted back to the ice plant and the sand. "How do I go about seeing the colors of these little guys? I remembered just now, when I was tiny, I saw them. How do I do it again?"

Chea nodded her head at me, "Yes. To the little plants. It's true about tiny children. The old ones tell us that babies see in this way. They have no masks to shut it out. To study the sense of sight, as we have been teaching you, is to reclaim that ability of your childhood and more. You will have to watch and watch and watch like it was all brand new. Don't let any other information distract you. Look and remember, over and over. Your way of looking is a habit of a lifetime. So don't be whipping yourself around the block. And don't be expecting that you will see like a baby all the time."

"What do you mean?" I asked. "Why can't I see that way all the time?"

"Because you will know both ways of seeing," Chea answered. "And both are part of you. Both serve you. It's a matter of how you turn and focus your attention, and why. This work on the senses is about more than what you came into this world with. It teaches you to use what you have spent a whole life collecting. It's a combination, a result that is more than the adding of the parts."

"Wait," I interrupted her. "What's the 'more?' I don't understand how it all fits. What does it have to do with the plant? What does it have to do with me?"

Chea spoke and gestured heavily with her hands, "When your people of the white culture look at the world, their eyes see only death. This is what you have to overcome in yourself. So you learn to use your eyes more and pay attention to what is out there, to broaden your field. You learn to let yourself see energies and medicines and to feel their intent. But you are also learning the other subtleties of sight. Each sense touches the world in a different way. Each has a totally different psychology. Information that comes to us through our sight is handled in terms of using and mastering the many levels of awareness and mind. It has to do with understanding that can come and ability to analyze and respond from the heart. There is a special tie there between the eyes and the heart. Do you see?"

I couldn't say anything. I had no direct knowing of this, only a vague whisper in my mind of something incredible that might be there.

She stared into me like a scientist with a microscope. I felt open to being observed but not uncomfortable. After a moment she said, "Understanding subtle information and the framework it rides on is crucial to your own healing and your ability to make the sacrament of the sacred links. As we have told you many times before, in order to help your planet heal into the next era you must learn for yourself first."

The rest of the afternoon we worked among the ice plant and sand. The Sun was low in the sky and it lit up the clouds near the water line when they had me stop everything and watch it. I never had the feeling so strongly before of standing on a living planet that was turning and revolving through space around an equally alive and mobile star.

"We need to go back quickly," Domano said after the last edge of the Sun sank beneath the surface. "Before it is too cold." We all quickly agreed and made our arrangements for our next meeting as we walked. I wanted to get home before it got completely dark so I could walk down through the meadow to meet my date for the night. I was about to go out again with the man Chea didn't approve of.

I got to my apartment just in time to grab my coat and head for the field. I climbed over the fence and began to jog around the boulders and holes. My mind kept slipping in and out of looking at the surroundings in the way of the practice. In flashes I would see the energy fields of things as I passed by. A buzzing feeling began to creep up my legs. Colors, shapes and shadows loomed up and darted out toward me. But as soon as I struggled to see them completely they would vanish.

I picked up speed. There were large dark forms in front of me in a place where nothing should be. I was becoming disoriented. I couldn't be sure what they were and I strained my eyes to focus clearly on them. My sight shifted again and again. There were rustling sounds and heavy steps in the low brush. I couldn't hold back my fear from gnawing away my clarity. I had to get away from there now.

The last light was leaving. A low grunting came from the dark shapes ahead. I hoped they were only the cows. Rumor had it that sometimes at night the farmers let the big bull in the field to protect

THEIR EYES SEE ONLY DEATH

the calves and cows from any roaming packs of wild dogs. One very large dark shape stepped out in front of the others.

I froze. It dug at the ground in front of me. I could hear its breath snorting in its nostrils. I didn't know what to do, I could hardly inhale. My vision was alternating completely out of my control. I couldn't see the beast, only a looming mass of energy that threatened violently closer in front of me. Strange light came from nearby and moved of its own accord. I had no idea what these things were.

A shadow came at me from my right. It felt vulgar and dangerous. I screamed involuntarily, darted to my left and ran back toward the road as fast as I could. My body trembled violently. I felt as though I was going to throw up. I tripped and stumbled across the broken ground, all the way to the buildings.

I ran into my apartment, turned all the lights on and locked the doors and windows. I didn't care about the date anymore or that I had no way to call him and let him know I wasn't coming. I only wanted the safety of being lost in a television program, huddled securely under every blanket and pillow in the house.

EIGHT

POWER OF THE FORBIDDEN FRUIT

On the spring equinox I was to meet Chea by the little waterfall. Our concentration had been on the many aspects of sight through these last months and the whole training of the senses was drawing to a close.

I rarely had the opportunity to spend time with Chea alone. Although I had no idea of what to expect I was really looking forward to it. She explained that it was time she taught me about women's knowledge; my culture had lost a tremendous amount of our understanding of not just sensual experience but of what that means in terms of femaleness and maleness. She was going to teach me the vision quest ways of a Bleeding or Moon Ceremony.

The day was warm and the moisture from the damp soil of the forest floor made the air thick and sweet. Chea asked to meet me at this location because she said the waters of our planet are the blood of the Mother Earth and in that way are similar to the blood within our own bodies. For a woman it can be a special benefit to her at her bleeding time.

As I walked down the middle of the little river I could see Chea sitting on the boulder near the fallen tree. She was quietly looking at the falls and dangling her feet into the water.

"Hi, Chea," I said as I got close enough to be heard. "This is sure a beautiful day."

"Come." She smiled and motioned for me to sit on the rock next to hers. "Here. Sit so you can see the white water as it tumbles down."

The rock was wet but I didn't care. My jeans were rolled up to my knees and I had slipped into the creek often enough that they were now soaked. We talked about my work at school, the weather, my family.

Chea looked around breathing deeply, taking in the banquet of smells the forest had to offer and went on to say, "In these days while we are here I'm going to tell you the knowledge my Grandmothers told to me and their Grandmothers told to them all the way back to the time of the land before. These are the things we learn in our Bleeding Ceremonies.

"To begin our time at this place we need to ask the folks who live here, our relatives here, for permission to share their home with us for our ceremony. We offer of our hearts and ask for their help."

Chea and I stood up on the bank. She pointed and said, "We walk all the way around the area this way, clockwise, and talk to every-body." She tapped her chest. "We talk to them this way."

When we finished the circling we sat back down on the big rocks at the edge of the waterfall. She studied my face the way she often does. "You've applied all your senses now but they only work as ful-ly as your awareness and acceptance is of your whole self. You must understand what it means to be a woman. You must perceive through your awareness of your body as female."

She paused as if giving me time to ask questions. I realized then that my conceptions of sexual roles, whether they were genetically defined or culturally mandated, were uncomfortably haphazard, but I could think of nothing to ask.

"Women," she said, "are the center. That is what it is to be a woman."

She waited again, splashing her feet in the water. Her words con-fused me even more. I still couldn't think of anything to say.

"We are the center of the family," she added. "And the center of the tribe, the nation, even our species. Everything moves around us.

It is the women who naturally set the rhythm, the mood, the pace. We are the fire that is at the center of the hut, the smoke that rises up like a pillar to the Creator and the spirit nations. For the generations of the Humans we are the source—the key to the future, the survival of our kind. We carry the future inside us and we mold the makers of the world of tomorrow."

I looked up at her, "How does that make us the center? Why do you say 'center?'"

"I say it because everything comes from a womb." She looked back at me as though I should understand her reference, but I didn't. "We start there and we return there. You knock the woman out of her place at the center and your world begins to spiral backwards into destroying itself."

I stuttered as I shook my head nervously, "I don't think I understand what you mean when you say 'center.' Please tell me you aren't saying I'm only supposed to do one job: make babies and chase them around all day."

"No," Chea laughed. "You can still wear your women's-lib hat. Nobody is going to make a breeding cow out of you. Jobs are just a product of a culture. Don't give them a priority they don't deserve. It means we are the way babies get here no matter what other tasks we find in our path. That gives us a certain way of thinking. Women think in terms of making life continue. In terms of creating. Of balancing."

"Women actually think differently than men? You're saying there's an actual difference?"

"You mean you haven't noticed?" she asked back.

"Well..." I hedged. Sometimes she still made me nervous. There was a quality about her, of her incredible knowledge and abilities that I was never quite sure how to relate to. I felt transparent and trite and was always a little afraid of saying something stupid. "Sure. Kind of. Do you mean a cultural thing or is this genetic?"

She raised an eyebrow at me. I wondered if she was amused at my reaction. "It is in our cells," she said. "In our spirits. It is in the design of things.

"To be the center means we are the first and biggest influence on the tiny newcomers from the time they are conceived. It is us who make the crucial shape of the generation being born and we keep affecting for seven generations to come. We are the biggest influence on our mates. That makes us the biggest influence within our group. You have to come to know that, to know the weight of that.

"I'll tell you about the way it is back home. A girl in our tribe, when she begins her first bleeding, the old Grammas give her a bleeding hut to carry out her first Moon Ceremony in. She takes only water and fruit and stays there for her whole blood time, praying. Praying night and day. She seeks her vision of who she is and what it is for her to now be a bringer of the next generation, a starter of a brand new life that wasn't there before. Her Grandmother instructs her to think on being the maker of life who protects life and protects the making of new life. She seeks to understand how it is she can live best to help herself and her people be healthy and happy. She is to begin to find her power as a woman. Her spirit helpers come and teach her. She talks to her Mother Earth. She learns that to be a woman is a great responsibility."

"More than a man's?" I asked. I was beginning to feel uneasy and pressured by the weight of her words.

"Sure," she said as if everyone knew this "truth."

I couldn't tell if she meant women just had a rotten deal in life and men were somehow not required to carry the big loads or if there was something I was missing. My frustration started to take my attention. I couldn't think of what to ask that would clarify it.

The Sun was getting hot. I leaned down and splashed some water on the top of my head. "Well," I babbled, not knowing what else to say, "what happened to this equality and fairness stuff?"

Chea pointed to her heart and to the things around us. "Equity in relating and loving and sharing does not take away the fact that all things are different from each other. Each with its own abilities, its own burdens, to be accepted and honored as such. With equity."

This time the way she stated the concept of different in structure, content and purpose but equal in acceptance made it more understandable and usable to me. I could see how it would become a basic cultural foundation. "And this girl is taught this from a very young age?"

"Yes."

"And they teach her about power?"

"Yes."

"How is that?" The Hetakas' whole use of the word "power" always confused me. It was something I had never grasped completely. "You've told me before that women are more powerful than men. What does that mean? Is that part of this difference and responsibility thing? What is it they teach her?"

Chea seemed to understand my difficulty and thought hard for the right words to use. "It has to do with ability to collect attention and to alter inner atmosphere. And about ability to connect with other beings. Because women bear and nurture the new life they have a greater need to do this. It is a matter of survival.

"In my tribe, as a girl grows into a woman, her Grammas will encourage her to take her right to be in her ceremony and pray alone at her bleeding times. They will help her to quest and discover her own center, her place as center, her place among the nations of the planet, her place among the star people. They will guide her to learn about her awareness and to see that during her blood time she can collect her attention even better. The dream that hides some things and beings from our notice most of the time is no longer a burden, and she can reach in. Her prayers have no blocks. What she prays for has great influence. And she learns that her thoughts and emotions can cause even more effect than at other times.

"Her task, Kay, is to take responsibility for this."

My immediate reaction was to judge this a grossly unreasonable weight to ask anyone to take on. The words jolted out of my mouth before I could think. "Good grief! That job's just too damn big for anyone! I sure wouldn't want it."

"It's yours anyway," she said with the power of great assurance. "When a woman doesn't stand up and honor herself and the center place where she belongs, then balance is lost. Just look around you. This struggle to get your power back isn't about getting fair wages or equal jobs. It's about learning how to pull yourself back to the center place. How to take responsibility for your woman power, your birthing power, your influence, and to see that when actions are taken they are to the benefit of the generations.

"It's about acting and living in such a way as to earn the honor and privileges of the center place—not force them to be given to you no matter what. A woman who doesn't have her head screwed on right trying to take the center place is only a little better than a man trying to force himself into the center place."

That seemed like an odd thing for her to say. I found myself feeling irritated by it, as though the rules for being "correct" were beginning to appear impossible to live up to. I turned to catch her eyes. "What do you mean? What kind of woman?"

"A woman who has been taught to override her natural way of being and think like a man of your white culture. To think with the same walking-dead masks that he is preoccupied with serving and imprisoning himself in.

"This is like you were telling me about your baby boy when he was born. You wanted to touch and hold him, feed him from your breast. But the white culture said, 'No, we have to take him away.' You knew it was not good. It was wrong. But you talked yourself into trying to believe they knew what was best for you, that they were right. Do you see?"

I hesitated. I didn't want to know about those things. It was too disturbing. "Yeah. I see what you mean. Well, then, you're going to have to describe a woman who is able to take the center place."

"She is all that I have been talking about," she answered. "I've told you before, my people say women are sacred. It is not just your men who need to live with this as their guide. The women need to discover this for themselves, to know and honor this sacredness within their own hearts. It is part of their Song, their identity as a unique individual and as a whole group."

"OK, Chea. If she is the center of the group how come she's kicked out of things when she's bleeding, like in the tribes up here? Do your people do that? Isn't she not allowed to be around ceremony things? Isn't she forced to keep away? I've got to confess. I have a real hard time with that!"

"This is how the white man chose to see us when he first came here. And he hasn't changed his idea since. It was the only way he could understand what he found. He carried on his heart, like a great spear in his chest, the belief that women's blood was something to be avoided, something dirty and evil. He was terrified of women and their blood. They were a threat to him. So he assumed everyone else thought these things too. His church is the one that condemned women in their blood. Cast them out and called them ungodly, a curse sent by the devil.

"Among my people it is just the opposite. Women's blood is the most sacred and powerful, the most beautiful, of all the medicines. Women usually choose to be apart from the other things happening at their blood time so they can honor their own natural ceremony that comes on them, each praying in her own way, seeking answers to her questions, giving thanks, restoring herself, maybe seeking counsel with the Grandmothers or the spirit nations. It is a source of wondrous joy and pleasure and honoring. My people cherish and nurture this because it is her nature and she is to be without distractions at this time if she chooses. She is to be honored."

Her entire premise was so foreign to me I was going to have to consider and weigh these things for a very long time. The "undesirable" concepts reminded me of the attitudes I had heard from church as a child. "I never did buy that 'unclean' stuff. Good god. It sounds like she has leprosy or something."

"Hmmm."

"Isn't that prejudice kind of dying off here with this century, though, Chea?"

"Is it? Why don't the Catholics have women as priests?"

"Well," I answered, "I don't know."

She gave me that "see what I mean" look.

"Now, wait a minute. I don't understand this," I said. "I met some Indian men here who acted like they were going to catch something from getting close to a woman when she was bleeding."

"What I can tell you," she answered, "is that across the lands here each of the peoples had their own rituals and customs around bleeding. But the one thing they all held in common was the belief that women and women's blood are sacred. Women are always to be highly honored and cared for. Without women they are nothing. They have no future. Shaming and shunning came here from the white culture; that fear and attitude is only one of the things that many Indians took on from the white people. It's had five hundred years to creep in on them and they don't even see it.

"In my world, down in the wilderness areas of the Amazon, when a man who is a holy man, a medicine man, wants to make the most powerful medicine and prayer that he will ever be able to make he uses the woman's blood. He must find a woman who is worthy and ask her for the most powerful medicine that can be given to him— her Moon blood with her special prayers on it for this one ceremony.

He offers her something sacred like tobacco or pollen and humbles himself greatly, more than at any other time, because she is very likely to refuse him. But, you see, it is done only very, very rarely. That is how special it is!

"And it is common that he, and other men sometimes too, will go to a strong and powerful woman when she is in her bleeding and offer her tobacco or pollen, asking of her only to pray his prayer for him. He does this because he knows where the real power lies. In the womb."

I had never heard ideas like these before and I just couldn't face them. They were so different from anything I was familiar with that even my body felt stressed. "Did your people always do this?" I asked. "Do you have stories about the women from the really old times?"

"Some."

"What did they do? What was the structure, the way they did things? Has it changed?"

"Yes." She looked up from the water at me. "It has. My Grammas told me that a long time ago, even on the homeland that was before, before things started to get knocked out of balance, they said the great medicine people were all women. The Grammas. They led all the ceremonies. And the most important ones were done when certain of these women who were still young enough were in their bleeding times. These women had to be very strong, clear and pure of intent. They had to control their attention completely. That means controlling all the thoughts and emotions so they would not abuse their power.

"People today are not that clear. Even among my tribe. They don't have that strength of their attention. That is the other reason a woman might choose to stay away. Maybe she had an argument that day, or something, so she doesn't take the chance of disrupting things with a bad thought or feeling. But you see, any of my people would choose to stay away from sacred things if they had bad thoughts or feelings. By doing this they honor the works and prayers of others."

I sat there silent for a time. All the things she had said were charging through my mind like animals stampeding in a wilderness.

Finally I asked, "You've only mentioned a little of this in all the time we've been together. Why haven't you ever told me these things before?"

"Because you wouldn't have heard me," she said softly.

"But..."

"You have a hard enough time to see these ideas today. They are very strange to you. Things that will just sit in your mind that you will toss back and forth until the day you have actual experience to show what they truly mean."

"Yeah..." I hesitated and stammered. "You're right...after all, that's a big jump. To go from slightly sub-Human to most-powerful. Even sacred. Wow. That's quite a turn around."

"Yes," she said. "These are interesting times we live in."

My muscles were getting tight. I couldn't sit in that one place so long. I was starting to ache all over. I got up and stretched out on the fallen tree trunk. "Well," I said. "If that's what the women did, what did the men do?"

"Men do what needs to be done to honor the women and keep women's lives fulfilled and safe," she said in a tone as if it was the most obvious and natural thing in the world.

Her words took me so much by surprise I think I stopped breathing.

"Their job," she went on, "is to make it possible for the women to continue bringing and caring for life in as much health and beauty as can be possible. She is the center. He operates around the center, *for* the center. Not the other way around.

"The woman by her nature is daring and devoted. She never gives up. Even to her death. This is what the birthing paint is all about. This is the way of women that comes with the womb. Men have no womb. They must earn their power. In this way they imitate the woman, her willingness to never give up. They put on their war paint and choose to take an action that maybe will be as grand and bold and complete as hers. There is power in the decision to take an action and not go back on it. A woman does this every time she decides to keep a man's seed and make a child. That is an action and commitment that is kept to her death.

"Do you know why heroes of big adventures are usually men in the old stories?"

"Not really," I answered. "I guess I just assumed that it was because men wrote the stories and it was their chauvinism."

Chea laughed under her breath. "That's from a Christian background. I mean older stories. And the ones from the Americas before the white man. Men are pictured often because women don't have to go out seeking to find themselves, their adulthood or their power. A woman is already on the quest, she is a hero, every time she bleeds, every time she bears a child. A man takes his Song in his hand and hunts for his own opportunity to create his change.

"In order for him to move best around the center woman he must take on a quest and be willing to challenge himself even to his death. Only in this way can he ever be of great value to his people and his generations."

I was afraid this was starting to sound like just another injustice that would result in the excluding of women and the elitism of men. I felt like I was being cheated again. "Can't she go off on an adventure if she wanted to?"

"You're whining. Of course she can," she answered. "This has nothing to do with leaving her out of things or denying her something. He absolutely must quest in order to find his uniqueness and his place in the universe—in order to push himself into his best potential. For a woman these things are already there and they become fully part of her as she searches into her bleeding. She can go on the same kind of adventure and quest but in the stories, if she goes, there's usually something else involved too. She doesn't go for all the same reasons he goes. In her adventures they always have something to do with the balancing and honoring of her as the center as well as the balancing and honoring of her medicines and Song as an individual."

"But how does she..."

Chea cut me off abruptly. "No more questions for today. We'll be quiet with the river and the Mother Earth in the old way. This is your bleeding time. And this is the spring—our relatives are birthing all around us. We have no way for you to do a whole Moon Quest in the way of my tribe. But we can re-create some of it. Today we will spend here together as my Grandmother sometimes spent days with me while I bled. Tomorrow you will return alone to seek the knowledge of a woman. The following day we will meet here together again.

"Keep in mind that the whole time of bleeding is a pursuit—a quest. A plea to Creator for understanding and visions so that you can help yourself and so help others. Always be very aware of your senses. Think on what it is to be in the body of a woman. Observe yourself. Observe your world."

I wanted to know the component parts of the female hero's quest but I was glad the talk had ended. I had so much new and outrageous information I was afraid I wouldn't remember it all. I nodded back at Chea then walked over the rocks in the river for a few yards and sat on the dirt with my feet in the water.

I wondered what thoughts would run through the mind of a girl in a primitive tribe as she went into her first Mooning Vision Quest. What would it be like to be raised with the concept that you were to be the center and heart of the family and the whole tribe?

It seemed to me you would always have the feeling of security and completely belonging because you would be the connecting element that the members of the family would be a part of. You would always be the base of a family, a center, and therefore would always have a place and a purpose. Your "at homeness" would become a part of all the members.

As I followed this thought along I could sense a strong unity and acceptance that would make a bond between all. With a woman at the center the way Chea described, the workings of the group would be a priority but not at the expense of developing the potential of the individuals.

A woman within a system such as this would aim for the actions that would best serve her people today and at the same time serve the potential of the generations. How can her group ever reach its highest potential if the highest potential of its individuals is wasted?

What would this girl find in her new solitude, in her private, private place of exploring and becoming? In trying to imagine myself in her role I could only guess what the old women of the tribe must have come to know with the possibility of many such quests every year for forty years. No wonder they were so highly revered and were the ones who always made the most important decisions of a tribe.

I wondered how differently that girl and I felt about experiencing the world from inside a woman's body. How keen were her senses? Did she detect the medicines of things?

Then a dream came to my mind that I had had over a year ago. In it I was walking along the banks of this same little creek when I noticed the water keeper standing there. She looked considerably older than when I had seen her last and was leaning on a cane. She said to me, "Young one, don't ever deny your aliveness—it surges like

POWER OF THE FORBIDDEN FRUIT

this river here. Give this rejoicing to your world in this way." And as I began to wake up I watched her walk the path into the woods.

I looked down at my belly. My womb was slightly contracted. I could feel my blood as it slowly left my cervix. I realized that I had never really paid any attention to it before. Usually I would go out of my way to not feel any part of the bleeding process at all. The less I had to deal with it and the prospect of becoming pregnant the better. I had shut out my femaleness. There was so much of me that I did not know.

Chea was right. How could I have success in sharing medicines, Songs and friendship with another being in the way of what they called the oldest sacrament when I was not in touch with what I was offering?

I turned my awareness back to my womb and began to find my center. It was time to work on accepting this part of my Humanness and observe.

I had to start over and over. I couldn't hold my attention to my purpose. I became increasingly ill at ease. An old fear I had never acknowledged before was growing and festering inside me. It felt dangerous to relate to myself as a woman. Being this aware of my uterus and vagina and the physical sensations they generated was so uncomfortable it was causing me to faint. I stopped and leaned over.

Here I was, a woman in my late twenties having given birth to two children and the feeling of the movements of my own uterus and its blood was an alien experience for me. It was untouchable, unthinkable, as though it were something that belonged to someone else and I had no business nosing around in it, trespassing, violating their unseemly property.

To feel these processes of my body or consider taking ownership of them seemed physically unsafe and somehow improper or unclean. I realized that in the white culture to notice one's femaleness this keenly was "taboo," and I felt as though I were about to reap the far-reaching repercussions of breaking it. From an academic standpoint, if I were observing this phenomenon from an individual in another culture, I would describe it as an irrational, automatic response to a cultural superstition.

I breathed deeply and splashed water on my face. I could see Chea watching me from the edge of the waterfall. When the dizziness left me I sat back on the dirt to rest a moment before trying again. Time after time the feelings of invading the unclean flesh, the forbidden fruit, overwhelmed me until I became familiar with it enough that it lost its power over me.

The day was gone. Chea motioned to me that it was time to leave. I finally noticed how tired I was and let myself relax. I didn't want to go but it would be dark soon and I still had many things to take care of at the apartment before I could go to sleep. We hiked out of the forest all the way to the bus stop without a word.

The next morning I arrived at the waterfall late. My mind was so full of the conflicting beliefs toward women that I had great difficulty putting any attention on observing anything. There was nothing else I could do but re-evaluate the worlds of womanhood that were now open to me. I was surprised to find that not just my female body sensations seemed uncomfortably alien but the entire subject was.

All day I fought with the images and concepts. I felt dislocated, separated from anything familiar and confused. From one cultural perspective to the next I found things unfamiliar, some full of beauty and all laced with great anguish.

On the following day I met Chea as we had planned at the waterfall. The air was warm and there were even more tiny wild flowers with their blossoms open to the sky. We gave each other a hug and I picked a spot in the sunlight to sit down.

She didn't waste any time and began talking again about the teachings of women's knowledge that had been passed down to her from her Grandmothers.

Her bluntness and lack of white culture modesty took me by surprise. "I'm talking about sex," she said shaking her head at me. "What could be more a part of women's knowledge than the acts that help her bring a new life into this world?"

"Chea, I know about sex. I'm not a kid. I have kids."

She wrinkled her forehead at me. "You had better know a lot about it. But the horror is that you don't. And you don't even know it.

"Your culture amazes me! It has taken even this away from you. How else do you think they could conquer the women and their power? Women's power reaches from inviting a man to her vagina, to the cradle, to the crops, to the building of villages, to what is decided at her table and in the councils."

POWER OF THE FORBIDDEN FRUIT

I looked up at her and started to say something but she wouldn't let me talk.

"Now don't interrupt." She pointed her finger at me and tried not to smile. "You just listen for a while. You get comfortable there and let your mouth rest. Just listen.

"Your sexuality is one of your most private treasures and it was slipped away from you. The white people that marched to conquer, what they could not take by force they conquered by words, ideas. *Beliefs*. They destroyed the power of the women and the place of the women by the use of poisoned words. *Blind beliefs*. The church of Rome wanted to conquer and rule the world and they figured out how."

Her comments were so generalized and encompassing I couldn't stop myself from interrupting her. "Now that's a pretty broad statement. The church has been around a long time, Chea. I don't think it was always doing that. I think there have been people who were sincere."

"Open your eyes and really look, Kay. Sincere is not the problem. It's *what* they teach the people. It's designed to take away their power, their ability to observe, feel and think for themselves. It's designed to take away their individual freedom. Especially from the women. And then give it to the ruling body. The church. Cripple the women and you cripple everything, the entire system."

Chea cleared her throat. "Why do you think they killed all your Grandmothers?"

"What..."

"And where they move in now, who do you think they get rid of first?

"Then the people are trained, they are 'educated,' to hand it over voluntarily. And they do. No weapons needed. The church, and now the state and industries, they just wait and then come in and take everything. Look at it. The words from Rome are still ruling the world.

"You told me about the different peoples you have studied, and histories. Think of what was there. When women are at the center place, and know how to be the center, then there is equity and balance. Each individual lives in their own power. They are connected to the life around them. Things can grow into harmony and continue and prosper. Things are there in a good way for the generations.

"Take the woman out of that and make everyone believe she is a thing unworthy and broken, then you have a world where something is always wrong from the start. There is no balance, no harmony, no connection, nothing of value, no equality, nothing fulfilled. Everything begins falling into destruction.

"You take her and her Mother Earth from being sacred and turn them into unclean devils, then you have made war on your women and the very land and planet that sustains you. You have made war on the foundation under your feet, the roof of sky above your head, the blood in your veins. You have made war on your own survival.

"This way of being cannot continue on itself. It has no ka ta see, no balance. It has no center. It destroys everything in its path. It's coming to the end of its course. Do you see? It could actually take everything with it."

"So how do we stop it?" I asked throwing a little pebble I had in my hand. "Who should I get pissed at first?"

"Remember what we've told you, 'It's not your fault but it is your responsibility.' There is no one thing or person to make into a target. The men are just as much victims as the women. You can't be wasting yourself throwing your anger around at them or any others. You don't need hate. You don't need violence.

"In order to be in your own power you cannot allow yourself to wallow in your anger or your self-pity. It's an entire system that has to change. And the only way it can happen is for each person within themselves to refuse to be blinded and used anymore.

"Stop believing in their poisoned words.

"Each one must take responsibility to change inside themselves. And each must start making decisions in favor of things that promote life and the well being of all things for generations to come.

"Start by taking what is yours back. Your ability to observe well without jumping to conclusions or judging. Your delight of meeting and maybe talking to the beings you share this world with. Your pleasure of filling yourself with your Song and maybe the Songs of others. The knowledge of your senses. Your ability to think for yourself. Your pleasure, the purity, of your sexuality."

Chea shook her fist in the air in front of her. "Now that's women's medicine!"

"How?" I asked jerking back.

Chea reached closer and braced herself on a river rock. "These things are a natural part of Human experience. They are things that help you learn and be caring and free. They honor the generations. And for a woman of your culture to reclaim them is an act worthy of the birthing paint."

I could feel the huge rift that existed between our two cultures. Sometimes I wished I could go and live with her tribe so I could truly come to understand them and their view of the world. I knew my culture had big gaps in its ability to understand these ways but I had almost no concept of what the missing pieces must have been. "The way you talk, Chea, I think maybe sex must be really different with your people. Is it?"

She nodded.

"What makes it like that?"

"They have almost no contact with the white world," she answered. "They keep apart from them. So the old ways are still there. You see, among my people a woman's sexual actions are a part of her medicine. It is part of how she prays. This is hers for her pleasure and expression of her love and excitement for life and Creation itself. This is hers to invite a man she chooses to share it with. Our women enjoy showing their sexual desire and for our people this is a very honorable thing.

"My Grammas said in the old times a man never refused a woman, forced a woman or attacked her. That was inconceivable. Absolutely inconceivable. It was a great honor for him to be asked to have sex with her and he did his best to live up to it. Now that doesn't mean he didn't show his interest first if that was the situation. He certainly would and with much respect. But it was part of her role and her power to have this choice."

"That sounds like something that could easily be abused," I interjected. "Did women abuse that right? Was there, is there, trouble with that?"

She shook her head. "The acts of sex among my people are considered sacred. They go to sex for different reasons than your people. These actions are a way to give thanks, to honor your life and the one you are with. My Grammas said that it has always been a sacred prayer, a giving, a sacrament. The sacred link. My people don't take this lightly. The pleasures attract them, sure. They are a very sensual and openly sexual people, but the acts are not a way just to get an orgasm. They are a give-away. A time of deep, lifelong bonding.

"I think these things are hard for the white mind to catch. You are taught with all aspects of your life to keep a distance, and to 'take it now,' instant gratification. Your people aren't taught to give deeply of themselves, especially your men. You have lost the ways of opening yourselves up and bonding so intimately with each other, of building an honest love and trust between each other that makes a family unbreakable and weaves the entire tribe together.

"For instance, two men who, along the way, happened to have sexual sharing with the same woman would not be rivals. They would be close allies, brothers. They would have an honoring and closeness between each other because they both had a deep sacred bond to the same woman. Two women who had been sexual with the same man become lifelong sisters. If there are children from these unions, the children make the adults all part of the same family. In a way those adults all become a parent or, you could say, aunt or uncle to the children. They are bonded emotionally to the children and have social responsibilities toward them as well."

"Do they have sex with both these partners the rest of their lives?" I asked.

Chea looked at me with curiosity for a moment. "It really doesn't matter whether they were sexual once or always. A deep bond is still there. The love and sacred medicine shared. The responsibilities to that and the person are there. Whether they are sexual again or not there is a desire to not harm the bond that was built. The bond is sacred. It was built in sacrament.

"You see, they don't run and hump with every member of the village. You couldn't live up to that. An adult is free to be with who they choose. When it's time to pick a mate, you pick very carefully because you will stay together all your life. Often there are situations where a person has more than one mate maybe for a little while or maybe for life. This is not done lightly. There is a lot of responsibility to this. And a lot of joy and closeness too."

"Your tribe isn't monogamous then? I always assumed you were."

"Many Native American tribes accept more than one mate when the circumstances are there."

"Really? I didn't know that. I guess they're pretty practical folks, huh?"

She nodded. "Yes. Why not?"

I shrugged my shoulders and tossed another pebble into the water. "You said a lot of things about your women being treated with such reverence. I've tried to imagine myself in a world where I was treated this way by everyone simply because I was female. And I just don't know how to imagine it. I don't even know what the pieces would be like. I never realized how poorly women in my world were treated. I guess I never had anything to compare it with before. Everywhere I look, everything I remember, I see a whole different thing now.

"In my culture, you know, a woman who bluntly shows her sexual desire could actually be arrested for prostitution if the situation seemed to fit.

"I don't know, Chea. Is the horror of it really as big as it feels?"

"Yes." She didn't move her eyes from me.

"Yes? Just yes?" I asked. "Aren't you going to tell me how?" There was an old sadness welling up inside me, a pain I now realized, I had always gone to great lengths to suppress. "How can that have happened? It scares me when I can't even picture what a scene would be like between me and a man where he truly treated me with honor in all situations."

"Kay. You are a product of your culture. Just like all the women here, and the men. From birth you have been taught to give your authority and your power away in every which direction. And you are all taught how to be a part in the taking of it from the others. But things are different now. Stop the cycles. Claim your right as a Human. No matter how long it's been gone it is still yours."

She grabbed into the air with her fist and said, "Take it back!"

"Just like that."

"Yes," she demanded. "Just like that."

"Oh god. Chea."

"Enough with the wimpy whining. Look at what has been stolen from you." She gestured with her hands and demanded again, "Look at it!

"Don't deny your pain and anger, trying to hide from it with your work, or cover it with sugar or alcohol or drugs. And don't waste the power of this on hurling it at some imagined target out there!"

She moved closer and her eyes bored into mine. "Use it to make yourself sensitive and strong. It will teach you if you let it.

"Can you see that part of the plan to conquer is to separate everyone? When you are high on drugs or alcohol you are separated. And when you have a target to vent your anger on you are separated. It doesn't matter who the target is, the fellow next door, the tribe next door, the 'other' country, the men, the women. *The devil.* As long as you are blaming and warring it keeps you divided and locked in the habit of your anger so you won't see what your part in it is or what the real target is.

"You won't see the way to stop the whole game. The secret is feeling and knowing your Song and the Songs of others."

My eyes filled with tears. "But..."

"Don't give me that self-pity crap, either. Are you ever going to stop that?" She wouldn't let me finish. "Nobody ever did anything while they're wallowing in the filth of their own self-pity. If you're knocked down then get up again.

"That's a woman's strength!

"That's women's medicine!

"Take your pain and your anger and hold them where you can see them hand in hand with your joys and passions. Never lose sight of your joys and passions. Come to know your pain and anger but don't let them overwhelm you. Learn what they have to teach you. And then let them go."

"But it frightens me," I said. I couldn't hold the crying back. "It frightens me to see just how much my people have lost. It reaches into everything, every part of our lives. It's very hard to accept. It's like living a lie. Like waking up from a nightmare and still being in the nightmare. You said don't let it overwhelm me. Well, the thought of it does overwhelm me. It's too big. Oh god!" I began to cry uncontrollably. "It's too big!"

She stared at me, moving her head from side to side. "What is yours to carry is never too big. A woman's power is to always be able to carry what is hers to carry. And sometimes a little more. The power of a woman is that she always picks up her pieces and keeps going."

"Birthing paint," I blurted out unconsciously.

"You're damn right, birthing paint! It's the only way," she said. "Like a journey begins with one step, a change in the world begins with a change inside a single person."

"How can that depend on one person?"

"The first step brings a momentum. And the second more. And so on. The change in one influences another person and they influence another and another. The change is repeated, expanded, improved. The influence spreads from one to ten to a thousand. Good or bad. Do you see?"

The Sun had gotten overbearingly hot. I squatted in the shallow water and splashed it on my head and back. It trickled down my face and into my eyes.

"Your culture," she added, "your Judeo-Christian culture, is a culture based on people not taking responsibility for their own actions, on not taking responsibility for their environment or their generations. They don't think they have to be responsible for anything they do. After all, their god gave them dominion and redemption, so to them they can do anything they want and they think it's OK. They think they have some kind of permission."

"I don't think I want to know this." I splashed more water over my head trying to take away the heat and the pressure.

"Don't you want your freedom? I mean real freedom? Real independence? Where do you think you are going to find peace inside yourself from out there in that craziness?"

"Yeah," I sulked. "OK. So, what do I look at? It's so huge, I don't have a clue how. I mean, what is it that's missing? Or what is it that needs to be eliminated? Just what do I go after?"

"You go after the most natural of things in the world. You go after your *IDENTITY*. Your connection to all around you, your place among Creation, your honor, your dignity. They're free, and they make you free. They are what keeps the power in the hands of each and every individual. This is what you come from. Your roots before Christianity came. Your heritage. Yes. Your identity. Who *are* you, Kay? Where does your heart aim you?"

I dug a Kleenex out of my pocket and blew my nose, mumbling, "How can words steal any of that? How can anything steal such things?"

"You were lied to. For centuries. They told you these things were not part of Creator but a trick of the devil—the monster created to control you and take all of your power and all of your people's power. They took away everything they could and pushed the people farther and farther into confusion and doubt. It is said among many Indians that these thieves try to 'steal your spirit.' If they could have actually stolen your Song they would have. They couldn't, so they buried it for you instead.

"You want to know what to do to stop it? Go after the excitement of your senses, Kay. Go after your Song. You have been isolated from your relatives and from your whole world. Separated. All of you from all of this and each other. And even from yourself. You remember their saying, 'Divide and conquer?'"

I couldn't say anything. I was afraid she was right, and the feeling of it choked the thoughts right in my throat.

"And what did their words give you?" she went on. "Fear, gnawing loneliness, guilt. The feeling of your whole Humanness and its beauty is carefully hidden from you. You are told that there is something wrong with you, even from your birth, that makes you shameful, untrustworthy. Not even your own god will have you. It's all been arranged for you to be lost from start to finish. What the hell kind of beliefs are those?

"Kay, the time can't be put off any longer. You don't have time to waste. Stand up and take your place in the center. Your body, your pleasure, your mind and emotions, your love of yourself and all things, your equity among Creation, your passion, your sexuality. These are yours by nature, by right of being alive. These are the way of women. Take them back! Stand up and own them! *Own* the truth of who you are!"

Chea stopped for a moment. Her silence was like a vacuum that sucked away even the sounds of the river.

"Do you see the will in your people?" she asked. "Their self-determination? It's crippled. The balance is gone. Your people live precarious lives full of boredom and frustration."

The more she spoke the less I wanted to face any of it. I shook my head and said, "It just seems so crazy. Maybe some of this stuff you say isn't there. Maybe you're seeing more into things than are actually there."

"Don't take my word for it." She stood up to move out of the sunlight, wiping the perspiration from her face. "Look at yourself.

Look at your own sexuality. Do you have sex in your life that pleases you? I don't mean just OK. I mean that makes you feel *alive* through every cell? Truly *full?* As though life itself was honoring you?

"When you are having sex with your friend does he treat you with dignity, caring, honor, great respect? Does he really value your pleasure? Does he value your orgasm? Your desires and needs and requests? Does he have deep pleasure in giving these things to you?

"Or does he act like his pleasures and orgasms are more interesting than yours? Like his are somehow more important than yours? Does he act like his needs are the only ones that have real significance? Or maybe he avoids acknowledging that you have needs at all? Is he one who carries the mask that says you are his sexual-servant-plaything and that it is not his place in life to have to give you any kind of sexual pleasures? That maybe you shouldn't even be wanting any sexual gratifications? I ask you, does he try to control just how much pleasure you actually get?"

Her questions hit me off guard. I felt as if my clothes had been ripped at in public and my neglected underwear was being exposed.

"If you really want to be free from the expectations and rules and restrictions of all parts of your culture and hold your center, to know balance and wholeness, then you had better take a long, hard look. Soon."

I could feel my embarrassment flushing through my face. I wanted to make her to stop and change the subject but I didn't know how. I was becoming frustrated and nervous.

"Is there anything you would change in your sex with that man you are sleeping with?" she kept on. "Or anyone else? If you could? Hmmm?"

I had no answer. I couldn't acknowledge having any anxiety about my sex life because then I'd have to admit to myself that it was empty. The horror of that was too much.

She kept studying me. I felt like an oddity on display. She finally said, "You don't even own your own sexuality. Can you see it? The church owns it. The society owns it. They've trained your man to own it. They are the ones who tell you exactly how to look, how to move, how to talk, how to have sex, how not to have sex. They even own your enjoyment of the sexual acts. They tell you what to enjoy and exactly how much. And you do it.

"Kay, they even manage to tell you what you can smell and what you can't. And if it is a good smell or bad. You know this now. The whole prescription of what your people are allowed to smell, taste, touch, hear, see. The whole society, they all follow along with no questions asked. You're all living half dead.

"I am hard on you with this because a woman's sexuality, not just her ability to bleed and the respect of that, but her profound pleasure of sex, her receiving honor, reverence and cherishing from sexual interactions is at the core, the very center of her place as center. Undermine this and you undermine the whole power structure of a people. Do you see this destroys her place and her power? You end up working on destroying her. As long as this continues your men won't be free and you won't be free."

Chea paused for a moment waiting for me to comment. I couldn't even look up at her. I had no defense against the realization that what I had held true and good was nothing but lies and excuses. I kicked the water nervously with my foot.

"I'll show you what I mean." She moved to the side just slightly to get a better view of my face and continued, "What would happen if you went out deep into the forest where no one ever goes and laid down on the loam and masturbated?"

I was utterly shocked! She had surprised me before with things she would say, but never this completely. I was offended! Outraged! That whole subject was not one I could easily face even in private, nor could I tolerate it at all in public.

I felt disgusted and so nervous I couldn't keep my hands from shaking. My voice tightened up. "That's perverted! What a weird thing to do. I would never do that. What if someone came along? I could be arrested."

Chea remained calm and at ease as if there was nothing unusual about anything she was saying. "I'm talking about some place very private, secluded, way back in the forest where no one hikes around. Not any place where people might walk through. This isn't about exposing yourself. I'm talking about being in a completely private place, all by yourself, alone with all the natural things and smells. Out on your Mother Earth. Feeling everything around you. Feeling yourself completely and freely. Enjoying where you are. Enjoying yourself. Appreciating every bit of information that comes to you through your senses. And doing the most natural thing in the world. In a most natural place. The way your ancient Grandmothers used to do. It is your heritage. Your right. These are things you should be proud of. And honor. Give dignity to. This great joy and beauty as a Human and most especially as a woman are what have been stripped away from you. Stolen. Tell me. Could you do that?"

"No way! It's weird, Chea. That's a weird thing to do."

"Masturbating is weird, huh? I suppose you never did that. That's what the prescription says, 'Thou shall not masturbate.' Especially women!"

My stomach was beginning to feel upset and there was a tightness in my throat like the feeling just before gagging.

"Look at your reactions. How uncomfortable you are to even think about such things and talk about them. This is what they've done to you."

I was starting to feel angry at everything. I wanted to just get up and leave.

"Don't get angry at me. The anger belongs to what has happened to you and your people. Use it to take back what has been denied, to live in your body again.

"Don't worry. I'm not telling you to go out in the forest and masturbate. Just think about what that means and why you react the way you do to even the idea of such freedom.

"You act like an animal who has lived its whole life in a cage and the cage door is left open—the animal is terrified of what is outside the cage and won't leave it."

We sat silent for a time. I didn't understand why I was reacting with such intense anxiety and anger. In reality, I actually envied the thought of being more sexually free, but I couldn't imagine myself ever taking actions such as Chea had described or being free of the guilt. I wondered how we got this way and who was right. I thought about what it was that I might be missing from my sex life. What would I change if I could have anything I wanted? I didn't even know. I realized I was not satisfied or, as she said, full. But I had no idea of what to do to change it.

Chea stood up and stretched. She looked as if she felt as tired as I did. She patted me on the shoulder and said, "Enough on that for today. You are in the last of your sensory training for the sacrament. And this is your Bleeding Ceremony. As I have said, your natural awareness builds from a knowing of your womanhood. So you must now find this knowing for yourself. When you do, then you take it like a foundation and aim your attention from it, evenly over all the senses. This is what you work on."

I agreed.

"I'll stay," she reassured me. "No questions, though, we'll be silent for now. Tomorrow we come again. OK. Let's do it."

I spent the rest of the day moving from dirt to rock and back. I was unable to get comfortable. My mind wouldn't let go of its death grip on my sexuality. I examined my womanhood and my state of freedom from every angle I could think of. I wanted to prove her wrong. It was extremely disturbing and painful to me to have to acknowledge that I did not have any of the freedoms that I thought I had. But I couldn't lie to myself any longer. She was right.

When the Sun was low Chea waved goodbye from a little way up the river and hiked off into the forest. I followed soon after, taking the wars of womanhood and power and freedom home for the night.

We were to meet again the next day as planned. I had hardly slept and my body ached all over. I was still so tortured from the battles and horrors surrounding womanhood within our culture that I walked all the way down to the waterfall without ever noticing or enjoying the sunlight and spring growth that was giving of its abundance everywhere.

Chea and I hugged and said hello and I gave her a bag of fresh fruits and rolls that I picked up to bring along.

"So," she looked at me with a little smirk. "You've been thinking about the women's medicine. Huh?"

"Chea. That's all I've been able to think about. I couldn't even sleep. I feel like a truck hit me. A big one. Honestly. I don't know how to deal with it all. I don't know where to put it in my mind. I just want to crawl away and hide from it somewhere. Only I can't 'cause it's stuck inside my head. And I just take it with me wherever I hide."

She laughed. "So don't hide. Examine it. Learn what yourself and the world are telling you about these things. To be effective as a

POWER OF THE FORBIDDEN FRUIT

woman and to be effective with the sacrament and as a kala keh nah seh you must come to know and understand these things for yourself. Examine it deep inside."

"How?" My voice choked off. "It's like a war in there in my head." Tears came to my eyes.

She wrinkled her eyebrows at me. "You're whining. Enough. Gather yourself and get to your business. There is a lot to be done yet. There's no time left for sniveling around. Let's get to what we came for."

She grinned at me. "It's women's knowledge of the medicines of romance and lovers that I will tell you about today."

My eyes opened wide. "That sounds a little more upbeat than the last stuff."

Chea shook her head and giggled at me. "Yes. This is a lot more fun. I know you will like this. When we finish here maybe you should go hunt down the pretty young man we found on the mall. Huh?" She nudged me in the side.

"Let's get good and comfy," she added, pointing with her chin. "How about over there. There's more grass and moss to sit on and it's in the sunlight."

"Good," I agreed. "There's no mud on that side. There aren't all those little sharp rocks either."

We spread out in the light that filtered from the trees. She handed me a peach and a roll and began to talk. "OK. These are the ways of my Grandmothers. They have been given to the daughters of each generation since we were in the land before.

"And as I have said, they taught that the medicines and acts of sex are very sacred. You have been learning about how to make yourself feel and hear and see the medicines and Songs of the relatives and spirits around you so that you can understand them. You've been learning how to purposely make medicines and atmospheres that are suitable so that you can share yourself with them in a good way."

I nodded and said, "Yeah. That's what the sensory work is all about, isn't it?"

"Yes. But it doesn't stop there." She gave me a big smile. "It can sure be a little crazy but you must learn how to observe the medicines of your fellow Humans as well. And learn the sexual arts of sharing medicines and Songs with a lover."

I grinned back. "Yeah! All right! This is getting better all the time."

Chea laughed. "This is what the whole of the sacrament is—the giving and accepting, the connecting with all those we share this world with. And in this way we talk with and come to know our Creator. These are all parts of the sacred links between all things.

"You are very aware now of how we Humans are sending out our thoughts and emotions all the time. These are the medicines we constantly make and feed out to the world."

"Yeah."

She added, "When we are thinking sexual thoughts we are calling on those parts of our body and the energies from there. If the thoughts are about a certain person then the energies go straight to that person no matter where they are, unless they are in ceremony.

"White people's minds are usually too crowded with something else and they don't notice so much. But the body sure isn't as dumb. It feels this coming to it. And it usually does something about it. It starts to like the interest and excitement. It wants to join in. If we aren't paying attention we may not know where it is coming from. We may think we started feeling this way all by ourselves first. Our reaction will be flavored with the signature of the one who first sent the medicine and so then we tend to feel we are attracted to this person.

"Our body becomes excited. Our mind turns to the feelings. The medicine escapes from us and goes to them. Their body feels it. They're aroused even more. And so the medicine builds between the two. It becomes a field that they are immersed in. The more erotic and detailed their images and feelings are the hotter the field becomes and the hotter they get. This is the medicine of flirting and courting."

Chea leaned her head over a little closer and looked at me with a big grin. "This will be your 'assignment.' You are to look for these medicines as they are sent to you. Follow them back to their maker. And if you like the maker, try sending these energies back and forth. Now be careful. I'm not telling you to go have sex with these men. OK?"

"OK," I answered.

"I'm telling you to study the medicines as they come and go and how they make your body feel and your emotions feel. See if you have impressions of exact sexual acts, or maybe the feeling of your body actually being touched. Observe all these things very carefully. And the energies you send out should be clean and clear of other issues. Yes?"

"I got it," I laughed. "This is the best homework assignment I ever had."

Chea laughed and agreed. "And try to catch their other medicines as well. The kind of person they are. See if you can observe any of those things."

"Like what we did with the sense of seeing? Looking at fields and colors?" I asked.

"Yes. And rely on the other senses when there is information there, if you are close enough. Trust in your ability to know."

I took a deep breath and nodded.

"Now don't forget to enjoy yourself." She looked over at me and giggled.

I laughed. "That I won't forget."

She patted my arm. "This is a serious thing but it is also light and joyful and beautiful. It is meant to be enjoyed. Keep both in mind."

"Yeah."

"As for the other part of your assignment, you are to pay attention to the medicines that are coming to you from the plants and trees. That's the nation you will be sending your voice to first in seeking the sacrament. You need to get very used to the way they feel and send medicine. When you practice observing with all your senses at once, aim at the plant nations."

"I bet that's going to be intense." Then I thought about it all for a moment and it dawned on me. "But the plant quest and the flirting, that's not the whole picture, huh? I'm right, huh? So tell me, what's with the rest of this sexual medicine? There's something else here. There's more to it than just the flirting, isn't there?"

Chea smiled. She was going to make me work for it. "What does it feel like? What seems like it might be there?"

"Well..."

"Go ahead," she encouraged me. "Say what you think. You have a sense of something there. What is it like?"

"It's something deeper that can happen," I said. The words to describe what I sensed were hard to find. I stopped and started several times. "It's like what you said. To make some kind of real connection or bond. It seems like maybe we should be able to join, or what you called it, merge, with somebody of our own species too. Not just keepers or other spirits. Is this right? Is there such a thing?"

"Yes." Her eyes never left me. "But there is a lot more than that. The things that bring deep, deep satisfaction and bonding. There is the giving back and forth of great energies and a great gift."

"What gift?" I asked.

"First I'll tell you of the energies," she said and gestured with her hands toward the air and the ground. "A man and a woman coming together are like two of the great forces here in our world, the sky above and the Mother Earth below, as they do their love dance to create excitement and fertilize and share their hearts. With a man and a woman it is the same.

"It is their natural state to come together in reverence for each other and for all Creation. He must come to her as he would come to prayer. And be overflowing with a need and desire to give to her. His senses alert to everything she does and wants.

"Sex is a time when you feel your Song very strongly and feel the Song of your lover. These are shared from a very deep place. You and your lover must have great trust in each other. Then the energy of life increases inside you. It builds like a thunderhead.

"When a couple is together, and have come to know the Earth Fire Serpent and the life energies that move with her, then this too swells up and through. It all rushes and bursts out to the lover. Back and forth. It carries their affection and lust and all the other medicines they have on their minds at the moment. It excites them. It nourishes them.

"My Grammas taught me that this can be aimed with your attention. It is offered and given through the touching of the skin or can be thrust out of the body in front of the action. Or directed to move out any part of the body you wish so that it can make contact with whichever part of your lover you wish. You can choose to send it as a steady flow or build it up and let it burst out or be pushed out into the partner in great surges and bolts like lightning.

"These energies in you are full of your heart and the hearts of the other three that they flow from—the heart of the Mother Earth, the heart of the Sun and the heart of the Milky Way. As they are given back and forth the caring and closeness grows intimately between you and your lover. Unbreakable bonds are made.

"This is an art of harmonics that is worthy of your most devoted attention. It can bring such joy and tremendous satisfaction. It's a thunderstorm that doesn't run dry and whose fires are never empty. And the pleasures are undreamt of.

"But whether you know the Earth Fire Serpent or not you can send the energies of life that move in your body in these ways. And you can use these to make the gift I mentioned. But once you know the Earth Fire Serpent there is no way to compare."

I interrupted. "The gift is something you make then?"

"Yes. From these energies." She accentuated with her hands as she spoke. "You take the life energy and build it inside yourself. You put into it every thought you carry at the time and every emotion and every precious sensation that your senses feel. All of your love and desire. The honoring. The passion. You offer your Song unguarded, to be cherished. Your thanksgiving to Creator. Everything. They are woven all together into the fabric of your orgasm and given to the beloved."

I sat up and scooted closer to Chea. This was so provocative I didn't want to miss anything she said. "But how is that given?"

"It is given as one would give a gift." She held her hands out as though they were filled with something large and delicate. "It is all these things as they have been made part of the energy and force of your orgasm. Whether you are aware of it or not you guide your orgasm with your attention. It is a very huge amount of energy. When you direct it into a gift it becomes even larger. It is from the very substance of your being. It is the most precious thing you can give someone.

"Your heart has to be very open to your lover to be able to give this and even more so to accept it when it is given to you. The bonds are like the foundation to a great temple."

"Do I need to be in my center to do any of these things?"

"No. But the closer you are, the clearer and more intense the experience is. It is not easy. Sometimes the distractions are pretty good." She giggled at me with a girlish grin. "The more you can keep the chatter of your thoughts out and experience without any masks then you have nothing blocking or distorting what is there. It is pure enjoyment and Songs and giving and accepting."

There was a stirring of leaves and branches off under the trees. We looked to see what was there. I could find nothing through the foliage but Chea acted as if she knew what was there. The branches stirred again and then I saw her, a beautiful doe. She stopped and looked at us for a few moments. There were sounds coming from behind her. I wondered if she had a fawn with her. She seemed satisfied with our presence and turned back into the forest.

"You see there?" Chea looked back at me. "She came to see how things were going with us. Our relatives are pleased that we are here having this bleeding time.

"Now, I want to tell you something about these ways. All of these things can be given to a person who is not with you at the time. Distance doesn't mean anything to medicines. They move in a different way. This can be nice if your lover is far away and you want to touch and exchange something special. It can be a very intense experience but being together in the flesh is always greater.

"And you don't want to be thinking of a different person than the one you are with. These energies follow your thoughts. They go to the one you are thinking of. You don't lay with one and send to the other. This is not a good thing. Do you see?"

I nodded.

"And when you are alone you have a responsibility to not invade on someone who doesn't want this. These energies are never to be given carelessly. There is responsibility that comes with the medicines you make in flirting, energy giving and gift giving. Do you understand this?"

"Yes," I answered. "Yes I do. My impact on the ones that would be my lovers is pretty big, huh?"

"It is. Whatever your mood is, whatever else you are carrying around with the masks you are wearing will affect them. So keep it clean. Keep it from the heart. Keep respect for them and yourself always."

I slapped my hands together and stood up. "Well, I'm ready to go try. Are we going to go find that handsome young gentleman on the mall now?"

Chea laughed. "You keep wanting to find that one again. You really liked his flirting medicines didn't you?"

"I did indeed. But you're going to have to tell me about the merging between Humans sometime too. Are we going to talk about it today?"

She sat up and reached for a piece of fruit. "I'll tell you something about it now because you are interested. But we will get into the whole part of it on another bleeding time. It is a very complex art and prayer. It is most sacred.

"Your intuition was correct, young one. In the same way you can merge a portion of your Song with a being like the wind keeper you can merge with a plant spirit or other such being. And in this same way you can merge for a few moments with another Human. It is more difficult between Humans and it involves the giving of the gifts in a very special way. But this all will be for another time."

I nodded and then stood there waiting for her to indicate that it was time to go.

She looked up and shook her head at me. "OK, eager beaver. Set yourself back down here for a while yet. You have to get the instructions clear in your head about giving out your energies and Song in quest to the plant nations. Your time to go and seek the friendship and sacrament with them is almost here. So get your mind back from the men now and listen."

I laughed and plopped myself down on my stomach.

She smiled at me. "It's the plants we have to talk about now. You don't have to look so burdened. We'll get back to the sex soon. Don't worry."

I blushed and giggled. "I'm listening. Really."

She raised an eyebrow at me. "Yes. This is easy to see. Too bad for you there is no tape recorder." We both laughed.

"OK now. You know to keep observing with all the senses as often as possible. It must become second nature to you. Notice the ones around from the other nations. Which ones are they? Are there a lot? Is there anyone you know? Like your friend the wind keeper. Or maybe you are in another location where your friend doesn't go too often but you feel another wind keeper there.

"Say hello. Be respectful. Always give your greetings and energies to the ones who live there, especially to the ones who are of a nation you are akin to already. This is the way we approach our relatives and friends."

She had me crawl over close to a small fern that was near our spot. She touched the leaves very lightly and said something to it under her breath. Turning to me she spoke, "One must always come gently to the plant nations. Come in peace and joy and respect. They are a most kind race and it is important that no matter how long it takes you always keep patient.

"It's good to remember that plants see right through your masks so you might as well leave them at the side of the road. Use the gifts of the four directions, stay in your center as well as you can. Make your quest clearly known to them. You want to feel into their medicines very keenly. See if you can copy the mood they make. Create it inside you.

"And always offer of yourself. Share the Earth Fire Serpent energy as it moves through you. Share the energy from your heart. Let them flood and fill the area and all the ones there. Remember, your body is an altar, it is a sacred thing. The energies and love and respect are your offering, your gift. Observe *everything*.

"You will do this daily until a member of the plant nation responds to you."

"But, Chea. How will they do that? Will I be doing this daily thing for a week or a year? Or how does this work?"

She said matter-of-factly, "However long it takes. Nobody can say. Don't worry. You will know when one has accepted you."

"I got a question. About making and singing the fibers to the plants. Remember when I did that by accident to the water keeper? Is this something that I should do or not?"

She seemed pleased with my question. Singing the fibers is something she always had a special liking for. "If it feels right to you and is something you want to do from your heart. Yes. Observe carefully. It should be an act of giving and offering and friendship from your heart. It should be unconditional. An honoring. The plant nations love gracefulness and melodic sounds. Sometimes you might even hear them singing back.

"This singing from your heart, you know, calls their attention like nothing else. It says to them, 'Hello, I'm here to show my gratitude and respect to you. I'm here as a friend. I seek to know you and share with you in the oldest way. The way of the sacrament.'"

"Chea. The way you talk about singing to the plants, you sound almost like you're courting."

"Of course." She smiled warmly. "When you are approaching any being for the sake of closeness, intimacy of one kind or another, it is a courting. Among my people singing to a prospective lover is always a part of the courting. It's a gift, an honoring. And singing to the other nations is a way to give, honor, court their attentions."

I smiled back. "That's so beautiful." The more I had the chance to think about it the more I was struck by the intensity of the gentleness and giving of this way of life. Tears came to my eyes. I had so much admiration and joy to express and no words that could carry it.

"So. You are ready now." She took my hand. I could feel her deep caring.

"I don't know if I feel ready. I guess I'm a little nervous."

She nodded and patted my hand the way she had often done to sooth and comfort me in times that were hard. Our eyes met. The love that had passed down through the countless generations of her family and people poured out of her ancient eyes to me. There was a bond there deeper than any I had ever experienced with a woman. She was my sister, my mother, my Grandmother, my teacher, my best friend.

"Our time for Moon Ceremony is ending," she said softly. "Your bleeding is over for this cycle. Now we go back to our other things. Next month we will get together again."

"Oh yes. Yes! I really want to. I'll make sure it fits into my schedule. I'll set it up tomorrow. These last few days have been something I could never have imagined. Even though it felt like you were tearing my guts out by the roots sometimes, I don't want it to end."

"I know." A sad look came to her face. "This kind of contact between the women and the Grammas is another thing your people have lost. It too is a part of women's power and growth, the assuring of the generations. There is nothing else that replaces it.

"Before you go you must give your offerings and thanks to all those who live here for all their hospitality and help. And you must show your thanks to Creator. I will do the same.

"This has been good." She looked very satisfied with the ceremony time we had spent together and with me.

I nodded.

She took both my hands in hers and reassured me, "We'll be together soon. In two weeks?"

"Yeah. At your place?"

Chea agreed.

We each gave our respects and offerings. I broke up the food I had left and scattered it over the entire area.

Chea and I hugged goodbye. And touching her hand to her chest, then toward the ground, then to my chest she said, "Manaole u manaole."

"Manaole u manaole," I answered, tears rolling down my face.

We stared at each other for another moment and then hiked out of the forest in our own directions.

When I finally got home it was time to start dinner. I was very tired and painfully sad that my Moon Ceremony was ended. My mind began to wrestle back and forth between the horrors in stripping the dignities from women and the possibilities of wondrous sharing and bonding. I felt so torn apart inside even food was not appealing.

I didn't bother cleaning the dishes after the meal or taking care of any other chores that were waiting for me. I staggered my way to bed and fell exhausted into a restless sleep.

I dreamed of a beautiful woman. She was intensely familiar but I couldn't quite place how I knew her. I was very fond of her. Her hair was long and full and dark. Her skin was fair and clear. She had eyes that caught the light and reached down deep inside me. She was adored and cherished by her people. She had built them their village; they took care of her and she took care of them.

She loved life so dearly and appreciated and honored everything it had to offer. She was sensuous, openly sexual, bold and free. She was the center of the people and did well and fairly by her responsibilities. Life was good for all and there was peace in her village. Her name was Lilith. They called her Lilith the Beloved. Lilith the Mother of Them All.

Then something happened. Suddenly everything was different. People were yelling and fighting. They were chasing someone down the street out of the village, throwing rocks and broken pieces of pottery at the exile.

I gasped. I hadn't recognized the chastised one at first. It was the same beautiful woman, Lilith. They had taken away her special robes and ripped at her hair and body.

Someone saw me and shouted to the others, "She stands with Lilith. She's unclean. Don't let her get away." The men started to run at me. Rocks hit me from all directions. I tried to get to Lilith to escape with her but she was far ahead of me and disappeared into the forest. The people shouted after her calling her a demon and corrupter of Humans.

Then they realized I was still within the city boundaries and turned to attack me. I couldn't make my body run. Terror paralyzed me completely.

I screamed and woke myself up with a jolt.

I was soaking with sweat. My heart was racing. I had a hard time catching my breath. As I watched Lilith running into the trees in my mind, I realized who she was. She wasn't just the Biblical Adam's first wife. She was the Mother of Us All—the Mother Earth. She was the uncontrollable one, raped, defiled, discarded, who was exiled from her children and the world she created and loved, accused of being the demon that ruins Human souls forever.

I knew who she was now. I loved her more than words can express. She was the presence, the Song that I had felt in the burning cave. She was the Many Breasted Mother. She was the Earth whose Song I touched those years ago on the beach cliff when the Hetakas gave me the Earth Fire Serpent Ceremony. She was the soil that glowed and sang to me when I was still a tiny child.

NINE

THE OLDEST SACRAMENT

THE first week of spring quarter at the University of California had begun. I left my apartment early in order to spend a few hours walking out in the fields to begin my plant questing process.

The weather in Santa Cruz continued to be dry and warm. Thinly scattered clouds were moving in slowly from the southwest over the ocean. There were birds and squirrels everywhere. Their voices chattered with the wind.

I began the work of observing and approaching the plants of the area as Chea had described. As I let the energies of the Earth Fire Serpent flow out of me into the surroundings I kept remembering the dream I had the night before. I watched the dirt becoming saturated with my offering and I could feel the Song of the Mother of Us All coming from it. She was a Holy Thing, a Holy Being. I knew in every cell of my body that I was a part of her, from her. I was her daughter; she gave me form as I gave form to my children.

Within her lavishly rich femaleness I found a sense of what it means inside myself to be a female, to be a woman. Everything around was intimately involved in interacting with her. She was the foundation and sustainer. All the hundreds of beings' lives moved around her. Through their actions they danced their joy in tune to her rhythms.

I stopped walking and sat down to observe more clearly. I found myself among a group of little pink flowers. I was intrigued by the atmosphere they created and they soon captured my full curiosity. I offered them my energies and Song and was able to observe with all my senses at once. Their open blossoms gave off a medicine remarkably similar to a state of erotic joy, they were in their time of mating. In a sense their medicine was like a celebration, a thanksgiving offered to all who cared to share. I stayed among them watching and feeling every nuance I could catch until my time ran short.

I needed to leave and get to my first class. I paid my respects to all those present and explained that I would be continuing my quest with all due respect as I coordinated it with my other obligations.

I walked on up the hill through the campus to the Merrill College buildings. This was the only opportunity I would have to attend a presentation by this visiting speaker. I had heard that everybody enjoyed his style very much. Unfortunately he was only going to be with us for a short lecture series this year in Santa Cruz. His popularity had spread by word of mouth and this class was standing room only. I was lucky I had arrived early enough to get a seat in the center of the front row.

As I was sitting there preparing my notebook and papers I felt a wave of energy pass over me. It was well focused and intensely sexual in nature. I wondered if I had not just been involved with the sensing of energies, particularly the ones of pollinating plants, if I would have ever noticed this occurring. I remembered Chea's "assignment" and decided to try to find out who it was coming from.

The room was quite crowded and I was going to have to be methodical in order to not make any mistakes. I decided to begin at my left. I concentrated on the feeling and signature of the medicine coming to me and then observed each man one at a time to see if I could find a match.

One after the other I studied them all the way around the room and there was no match. I wondered if I had done something wrong and then I realized I had left one man out, the speaker. It never occurred to me that he might be the one. I pulled myself to my center to make sure my observations would be accurate and made the comparison. The medicine was his.

My jaw dropped unconsciously and I found myself staring at him. He must have realized on some level that I was aware of his thoughts and feelings toward me. He looked like a kid that just got caught with his hand in the cookie jar.

I turned away but his medicines kept coming to me unchanged. I needed to decide whether I would send flirting medicines of my own back to him. I considered the responsibilities involved and the risk of becoming emotionally attached to him.

From what I knew about him already he was supposed to be considerate, conscientious and fun loving. Lecturers and staff were not allowed by campus rules to be sexual with the students and this man's energy seemed honorable. So that made him seem completely safe. I voted to make him part of my homework assignment.

The lecture began. True to his reputation he was dynamic and knowledgeable, well spoken and in complete control of his presentation and his audience. While I listened I collected the different energies as they flowed to me and let the erotic nature build within them.

After about ten minutes I figured I must have enough of them amassed by now and I propelled them with all my attention into the lecturer. I had no idea what to expect.

This unshakable professional whose control of himself and his work had been impeccable stopped in mid-sentence with his hand up to the chalkboard and forgot where he was in his delivery. He stood there with his hand in the air staring at me for a moment. There was a knowing between us and I could feel that a delightful game was about to begin. Not only was this to be a dance of flirting energies but he took it as a kind of challenge.

As class went on he asked questions of the students in a seminar style format. While they were giving their responses he was sending me his courting medicines. Then he asked me a particularly difficult question and sent a remarkably intense charge of energies.

They overtook my attention. I couldn't concentrate on what I needed to say. I was having a very difficult time. He leaned back and

THE OLDEST SACRAMENT

chewed on the end of a matchstick and gave me his sexy grin. I loved it. I have no idea what I babbled for an answer. He seemed perfectly delighted with himself. The score was now one to one.

The class ended. He watched me as I got my things together and stood up to go. We smiled at each other and he said he would see me tomorrow in class.

The feeling of him was delightful. He was exciting and unpredictable. I could feel his attention touching me affectionately on my face and my hair. Then I felt it slide around my hips and I got scared. I didn't know what to do. I was afraid it was becoming something I hadn't intended and I would lose control over it. I smiled and said I had to get to another class fast. I would see him tomorrow. And I left.

I practically ran out into the forest that surrounded the classrooms. His medicines felt better than anything I had ever imagined. I was truly frightened. It hadn't occurred to me that I might come to really want him in my bed. But to my great distress I felt myself wanting even more of him than that. I certainly never expected to respond this way to someone I was fulfilling this "assignment" with. I picked him because I thought he was safe, that we could playfully flirt back and forth and it wouldn't lead to anything else. But now I wasn't so sure.

I walked up beyond the last college buildings and sat down in the middle of a circle of redwood trees. I still felt as if his medicines were wooing me. There were sexual sensations. My body had a tingling excitement at the elbows and up my arms as if something electrical were touching them. There was a pressure, almost like a longing, on my tongue that reached all the way up into the roof of my mouth. I could see his eyes reaching to be inside me.

I looked at the top of the trees. They seemed to reach forever into the heavens. Leaning back against one of the trunks I tried to make the sensations stop. What was I going to do now? I had started something I wasn't sure I knew how to manage. Chea's words about the responsibilities of sending out medicines were beginning to make strikingly clear sense to me.

It was another two hours before I had to be at my next class. I didn't want to go anywhere or see anyone until then. I needed to be separated from the jumbled confusion other people's energies sometimes caused in me. The steady uncluttered atmospheres of the forest and meadows had become my sanctuary.

I looked around to all the variety of beings and forms. There were hundreds, perhaps thousands of different species right there. I decided to spend the time talking to them and observing in the way of my quest.

As I stilled myself the Songs of the big trees came into focus. I offered them the life energies that flowed through me. The presence of Mother Earth was permeating everywhere. I could feel my Song reaching out to mingle among the many different beings. I was cared for, surrounded, protected. They invited me to join their chorus and one by one another Song added into my awareness. We were an interdependent family. I felt them with my entire body, each one tending to concentrate in a different area. Their abandonment to the pleasures of interaction consumed me and time slipped away.

The next day I had materials I needed to get ready for the class. I arrived at the large seminar room more than an hour before it was to begin. At the moment the space was a series of areas being defined by temporary partitions left there from the previous group. I went and sat in the last section entirely separated from the door.

I began to feel the medicines of the guest lecturer. They were playful and sensuous. My stomach got nervous. I felt the same anxious tingling in my arms and mouth only stronger. I knew he was nearby.

The door opened. I waited a moment to give him the chance to find me. Nobody walked through the divided areas but the energies were increasing. I went into the partition where the door was to see if it had been the lecturer. There was only the same student sitting there just as he had been when I arrived.

"Who came in?" I asked.

He seemed involved in his work and it took him a moment to look up and answer. "The janitor."

The medicines were very strong now. My hands were actually shaking. I had expected it to be the lecturer. I didn't understand how to interpret what I was feeling. I went back on the other side to my chair and continued to work on my notes.

The door opened again. My stomach jumped into my throat. I waited for a moment until I couldn't stand it any longer and went around the partition.

"Who was that?" I asked the young man again. "Who just came in?"

"Oh," he answered. "Somebody who looked like they had the wrong room."

"Nobody else has come in?" My voice was becoming louder and strained.

"No," the student answered.

It seemed as though the lecturer should be only a few feet away from me. My knees were weak and buzzing. I felt the medicine touch along my face and down my side. Then a large wave of it hit me. My stomach rolled. I couldn't think straight.

"Well," I asked again. "Have you seen the guest speaker yet today?" I was feeling desperate. I had to find out whatever I could to understand the sensations of his medicines.

"No." The young man looked up from his work as though he wished I would stop bothering him.

A few students started to wander into class.

The energy increased even more. I heard footsteps from behind a partition near the window. There was someone back in the other part of the room where I hadn't looked. I was so nervous I couldn't move. And then there he was coming around that other divider, smiling like a cat that just swallowed a fish. I loved feeling the medicines this way. Oh god! I loved it!

"Hello, Kay." He stood there with his hands in his jean pockets leaning the way he does.

"Hello." The energies were doing somersaults in my throat and belly. I could hardly get the word out. I tried my best to sound normal and unaffected.

"We have a good chance to talk at lunch today," he said. "Shall I meet you here at noon?" He could have pushed me over with a feather.

"That would be good. I'll be ready." I tried to keep it all as businesslike as I could so that no one would notice the real interactions that were going on. The score was now two to one.

For the rest of his visit we volleyed our flirting medicines back and forth. It was a beautiful and exciting dance that built a very special friendship. In this play we shared our Songs and concerns and appreciations. He always respected me and I knew I could count on him. I was going to miss him when he was gone.

Every day I had been spending some time actively involved in my plant quest even if it was only for an hour. I found that my sensitivity varied a great deal. Sometimes my mind would be so full of events and problems from the rest of my life that I was barely able to detect the delicate medicines of the plant nations. Near the end of the quarter I was able to take a whole day to be in the fields among them. I set aside this particular Monday in hopes of removing as many of those distractions as possible.

I decided to go above the campus to the little meadow that I had been at with Domano and Chea. I walked all around the outer edge giving my greetings and offerings to all those present. Near the middle of the clearing was a spot where the grass had been pressed down by an animal. I went over to it and touched the blades. The place was comforting. There was a lightness there.

Many tiny wild flowers were growing between the grasses. I gave out the Earth Fire Serpent energies as they rushed through my body. It occurred to me that this little area was a circle. The Hetakas had always said that the best kind of place to be in when performing a ceremony was a circle. It made me feel connected to tradition.

I sat there on the bent grass for many hours making my offerings and observing with all my senses at once. The Song of each little individual came to my attention but one stood out above all the rest. It belonged to a plant about four inches high with bright emerald green stems and leaves. Covering the top were many blossoms composed of four silvery white petals. It was the only one of its kind that I could see.

I kept being drawn back to it until I became so enraptured that I forgot about the others. Its Song became stronger and stronger. I lay down on my elbows with my face in my hands. I had to be closer to it. Without thinking I began to sing out loud making the fibers from my heart as the Hetakas had taught me those years before. All I wanted was to give to this wondrous being.

I reached out to it with my Song. Something changed. My awareness shifted and I could feel this one searching and delving into me. There were sounds that it was making like many low and secret voices. A gentle feminine quality pervaded its whole nature. I knew this silver blossomed creature and she knew me. She was my elder and mentor. There was nothing that I needed to hide from her, whatever was there inside me she understood and accepted.

I had no fear. Our inner atmospheres and rhythms composed themselves anew to be in accord with one another. Her beingness began to move through me. She gave her Song to me and her medicines flowed in on my breath. I merged into her vastness. She was connected in ways I could never have imagined to ancient things and peoples long since past. She had so much she wanted to give away, so much she wanted to tell me about health and happiness for women.

Time lost its meaning. We were together a moment, a day. My trust in her was complete, I knew she would always be there for me asking nothing but my mutual respect. I could hear our Songs as they poured out together harmonizing and weaving one into the other. Then Songs and sounds from around us mixed and played intertwining. I gave them all my heart and they gave me theirs.

Through the next two months I continued to go out among the plant nations and down by the waterfall to observe, share and seek the sacrament with those beings I had come to know and care for so intensely. They were always curious and endlessly generous.

Chea and I met alone again at my bleeding time. She continued teaching me the ways of her Grandmothers on the meanings of women's cycles and sexuality. I asked her if I could share some of the information about the giving of the sexual energies. Even though Chea didn't approve of him I was becoming sexually active with the man I had been seeing and wanted very much to have this special sharing and bonding between us.

To say Chea wasn't pleased with my choice was an understatement, but she finally consented to let me instruct him on the concept of making a gift of one's sexual and orgasmic energies. I was not to divulge any other information about it or my source.

Chea and Domano had talked with me a great deal about the sacred link teachings through the last months. My observing abilities among the plant nations was steadily increasing. I was becoming eager to extend that sensitivity to my own species.

The time finally came when I was to spend the evening with the man of my choosing. I fixed clam chowder and fresh warm French bread. Candles were lit throughout the room. He brought gentle classical music and a single red rose. We touched and kissed all evening. I told him about the gifts and how I wanted to share them with him. He was delightfully interested and excited to try.

The evening moved with tenderness and sharing until we made love. His attention remained on himself. He gave of no energies. My sensitivity was wide open and I watched as he pulled all of his medicines and then his own gift back into himself, rolled over and went to sleep.

I was devastated. How could anybody do such a thing? What could possibly make somebody that selfish? I doubled up in pain and cried myself into an uneasy sleep. He never noticed.

I dreamed I was on another land, an island perhaps. There were men there with the legs of deer and little antlers on the tops of their heads. They wore no dressings or decorations except a single medallion around their necks.

I watched as they talked warmly among themselves, laughing and teasing each other. They called themselves satyrs and greeted me as if I was a beloved friend they hadn't seen for a long while. Their voices were like exquisite sounds of music from a forgotten time. We walked through wide open gardens in the sunlight together. They offered me their fruits and their water from a sacred spring.

I felt a great ease and comfort. Their Songs and love poured out to me in such abundance as I had never observed or felt before. I loved them endlessly. They showed me every honor and respect. I felt revered, cherished.

All through the night till the Sun rose again they played their music and danced for me. All through the dark of nights and the light of days they gave their Songs to me.

THE END